THE TRUTH
ABOUT THE
O. J. SIMPSON
TRIAL

Other books by F. Lee Bailey

The Defense Never Rests, 1971.

For the Defense, 1975.

Cleared for the Approach, 1977.

Secrets, 1979.

To Be A Trial Lawyer, 1982.

Criminal Law Library (West), 11 Volumes.

THE TRUTH ABOUT THE

O. J. SIMPSON

TRIAL

BY THE ARCHITECT OF THE DEFENSE

F. LEE BAILEY

Skyhorse Publishing

Skyhorse Publishing books may be purchased in bulk at special discounts for sales promotion, corporate gifts, fund-raising, or educational purposes. Special editions can also be created to specifications. For details, contact the Special Sales Department, Arcade Publishing, 307 West 36th Street, 11th Floor, New York, NY 10018 or info@skyhorsepublishing.com.

Skyhorse® and Skyhorse Publishing® is a registered trademark of Skyhorse Publishing, Inc.®, a Delaware corporation.

Visit our website at www.skyhorsepublishing.com.

10 9 8 7 6 5 4 3 2 1

Library of Congress Cataloging-in-Publication Data is available on file.

Cover design by Brian Peterson

Cover photograph by Getty Images

Print ISBN: 978-1-5107-6584-9
Ebook ISBN: 978-1-5107-6585-6

Printed in the United States of America

After sixty-five years of bumping heads and rubbing shoulders with genuine courtroom lawyers, I am pleased to report that the United States has a good inventory of legal sharpshooters. Very few are a cut above the rest. Such a person is my friend **Joseph J. Balliro, Sr.,** a Boston legal warrior, for more than seven decades. He has been a mentor, colleague, co-counsel, my lawyer and trusted advisor. This book is dedicated to him.

Contents

Foreword

I have had the honor of knowing F. Lee Bailey for several years. We first met more than two decades ago via a satellite video hookup on the *CBS Early Show* hosted by Bryant Gumbel. The topic was the notorious Boston Strangler case. Mr. Bailey had defended Albert Henry DeSalvo, the self-proclaimed Boston Strangler, while I was re-investigating the murder of my aunt, Mary Sullivan, who at nineteen years old was the youngest and last victim of the notorious 1960s murder spree. We sparred over our strong beliefs in the case, and as a young and cocky journalist, I admit that I was unwilling to entertain Lee's assertion that DeSalvo had committed the murders.

It wasn't until years later, during a luncheon with Lee, which had been set up by a mutual friend, that I opened my mind to the evidence he presented, and more importantly, to his critical thinking. There is a reason that the name F. Lee Bailey is synonymous with jurisprudence in America. He is an iconic figure who is no-nonsense and completely unafraid to share his theories about a case he has been involved in—which brings me to this book chronicling his work in the O. J. Simpson case.

Like many of you, I have read a number of different books and have watched several documentaries pointing to Simpson's guilt in the murders of his ex-wife Nicole Brown and Ronald Goldman. My mind was made up a long time ago. But, as an investigative journalist and true crime author, I figured it was my responsibility to read what Mr. Bailey had to say about the subject. After all, he was there as a member of Simpson's Dream Team, standing resolutely in the eye of the hurricane.

I read Lee's book with a set of open eyes and I learned a great deal more about this celebrated murder case and the so-called Trial of the Century that followed. Bailey, who performed so brilliantly in the courtroom and behind the scenes in high profile cases, makes strong arguments here, which you'll no doubt debate with others long after you've finished this book. No study of O. J. Simpson and the crimes that he has been accused of is complete without reading *The Truth about the O. J. Simpson Trial*.

Casey Sherman
New York Times, USA Today, and *Wall Street Journal*
best-selling author of *Hunting Whitey: The Inside Story of the Capture and Killing of America's Most Wanted Crime Boss.*

Acknowledgments

I n most books published over the years, a nod of thanks is given by the author to those who chipped in in some way or another to the finished product. Some of these contributions have been admittedly modest. Not so in this case. My longtime friend and sometime co-author framed out the original story and got us around first base. **John Greenya** has written books with me before and is always a joy to work with.

The backbone of this tale—somewhere between stainless steel and titanium—is **Patrick McKenna**, my chief investigator and valued friend. And he knows the case better than Donald Trump knows his coiffeur.

I am sad to say that although begun in November 2017, this manuscript had pretty much fallen by the wayside for more than two years. Then I began working with a young lady in early 2020 who expressed interest in bringing it back to life. She is articulate, has a stunning memory and a deep vocabulary. Within a short time, she had memorized the existing manuscript nearly *haec verba*. She took over the project, and she made this book happen. You will be seeing the name **Jenny Sisson** frequently in this industry. She has "The Right Stuff."

Brian Heiss and his associate, **Jonathan Dallavalle**, did some excellent research, assembled the certified transcript of evidence, and produced the most accurate animation of the timeline of the events of June 12, 1994 which was released in conjunction with publication of this book. (www.TruthAboutTheOJSimpsonTrial. com)

Every author crosses his fingers against the hope that the publisher will provide a first-class editor to help boost the story to some form of stardom. We hit a home run with **Lilly Golden**: Sharp, challenging, skeptical but always solid. Lilly is a joy to work with, and this a better book on her account.

PROLOGUE

June 12, 1994: The Murders of Nicole Brown Simpson and Ron Goldman

On the evening of June 12, 1994, just before 10:30 p.m., all was quiet in the vicinity of the condominium residence located at 875 South Bundy Drive in upscale Brentwood, California, a section of western Los Angeles.

Danny Mandel[1] and Ellen Aaronson[2] had just finished dinner—their first date—at the nearby Mezzaluna Restaurant and were walking south on South Bundy. They passed by the gated entrance to number 875 at 10:25 p.m.[3] They saw no blood on the sidewalk. No dogs were barking, no human voices were heard. Aside from their conversation and their footfalls on the concrete sidewalk, there was silence.

In her home at 918 South Bundy—across from and south of 875 by three hundred feet—Denise Pilnak[4] had just said good night to her friend, Judy Telander,[5] who had been using Denise's computer. As Telander and Pilnak bid each other farewell, the women discussed how uncommonly quiet the night was. As Telander departed, Pilnak called her mother on the phone. The record shows the call ended at 10:28.[6]

At approximately 10:35,[7] there erupted a series of barks from what sounded like a large dog. Pilnak mentally noted the unusual volume of the bark and would later testify the barking lasted up to forty-five minutes.[8]

Meanwhile, Robert Heidstra[9], a self-employed detailer of automobiles and a naturalized Frenchman who lived on Dorothy Street, near the corner of Westgate Avenue, was walking his dogs in the vicinity. Weather permitting, he walked his two dogs almost every evening. His usual route took him from his home in a westerly direction on Gorham Avenue to Bundy Drive, then south to Dorothy Street, then home. But on this night the dog—whom Heidstra knew to be the Akita at 875 South Bundy—sounded unusually agitated. Heidstra wanted no skirmishes between the animals, so he turned south into an unmarked alley which ran parallel to South Bundy, then he emerged on Dorothy and went home.

But in the course of doing so, two occurrences came to Heidstra's attention from his position in the alley across from Bundy Drive. At 10:40 p.m. he heard a male voice yelling, "Hey! Hey! Hey!"[10], followed immediately by the sound of the clanging of a gate. At 10:50 p.m., Heidstra then noticed a white or light-colored automobile turn south from Dorothy Street to South Bundy Drive.[11]

At 10:55 p.m.[12], Steven Schwab, a neighbor, took a stroll with *his* dog, a nightly ritual keyed to the broadcast of the *Dick Van Dyke Show* which aired at 11:30 p.m. on weekdays. On Sunday, however, it aired an hour earlier, at 10:30. On his walk, Schwab spotted an Akita standing on the sidewalk near the gate of 875 South Bundy, its paws appearing muddy or bloody. Schwab, finding no identification on the dog, brought the Akita back to his apartment building and a neighbor in the building, Sukru Boztepe,[13] offered to take the dog in for the night. But at about midnight, Boztepe and his wife took the restless dog back out, in hopes of finding the dog's owner. The dog pulled them along the sidewalk and stopped at the gates of 875 South Bundy. The Boztepes were the first to discover the brutally stabbed, lifeless body of Nicole Brown.

At 12:30 a.m. on June 13, 1994, officers arrive on the scene.

From there, the biggest homicide case in Los Angeles of the twentieth century blasts off like a rocket.

CHAPTER 1
The Beginning
June 13, 1994

Like most people who tuned into the news midday on Monday, June 13, 1994, I can recall being startled to hear that Pro Football Hall of Famer O. J. Simpson's former wife, Nicole Brown Simpson, had been found slaughtered outside her home in Brentwood, California. (That day had special meaning to me, since my father was born on June 13, 1900, and would have turned ninety-four had he not passed away in 1981.) The media reports mentioned that a male victim was also found at the scene and that O. J. Simpson, who was in Chicago at the time, was hurrying back to Los Angeles to confer with law enforcement authorities.

The *Los Angeles Times* quoted unidentified police sources saying Simpson was under investigation and that a bloody glove was found at his estate on Rockingham Avenue. The *Los Angeles Daily News* went further, reporting the glove matched another found at the murder scene. (Details about *who* found the glove and the manner in which it was found were yet to be known to the public.)

By Monday, just a day after the murders, O. J. told reporters upon his return to LA that he knew nothing about the incident. An Associated Press article stated that family and friends streamed to Simpson's Brentwood home in support. His friend and criminal and entertainment attorney, Howard Weitzman, described Simpson as "distraught."

"It's difficult enough with the shock that your wife's been murdered, but to hear that you may be accused of it, well, it's awful," Weitzman told the press.

Although it was not my habit to analyze reported homicides for which I had not been consulted or retained, this case was a little different. I remember wondering vaguely what sort of rash conflicts had led to this violence. In the seventies, as a dedicated fan of the then-struggling New England Patriots football team, I had come to dread each game we played against the Buffalo Bills, because O. J. Simpson, the Bills' star running back, ran roughshod over our defensive line on a regular basis. Nonetheless, no amount of rabid partisanship could prevent my admiration for Simpson when, in December 1973, he broke a National Football League record by gaining more than two thousand yards in just fourteen games. Yet despite his stardom in a backbreaking sport, wherein many games result in multiple penalties against those who cross the line with physical aggression, Simpson had a spotless nonconfrontational history.

While Simpson was basking in the limelight at the peak of his football career, I was, at the time, unhappily sitting in a federal court in Jacksonville, Florida, as one of thirteen defendants in a criminal prosecution for conspiracy and mail fraud. To add to the depression of the moment, I had information that at a cocktail party the trial judge had boasted—*before the trial had opened*—as to what sentence he would impose if and when the jury convicted me.

Ultimately, the case was dismissed by another judge without a jury verdict, but December 1973 was as low a point for me as it was a highlight for O. J. Simpson.

Some years later, in one "green room" or other, I met O. J. while we were waiting to appear on a television show. We spoke only briefly, but I was impressed that unlike some star athletes and many rock stars, Simpson did not seem to be full of himself. He was pleasant if somewhat garrulous, and, I thought, rather interesting—the kind of guy you would like to invite to your home for dinner.

So when I received the call from my then-friend Robert Shapiro, who had been retained by Simpson as his attorney following his ex-wife's tragic murder, I was happy to lend whatever advice or services might be beneficial.

At the request of Shapiro, I entered the O. J. Simpson case on June 14, two days after the homicides. I have frequently asked myself what I might have done differently in those earliest days had I joined the defense team as lead counsel, rather than as an adjunct, a role that did not change until after the preliminary hearing was completed two weeks later. Most certainly, my investigators would have discovered much earlier that the lead detective in the case, Mark Fuhrman, filed a lawsuit years before that effectively labelled him as a racist, a liar, and a malingerer. A further inquiry would have upended a veritable cornucopia of impeachment materials, history has shown. But I wasn't in a position to call the shots in the early days of the case.

* * *

I had known Robert Shapiro since 1976 when we represented codefendants in a major drug case in Honolulu. I had a client named Samango, the alleged ringleader, and Bob represented one of the underlings. It was an extraordinary case.

Grand jury proceedings resulted in the indictment against Samango for drug importation. However, a DEA officer who'd worked the case had unjustifiably described my client as a person suspected of having also committed a number of homicides. Besmirching a criminal defendant before a grand jury in this manner is completely improper, and after reviewing the offensive section of the grand jury minutes with Chief Judge Samuel King, I got him to agree that the indictment was defective, so he dismissed it.

Unbelievably, when the federal prosecutor went back to a new grand jury to again seek an indictment against Samango, he did not call witnesses; he simply *read the prior grand jury minutes,* thus replicating the harm that had been done in the first instance.

I once again brought this to the attention of Judge King, who was not pleased. He quashed the indictment and dismissed it. The United States appealed to the Ninth Circuit Court of Appeals, but the dismissal was upheld.

Thereafter, Bob and I would see each other from time to time and talk about working on more cases together. At one point, he asked if he could put my name on the upper right-hand corner of his letterhead as "of counsel." (I agreed, not realizing at the time that one who accepts of counsel status in a law firm becomes liable for the mistakes of any of the lawyers, just as if he were a partner.) This was a binding commitment that would later tie me to the Simpson case without fees, although I had no way of knowing it then.

* * *

That first call from Shapiro on the Simpson case, in hindsight, was a harbinger of what trouble lay ahead—not only of what would become of our friendship and professional relationship, but also of his future ham-fisted handling in the Simpson case.

On the evening of June 14, two days after the murders, Bob called to informed me that he'd just been retained to take over the defense of the Simpson case from Howard Weitzman—*and* that he was at the offices of the polygraph company Intercept's owner and chief examiner, Ed Gelb, trying to get Simpson tested on the polygraph.

I was quite taken aback by this news—not that Bob was retained in the case, but that he was attempting to subject O. J. to a polygraph examination two days after the murder of his ex-wife. One of the critical aspects of administering a reliable polygraph test is that it not be given to a surviving marriage partner hard on the heels of the traumatic loss of the spouse, and the fact that Simpson and Nicole were separated and divorced would not change this principle. Research shows the results are wild and inconclusive. With more than fifty years of polygraph experience under my belt, I felt Bob's timing of the test was critically inappropriate—something that even the polygraph examiner had warned him about before proceeding.

Ten years earlier, I had been the host of a syndicated television program called *Lie Detector*. Its format was to invite volunteers whose credibility had been questioned on some issue, criminal or otherwise, and who were anxious to be vindicated as truth-tellers by a live appearance on the show where we had some top-level polygraph examiners.

On many occasions when I was taping the show in studios in Los Angeles, Bob would come, with his wife, to sit on the set and enjoy the excitement of doing a television program. During those visits, he picked up some of the rudiments of the highly complex polygraph testing business (I thought), simply from hearing the on-screen explanations given by me and the co-host, the aforementioned Ed Gelb.

A fundamental rule in polygraph examination of a homicide suspect involves the *timing* of the test on the subject. The degree of anxiety and grief that arises from an uxoricide—the killing of one's wife—will have a decidedly negative effect on the tests.

When I learned that Bob had rendered this test to O. J., I remonstrated him for this blunder as I believed he should have known better. Shapiro replied that right at the outset of their interview, Dennis Nunnally, the examiner handling the Simpson test, had told him precisely the same thing. But Bob reasoned that he expected O. J. was going to have to surrender the following morning by 11:00 a.m. and Bob wanted to use the prestige of a polygraph test conducted by a former high ranking LAPD examiner, Lieutenant Gelb, because he believed that if the results were favorable for Simpson, they could be used to slow the momentum of the detectives who were advocating Simpson's arrest. Shapiro's sense of urgency was justified in part because no one likes to give polygraphs in a jail facility.

But Gelb was in Spain and unavailable. And reluctantly, Dennis Nunnally stepped in to conduct the examination.

When Bob called me from the polygraph lab, I asked to speak to the examiner. Nunnally told me that the charts were wild and ragged, which is exactly what one should expect when testing a subject who was in an agitated state of mind. I strongly suggested that the test be terminated and that it be run another day somewhere down the road even though that retry might very well have to be in a Los Angeles County jail facility.

When Nunnally stopped the test, Shapiro grabbed the paper charts which record the responses of the suspect and left the office building. Nunnally was shocked and dismayed, because in those days, there were no copies or electronic records of results. No examiner ever wanted to lose his polygrams, and thus have no reference if questioned about the nature of the test and its consequences. (I later saw the charts in Shapiro's office. I am the only person other than Dennis who has seen these charts *and* knows how to read them. In my opinion, they were unreadable. When ordered to produce them in the later civil trial, Shapiro said he had destroyed them.)

* * *

Early the following day, the news media eagerly awaited the surrender of Simpson at LAPD headquarters in the Parker Center in downtown Los Angeles.

But Simpson did not appear.

On the evening of June 17, while I was at home in Palm Beach, Florida, a friend called and told me to turn on my television set. Helicopter-borne aerial cameras were focused on a white Ford Bronco headed north on California's Interstate Highway 405 at a deliberate, but not hurried pace. Surrounding this Bronco were six or seven police vehicles, comprising what the press would later label as the "low-speed chase," perhaps the greatest oxymoron in media history. We learned that O. J.'s longtime loyal friend, Al Cowlings, who had played with him in both Buffalo and San Francisco, was driving his own white Bronco while O. J. was in the back seat with a loaded weapon in his hand.

Using his cell phone, Cowlings repeatedly exhorted the police not to come any closer because Simpson was, he said, very distraught, and if provoked might well commit suicide. Cowlings said he was taking Simpson back to his home in Brentwood to help keep him from panicking further. In due course, Simpson arrived, abandoned the weapon, and was escorted into his home where he made a phone call to his mother.

It was a shocking scene.

Matters were further intensified by the fact that Simpson had left, in his own handwriting, a letter that had all the earmarks of a suicide note. Another longtime friend, Robert Kardashian, read it—on national television—while Simpson was riding in the Bronco. With all of the action, I think the public did not really hear or focus on the initial phrase in that otherwise hopeless message, "First, everyone understand I had nothing to do with Nicole's murder."

I now think that, based on the events alone, many people decided then and there that Simpson was guilty. And even though later developments strongly supported the notion that he had neither the opportunity nor the motive to commit the murders, they were not inclined to reevaluate that position.

The day after Simpson's surrender, Shapiro called me and told me that the cops had absolutely nothing in the way of evidence except for a glove which had been illegally seized at Simpson's home without a warrant, and "would be easily suppressed." That glove, which would turn out not to be "easily suppressed," became the linchpin of the entire case.

On Saturday, June 18, I was in the Bahamas aboard a client's yacht when I got another call from Shapiro: "I had the wrong information," he said. "It looks like they have Simpson's blood everywhere, along with Nicole's—and we don't have a shot in this case, so please explore an insanity defense."

What I didn't know then but would soon find out, this kind of unpredictable, uninformed, half-cocked behavior became Bob's way as the case progressed.

Acting on Bob's misinformation, I immediately placed calls

to two of the leading forensic psychiatrists then in practice: Dr. Louis Jolyon West of Los Angeles and Dr. Bernard Yudowitz of Arlington, Massachusetts (now deceased). Both had, of course, been reading about the Simpson case, and when I explained that, according to Shapiro, the evidence of his participation in the homicide was overwhelming, both began to ask for more facts which would enable them to pursue the issue of legal insanity or its absence.

It developed, however, that the blood evidence that Shapiro claimed was "everywhere" would prove to be all but meaningless.

Despite Bob's mistaken information about the blood, enlisting the help of Dr. Yudowitz proved to be very helpful in analyzing Simpson and explaining the psychological dynamics behind his Highway 405 excursion.

* * *

In truth, the biggest problem the defense had during the fifteen-month period that elapsed from arrest to verdict was not the evidence, or the defendant, but Robert Shapiro. His brief tenure as lead counsel was a fluke that never should have occurred. O. J. already had one of the best lawyers in California, Howard Weitzman. Weitzman had represented him successfully in 1987 when he was charged with assaulting Nicole and had won a particularly tough case for automotive executive John DeLorean, who was accused of trafficking in cocaine.

Weitzman had been with O. J. from the onset of the case. He was the one who met him when he arrived back home in Los Angeles the day after the murders. Weitzman was with O. J. when LAPD Detectives Tom Lange and Philip Vannatter arrived at his home to take him to the station in handcuffs. Weitzman had told the detectives to take off the handcuffs they had clamped on Simpson's wrist since he was not then under arrest. They complied, but it was an indicator of the general police attitude toward Simpson. They were so anxious to accuse him that they had needlessly handcuffed him, without an arrest warrant or probable cause to believe he had connection with the crimes.

The detectives announced that they were taking Simpson "downtown" for questioning. O. J. agreed. Weitzman agreed as well and said that he would sit in on the interrogation. Lange told him he could not be in the room during the interview. Weitzman said, "Okay, there will be no questioning." The matter might have stonewalled then and there, but O. J. stepped in and overruled his own lawyer, and said he would talk without his attorney present. He said he felt that he had a duty to help the investigators any way that he could.

That afternoon, Leroy "Skip" Taft—a civil lawyer who handled O. J.'s business affairs—and Robert Kardashian, a former practicing lawyer and friend of Simpson's, fired Weitzman (without consulting O. J.) for letting the cops have access to the defendant. Then they hired Robert Shapiro. They thought Bob was a guy who could "fix things." They heard he had substantial influence in the law enforcement community and could slow down the process, enabling Simpson to show his innocence.

What they didn't know was that Shapiro's principal practice as a defense lawyer was that of "copping pleas" for clients—pleading clients guilty in exchange for supposedly lenient sentences. He had conducted no murder trials that I knew of and had—in the view of many—butchered the case against Christian Brando—actor Marlon Brando's son—for killing his sister's boyfriend.

That Taft and Kardashian made this switch—wrongly informed, ignorant of the intricate folds and turns of high-level criminal cases, and generally with no idea what they were doing—is perhaps the most twisted moment of the whole affair. Had Weitzman remained as chief or had some other well-credentialed defense lawyer been hired, there is a good chance that the case would have gotten no further than the preliminary hearing and the case would have ended unless, and until, new evidence was developed.

CHAPTER 2
The Preliminary Hearing

The preliminary hearing was where the case should have started and ended.

A preliminary hearing is a minitrial without a jury wherein the prosecution must show *probable cause* that a crime has been committed, and that the defendant committed it. During a preliminary hearing, usually conducted by a lower-court judge, the prosecution presents such witnesses as it thinks may be necessary to establish "probable cause" and thus bind the case over for trial. (A bindover is defined as setting the case on a course for a full trial.) At a preliminary hearing, the defense gets a look at—and a chance to cross-examine those witnesses. Unlike Grand Jury testimony, which is often turned over to the defense just prior to or even during the trial, a transcript of the Preliminary Hearing is kept of everything that is said, and it becomes part of the record and part of the defense file immediately.

In a preliminary hearing, beyond cross-examining the prosecution's witnesses, the defense can present its own witnesses. In some cases the defense can poke a large enough hole in the prosecution's proof to justify denying a bindover. Had this happened in the preliminary hearing against O. J. Simpson, the case may well have died there and then. After all, if Judge Kathleen Kennedy-Powell, who presided over the preliminary hearing, had entertained severe doubts that Simpson was connected in some way to the "Rockingham glove," she had little basis to keep him in jail. But since Bob Shapiro and defense attorney Gerry Uelmen lacked the experience, the expertise, and the preparation to skewer Fuhrman's story, the case went forward. But I'm getting ahead of myself.

The preliminary hearing was set for June 29, 1994.

Bob had not asked me to be involved in the preliminary hearing. I hadn't been involved with the Simpson case beyond recommending the two lead investigators working the case, Patrick McKenna of Florida and John McNally from New York. I also selected proposed psychiatrist witnesses after Shapiro told me, quite incorrectly, that the evidence against Simpson was overwhelming. The two investigators, at that time, didn't report to me.

I didn't attend the preliminary hearing in person, but Shapiro had asked me to come to LA for the hearing and watch it on TV from the comfort of his friend Michael Klein's plush home. He wanted me close by for consultation. As I watched, I became increasingly alarmed by the flaws in the way the case was being handled, by both sides. On the part of the police, there were strong signs of ineptitude—and equally strong signs of what appeared to be dishonesty. The key witnesses that the prosecution called were:

Allan Park, the limo driver who testified he first saw Simpson in the entryway of his residence at 10:55 p.m. the evening of the murders. Simpson had not been seen prior until about 9:40 p.m. to 9:45 p.m. by Simpson's houseguest.

Kato Kaelin, who lived in Simpson's guesthouse and had dinner with him that night, testified that he heard several thumps behind his room at about 10:40 p.m. After going to investigate several minutes later, he said he saw Park's limo and Simpson in the entryway of his home with bags. Simpson and Park left the Rockingham property at about 11:05 p.m., heading to the airport.

Pablo Fenjves, a neighbor of Nicole Brown Simpson's, testified he heard the "plaintive wail" of a dog at 10:15 to 10:20 p.m. He was the only person at the preliminary hearing who offered a potential timeline for the murders. (The defense was still conducting its investigation of potential witnesses of others who had seen or heard anything around the Bundy Drive property.)

Detectives Mark Fuhrman and Philip Vannatter described their investigation of the Bundy Drive crime scene, which included finding a knit hat, a left-hand glove, bloody shoeprints leading away from the victims, several blood droplets, and blood on the rear gate of the property.

Investigators then moved to Simpson's Rockingham estate where Fuhrman said he noted blood on the driver's side door of a white Bronco parked on the street. Upon entering the property, Fuhrman reported finding a right-hand glove behind Kaelin's room. Detectives also reported blood drops on the driveway.

Dennis Fung, LAPD criminalist, testified he was called to first collect evidence from the outside of the Rockingham property, which included the glove found by Fuhrman. (Criminalist Andrea Mazzola was also at the scene to "learn" how to collect blood samples.) Fung then visited the premises on Bundy Drive to collect evidence.

When Simpson returned from Chicago the day after the murders, Vannatter testified that a "small laceration" was noted on the middle finger of Simpson's left hand. An unknown amount of blood was drawn from Simpson by investigators and placed into a 10cc vial. Vannatter took the blood to hand over to Dennis Fung. (No one asked where Fung was when Vannatter handed him the sample. *At the criminal trial, it came out that Vannatter took it to Rockingham.*)

Dr. Irwin Golden testified that there were two morphologically different types of stab wounds on the victims. Two knives could have been used in the killings: a single-edged blade and a double-edged blade. Vannatter brought Golden a knife and asked if it could be similar to one used in the murders. Golden said "it could be." (Golden *did not* testify at the criminal trial. Prosecutors chose to use his superior, Dr. Lakshmanan Sathyavagiswaran, LA County chief medical examiner.)

The prosecution's case presented in the preliminary hearing hinged principally on two things: their version of the timeline the night of the murders based on their witness testimony and the evidence gathered from both the Bundy Drive crime scene where the murders occurred and Simpson's Rockingham estate.

It was evident that the key player as it pertained to the evidence found for the prosecution was Detective Fuhrman. As I settled into Klein's leather couch, it was the first time in my life I had laid eyes on Fuhrman. As I watched him testify, he initially struck me as polished and professional—not out of character for a former Marine. But listening closely, I started to feel that his words didn't match his mannerisms, and the hackles on the back of my neck began to rise. His testimony regarding how the investigation unfolded and his lone participation—on several occasions—in finding and gathering evidence did not resonate with any police protocol. He also suffered small deviances between his testimony and the investigation records. For example, when answering questions about the Bundy Drive crime scene, he referred to *they* when describing the glove, not *it*. While this might seem to be a mere slip of the tongue to most people, I felt it was odd coming from a detective whose job it is to scrutinize a crime scene, make careful notations, and give precise testimony as to what he had seen. If my experience has taught me one thing, it's that seemingly slight anomalies often deserve a closer look. And there was no doubt that Fuhrman's story needed further investigation.

But the defense was neither prepared nor equipped to maximize their good fortune at being afforded a view of the State's case at the hearing. In fact, they did not yet know that Fuhrman's own history as a racist and a liar would blow up in the prosecution's face.

What the defense team would soon discover was this: *The pivotal witness in the prosecution's case, Mark Fuhrman, had filed a lawsuit in 1983 seeking early retirement on the grounds that he was no longer able to deal with minorities because of his strong bias against them.*

The failure of the defense to discover and surface Fuhrman's file, with its many references to his poor character, probably squandered a golden opportunity to put the case against Simpson to rest before it reached first base. But once Fuhrman testified that he'd found a glove at Rockingham, it would have taken the courage of a lion to throw the glove out considering that Fuhrman's credibility went unchallenged. Judge Kennedy-Powell did not strike me as a shrinking violet. Had the defense known about the 1983 Fuhrman file and presented it, the judge might well have directed the defense to further explore that litigation, and particularly the resulting expert opinions describing Fuhrman's instability, and ultimately she might have declined to bind the case over for trial unless some additional corroboration could be shown. If she had excluded the evidence and refused to bind Simpson over for trial unless and until additional facts were presented, the case against Simpson would have ended. However, unless and until he was charged formally in the Superior Court, and a trial jury was in the box—already sworn, *and the first prosecution witness had been called and at least sworn,* no "jeopardy" would have attached to the proceedings. That means that if a mistrial should occur for any reason other than being triggered by the defense, "double jeopardy" would have barred any further prosecution of the charges for which the jury was sworn to decide.

Therefore, there was no need for the rush to judgment which caused this case to become a shambles. The cops had plenty of time, because a public personality such as Simpson was at the time hardly a risk of flight. But the prosecution chose sensationalism and favorable publicity over professionalism.

By the time the court took a break for the day, and before Fuhrman's evidence was complete, I got Shapiro on the phone.

"This guy is rotten," I said of Fuhrman. "I can feel it in my bones. If Gerry Uelmen [the defense attorney who was conducting the cross-examination] doesn't dismantle him, this witness is going to be the one who'll cause Simpson to be tried, and to carry the case to a jury. Fuhrman's glove story is full of holes, and I suspect the prosecutors know it. You had better take him apart!"

Unfortunately, despite my warning, Fuhrman skated through his cross-examination with hardly a ripple. To make matters worse, I could see that Uelmen was somewhat hard of hearing, which probably explained, in part, why he failed utterly to catch some of this witness's important missteps. (I did not realize until later that neither Shapiro nor Uelmen had any meaningful experience cross-examining slippery cop witnesses in a homicide case.)

As it turned out, my instincts about Mark Fuhrman were solidly grounded. We didn't know all of it then, but two key findings that unfolded before and during the trial would prove him to be a bigot, a liar, and a dirty detective who supported brutality against minority suspects and planting evidence:

1. As mentioned, in 1983, Fuhrman filed a lawsuit for a stress disability pension because of his penchant for violence against minorities.[1]
2. During the trial, the infamous "Fuhrman Tapes" emerged—thirteen hours of recorded conversations whereby Fuhrman hurled racial insults and spoke favorably of violence against people of color.[2]

Unfortunately, except for two minor racial slurs, the gravamen of his contempt for African Americans would never reach the jury.

* * *

The next key component of the preliminary trial was the prosecution's proposed timeline for the murders.

To reconstruct a murder scenario in which Simpson was the killer, the police and the prosecution had to perform some serious metamorphosis of the facts. Bear in mind that the prosecution team was acutely aware from the outset that the timeline presented a problem. Therefore, to present a plausible theory of guilt to Judge Kennedy-Powell at the preliminary hearing, the time available for O. J. to perform the grisly deed had to be altered. Although it knew otherwise prior to June 17, the prosecution fixed upon the time of the murders as **10:15 p.m.** because Simpson was not seen (at his residence) until about *10:55*. This gave the prosecution forty minutes within which—it contended—Simpson could have left the scene, hid the bloodied clothes and knife, and rid his body and vehicle of all traces of blood, before leaving for Chicago that night. As every detective knows, getting rid of blood evidence completely is very, very difficult.

But establishing the murders as having occurred at 10:15 p.m. posed many problems: This time did not square with the testimony of several other witnesses who were nearby the scene, who consistently reported hearing a commotion beginning for the first time about twenty minutes later. Additionally, Mr. Fenjves's ability to fix the time was vague, and he offered no corroborating circumstances, such as the nature of the news being reported on the TV he was watching when he heard the "plaintive wail" of a dog. Fenjves was the only prosecution witness to be called to testify at the preliminary hearing about the time of the onset of the disturbance.

It was settled as a necessary strategy, apparently. The prosecution had decided which witnesses to avoid in their presentation. Tragically, counsel for the defense were not far enough along in their own investigation of the neighborhood witnesses to take advantage of the judge's invitation to call their own.[3]

Although we will never learn to what extent the police orchestrated the "changes from reality" which had to be accomplished to accommodate the 10:15 p.m. murder time, and to what extent they were directed along the way by lawyers working for District Attorney Gil Garcetti, the finger of suspicion points heavily at the latter.

Later that summer, the defense team would get busy doing its own very intense investigation of the timeline surrounding the murders. McKenna and McNally had found witnesses that made the prosecution's claim that the murders began at 10:15 p.m. highly doubtful. *And* at least one of those witnesses had a *precise time record* from a phone and computer log.

But at the time the preliminary hearing ended, the defense

didn't yet have the benefit of this evidence. Without it, the six-day preliminary hearing concluded with Judge Kennedy-Powell citing "ample evidence" for trial.

On July 22, Simpson entered his plea: "Absolutely one hundred percent not guilty."

CHAPTER 3
The Team Assembles

On June 14, 1994, the night of O. J. Simpson's aborted polygraph examination, when Shapiro and I first discussed the case, there was no talk of any further involvement on my part. But as the days went by, he asked for additional bits of help. First, I was invited to be the spokesperson to the national news media for the Simpson defense team. And after the preliminary hearing was completed, Shapiro wanted me to assist him in preparing the case *and* to supervise the activities of the various investigators who had been retained.

After the publication of two magazine articles which trumpeted the fact Mark Fuhrman had attempted to get an early pension by claiming that he was disabled, essentially from having been forced to deal with minority gang members (which had supposedly "burned him out" to the point where he could no longer function as an effective police officer), Shapiro reluctantly admitted that the investigator he hired dropped the ball by not discovering this explosive piece of evidence, which was a matter of public record, before the preliminary hearing. He also asked whether I would take over responsibility for the preparation of the entire case, and make sure that no other critical pieces of information were overlooked.

At that point, I got very, very busy.

Soon after, I appeared on *Face the Nation*. The host asked if we planned to use the insanity defense. I assured him we would not and said that O. J. would plead not guilty and the prosecution would have to prove otherwise to win their case. Another guest was Bob Bennett, who would later become President Clinton's lawyer in the Paula Jones lawsuit. Years earlier, Bennett and I had worked together, defending Saddam Hussein in a mock trial for the American Bar Association. Bennett's brother, Bill, one-time secretary of education, had already told the press that Simpson was clearly guilty. I chided Bennett, speculating that during his time at Harvard Law School, his brother had somehow escaped the teachings of famed legal professor Alan Dershowitz about the presumption of innocence. Bennett simply shook his head and said, "I am not my brother's keeper."

Not long after that, I did a morning TV segment by remote from Burlington, Vermont, where I was handling a federal criminal case. The other guest on the show was Alan Dershowitz himself, a longtime friend and Harvard Law School professor. During the interview, Dershowitz suggested that Bob Shapiro had better make up his mind rather quickly as to whether he was defending his client on the grounds of innocence or whether he was defending him on the grounds of insanity. Right after his appearance, which had been remote from Boston, Alan boarded a flight to Israel. Within the next twenty-four hours, Shapiro had tracked him down there and hired him as appellate defense counsel should the case find itself in need of an appeal.

Despite the fact that Shapiro and I are no longer friends, I must admit that while he was certainly spending Simpson's money at a very brisk pace, he made some good decisions early on. Hiring Dershowitz was one of those decisions.

He also hired Dr. Henry Lee, for many years the head of criminalistics for the Connecticut State Police, and one of the most formidable witnesses ever to take the stand. His purpose was to analyze the physical evidence, the way it had been gathered and the way it had been preserved, tested, and stored. At the same time, he also brought Dr. Michael Baden, former head of the Office of the Medical Examiner of the City of New York—and subsequently chief medical examiner for the New York State Police—on board. Both were top-notch experts in their field, and both proved to be assets when the trial rolled round.

And, at O. J.'s insistence, Shapiro brought in former LA prosecutor-turned-defense attorney Johnnie Cochran. He was handsome, very well-spoken, and had made a career out of suing police officers for brutality, discrimination, and other bad conduct. When LA District Attorney Gil Garcetti decided that the trial would be moved to downtown LA rather than the predominately white Santa Monica where the murders occurred, it meant that the constituency in the jury box would be primarily black. Johnnie, with years of representing underserved minorities, felt like the perfect fit for the defense team.

However, at the time Simpson was charged with the murders of his ex-wife and her friend, Johnnie was already representing pop singer Michael Jackson against allegations of child abuse—charges Jackson denied. Jackson was uncomfortable with whatever unwanted or unnecessary publicity might arise from Johnnie taking the high-profile Simpson case, thus relating the two of them. Ultimately, Johnnie could not resist the opportunity to confront the greatest challenge of his lengthy and distinguished career as a trial lawyer. So, Jackson hired other very competent counsel, and Cochran came into the Simpson camp.

Prior to adding Johnnie Cochran to the case, lawyers of demonstrated prominence—both within California and elsewhere—had given indications that they would be more than willing to step in and take over, or even just participate. Prominent among these was Gerry Spence of Wyoming, a colorful lawyer who was a regular on *The Larry King Show*. Bob Shapiro thought Spence was pushing overtly to be hired as chief counsel. When O. J. raised a question about Spence's offer to come aboard, Bob sought to close the door by saying dismissively, "We've got the best, Lee Bailey. Why would you want to downgrade?" Effectively, he wanted me posted at the palace gate to ward off the competition.

My position on the team also gave Bob something else he wanted and needed: a spokesman with legitimate credentials. I had gotten a call from David Margolick of the *New York Times* who asked me "what the hell" Bob Shapiro was doing as lead defense counsel, given his dearth of felony trial experience. I tried to duck the question, for which there was no good answer. "Why don't you ask Bob?" I suggested. David said he had, several times, but Shapiro wasn't returning phone calls.

As things worked out, another important element in the case was the jurist who presided over it. The matter had been assigned for trial to Judge Lance Ito, a former prosecutor who happened to be married to the most senior female officer in the LAPD, a captain named Peggy York. Based on this relationship, and to avoid any suspicion that he might try to give the police a helping hand with his rulings, Judge Ito offered to recuse himself.

Most defense lawyers would have quickly accepted this offer with a certain amount of grace, but not Bob Shapiro. He told Judge Ito that the defense would be more than happy to have him preside.

Upon learning of this development, I asked Shapiro why he had done this, pointing out that no matter the solid reputations of the people involved, pillow talk between a presiding trial judge and a senior captain of police, whose department's reputation was seriously on the line in the wake of the Rodney King beating that occurred three years earlier and sparked riots all over the city, was all but inevitable. When I asked Shapiro why in the world he didn't let him disappear, Bob's answer was, "Ito loves me."

I groaned internally. It's one of the cheapest shots in trial work: Tell the client the judge is very partial to you, and you are likely to survive as counsel no matter how egregious your blunders. By allowing Judge Ito to remain, Shapiro passed up the next judge in line, Paul Flynn, described by many of our colleagues as the best on the bench. I felt that could be a steep price to pay, but Shapiro was adamant that Judge Ito's affection for him would be a solid counterpoint to any sympathies he might have for his wife's organization.

It turned out, Shapiro's romance with Judge Ito was short-lived. Less than a month later, Judge Ito made an unfavorable ruling regarding a small knife found in Simpson's home, and Shapiro became impatient and described the judge as "disingenuous." Because of his modest speech skills and limited inventory of fifty-cent words, I believe that Bob did not know the meaning of the word, and that he had not meant to call the Judge a liar in open court.

Judge Ito was not pleased, but all he said was, "Mr. Shapiro, you better take a very deep breath and count to ten."

Some judges would have exacted an apology for an insult that blatant. Judge Ito chose to let it ride.

Reporters were asking, "Why offend the trial judge even before there's a jury in the box?"

Why, indeed . . .

* * *

Before the trial, Bob appeared to be calling the shots. To bring the team together, he'd rented a beautiful, spacious conference room in a Beverly Hills law firm, inviting me, Johnnie, Alan Dershowitz, and Drs. Lee and Baden for weekly meetings on the case. He paid $7,500 a day for the room, a foolish extravagance, in my opinion. But, it was easy to spend his client's cash and, for Bob, appearances are everything.

When Johnnie joined the team in August, Shapiro immediately began to wage a power struggle as to who the *real* leader of the team would be. Cochran, whom I liked immediately and who was a fellow of cool judgment, did not push the issue, but waited patiently until he felt he was thoroughly entrenched.

Meanwhile, I was busy managing the lead investigators who were unearthing and documenting critical witness statements and piecing together the timeline and other details that would support Simpson's innocence.

What they were uncovering proved to be startling.

CHAPTER 4

CHAPTER 4

The Night of the Murders and What Happened Next

The first part of any criminal defense investigation is to start at the beginning.

Orenthal James Simpson had spent the afternoon of Sunday, June 12, 1994, at the dance recital of his youngest daughter, Sydney. That night, he was scheduled to take a red-eye flight from Los Angeles to Chicago to participate in a round of golf the following day at the behest of his "he runs through airports" sponsor, Hertz Rent-A-Car. Simpson was booked on American Airlines flight 668 departing Los Angeles International Airport (LAX) at 11:45 p.m.

Simpson had expected his usual hired limousine driver to pick him up at about 10:45 p.m., but a new driver, Allan Park, who had never been to Simpson's home at 360 North Rockingham Avenue in Brentwood came instead. Park wanted to make sure that he was not late, and arrived at the locked gate on the Ashford Street side of Simpson's home early, at about 10:25 p.m. He saw no one. Not knowing how to gain access to the gate to pull up in front of the door, he sat just outside it with his headlights on, illuminating the front door area for half an hour. During that time, he did not see any people or vehicles arriving or leaving.

At 10:55 p.m., Park noticed a figure in the entryway of Simpson's home heading into the house. He noticed a bag in the entryway. Park buzzed the intercom and spoke to Simpson, who said he'd overslept. Park was let in through the gate, where he parked in front of the entryway. Simpson brought out more bags, including his golf bag, and he and Park loaded his luggage into the limo.

Kato Kaelin testified that he also helped load the bags, and he noticed a small, dark bag on the driveway, and offered to grab it. Simpson told him, "That's okay, I'll get it," and loaded the bag into the vehicle. Prosecutors would later refer to this "mysterious bag" that Simpson didn't want anyone touching because it contained items related to the murders.

With the bags loaded, Park drove as rapidly as he could to the Los Angeles International Airport's American Airlines terminal. At one point, he got lost and Simpson directed him back on course. The divider between the front and back seats in the limo was down for the entire trip, and Simpson and Park talked back and forth for most of the ride.

When the limo arrived at the curb, two baggage handlers—Michael Gladden and Michael Norris—appeared and asked for Simpson's autograph. Even though his flight was about to close its doors, Simpson, following his generally affable custom, agreed. After signing the autographs, he walked quickly to the gate.

Despite his Hertz pitchman persona, Simpson did not *run* through airports. In this case, he hurried on board as the last passenger, and took his seat in first class. Once he was settled in, Simpson spotted an old friend—Howard Bingham—a well-known photographer. (When he testified at the criminal trial, Bingham referred to himself as "the world's greatest photographer.") Bingham and Simpson exchanged small talk. In his usual pleasant and chatty mood, Simpson was smiling comfortably throughout the flight.

After the aircraft was leveled and cruising, the captain, Wayne Stansfield, emerged from the cockpit with his logbook in hand and sat next to Simpson. He wanted Simpson's autograph in the logbook, and they talked together for fifteen or twenty minutes before the captain returned to his station.

Meanwhile, back at Nicole's condo at about 10:55 p.m., a neighbor, Steven Schwab, was walking his dog when he spotted on the corners of Bundy Drive and Dorothy Street what would turn out to be Nicole's Akita. The dog was acting very agitated and had what appeared to be blood or mud on its paws. Schwab checked the dog's collar and found it had no name or address so he decided to take the dog home until he could determine the next best step in how to reunite the animal with its owner.

As Schwab and his wife were determining their options, their neighbors, Sukru Boztepe and his wife, who lived in the same apartment building, arrived. To be helpful, Boztepe agreed to take the dog for the evening. But once in their apartment, the Akita was still disconcerted so at about midnight they decided to walk the dog around the neighborhood in an attempt to soothe the animal and hopefully find its owner. They walked the dog up Bundy Drive, and it paused directly in front of Nicole Brown Simpson's condo. Boztepe followed the dog's gaze and saw what appeared to be a body on the ground on the condo's walkway. Boztepe and his wife immediately notified a neighbor, who called the police.

At about 12:30 a.m., Officer Robert Riske of the Los Angeles Police Department was dispatched to 875 South Bundy Drive. When the officer arrived at the residence, he saw two dead bodies inside the main gate to Nicole Brown Simpson's condominium, and called for help. Detectives Ron Phillips and Mark Fuhrman were awakened and sent to the scene. When they arrived at about 2:00 a.m., Fuhrman quickly realized that the female victim was the ex-wife of football legend O. J. Simpson. He had in 1984 once responded to a "415 call—Family Dispute" and had spoken with both parties at their home at 360 Rockingham, a property just a couple of miles away.

Mark Fuhrman must have realized that he was working the biggest case of his career. But that glory was almost fleeting, because a short time later, a call came from Parker Center, LAPD headquarters. Two of the most experienced homicide detectives on the force—Tom Lange and Philip Vannatter—would be taking over. Fuhrman and Phillips would be relieved as soon as they arrived.

The detectives examined the Bundy crime scene and its surrounding area. Nicole's children were found to be sound asleep alone inside her condo. They were taken into police protective custody.

Shortly after 5:00 a.m., Fuhrman suggested[1] the investigators go to Simpson's house to see who was there and whether they were in any peril. Fuhrman, Phillips, Lange, and Vannatter went to the Rockingham home in two separate vehicles. When they arrived, they found that the front entrance gate—the same gate that had blocked driver Allan Park from entry several hours before—was locked. As Detectives Lange and Vannatter pondered how they might gain entrance, Fuhrman, who said he had noticed blood on the driver's side of a white Bronco parked on Rockingham, jumped the wall and let them all enter through the Ashford gate.[2]

The detectives did not immediately approach the house. They went first to the attached bungalow and knocked on its door, where they were greeted by Kato Kaelin, a houseguest who lived there. Before moving to Rockingham as O. J's guest, the young man, an aspiring actor, had lived with Nicole in her condo and traded occasional babysitting and other chores for rent. As there wasn't a separate residence at the Bundy Drive home, O. J. offered Kaelin the bungalow at his Rockingham estate, basically rent-free.

After the two senior detectives, Vannatter and Lange, had spoken with Kaelin briefly, Kaelin directed them to Simpson's twenty-five-year-old daughter Arnelle's room, which was also a guest room with a separate entrance. She let them into the main house, and Fuhrman stayed with Kaelin at the bungalow and engaged him in conversation, questioning him about any observations he might have made during the prior evening. Kaelin stated that at about 9 p.m. on June 12, he had gone with Simpson in Simpson's Bentley to get some fast food, and that they had returned to the house at 9:37 p.m. He said he did not see or hear Simpson after that time; however, Kaelin did recall that while talking to a friend on the telephone at around 10:40 p.m. he heard three "thump" noises that apparently came from the vicinity of the air conditioner which was fitted into the wall of his bedroom. The compressor and condenser portion of that unit protruded into a very narrow alley located between the house and a chain link fence that marked the Simpson property line. Kaelin said he had made no effort to investigate the source of the thumps.

Meanwhile, Detective Phillips had learned from Arnelle Simpson that her father had left for a business meeting in Chicago the prior evening, and that he would be staying at the O'Hare Plaza Hotel. As Phillips was trying to reach Simpson by phone, Fuhrman escorted Kaelin from his bedroom to the kitchen where the other detectives were gathered and said to Vannatter, "You need to talk to this guy."[3]

Then Fuhrman disappeared, alone, for about fifteen minutes. During that time, Phillips reached Simpson in his hotel room and gave him the grim news. Fuhrman returned to the kitchen and announced that he had found "something which might be of significance." Fuhrman took the detectives—one by one—to a place in the alleyway on the north side of the house that was close to the protruding air conditioner. There, he illuminated with his penlight, lying on the ground among some dried leaves, a leather glove—apparently made for an adult right hand—which was glistening with some substance on its surface. The glove was collected sometime thereafter by the crime scene lab crew and marked as evidence. It turned out to be an Aris Isotoner Lite, a glove of medium quality, manufactured in the Philippines. For some reason unexplained to this day, that glove was not subjected to DNA testing until October 1994, four months later. And that testing only involved blood on the exterior of the glove. The *interior* of the gloves has *never*—as of this writing—been subjected to DNA testing for traces of human skin, hair, or sweat such as might ordinarily be found in the lining of gloves, *unless* the prosecution tested that area, got an adverse result (either no Simpson, or a third party's DNA), and concealed it.

* * *

When Simpson landed in Chicago at about 6 a.m., on Monday, June 13, a driver and Hertz junior executive named Jim Merrill was on hand to take him to the O'Hare Plaza Hotel where Hertz had booked him a room. Simpson., who checked in at 6:18 a.m., hoped to get a nap prior to being picked up to go to the golf course later that morning.

Shortly after 8:00 a.m. CST, the phone rang in Simpson's hotel room. A male voice, who identified himself as Ron Phillips, said that he was a detective with the Los Angeles Police Department, and told Simpson he had unfortunate news. He said that Nicole Brown Simpson, O. J.'s former wife and the mother of his two younger children, had been killed.

Frantic to get home, Simpson immediately contacted Hertz for assistance in getting back to Los Angeles. He was then connected to Thomas Cook Emergency Travel, and he spoke with an agent there named Lori Menzione. Simpson explained that he had a death in the family and needed to get home. As they were making arrangements for an immediate return flight, Menzione heard a crash and the sound of a phone dropping.

According to Simpson, he had a glass of water in his hands at the time, which he dropped in the shock of the moment. It shattered, resulting in him cutting his hand.

These are her notes from that call:

Caller: The first name is Orenthal.

(Noise in background. Then he asked me to hold on if I could. He returned, apologized, then another phone rang. He asked me to hold for a quick moment. Working in all systems to locate current reservation... I could hear caller speaking in background.)

Caller: I am so sorry but I am trying to get the few items I unpacked re-packed.

(He was moving around room. I could hear a crash like the phone fell on floor.)

Caller: *Hold on.*

(I heard him making a sound water running. He returned in sort of disgust. In meantime, found a few past date records. Nothing for day of travel. Mr. Simpson came back online. I asked is everything alright.)

Caller: *Yeah, I just cut myself and I am bleeding. I am sorry but I received a call and was told my wife is dead.*

It's important to note here that, while Menzione's statement is part of the State of California v. Orenthal James Simpson trial record as an offer of proof, Judge Ito *excluded* her testimony on the grounds of incomplete authentication. That was a harsh, unbalanced ruling. There was enough authentication for her testimony to sink a battleship, but Judge Ito felt there was a defect in the chain of custody.[4]

After finally making flight arrangements to return back to Los Angeles, Simpson packed his bags and went to the lobby where—at the side of the counter—one of the front desk clerks tried to stop the bleeding in his hand, first with a compress by wrapping it and then applying a bandage. Later various hotel personnel said they noticed Simpson was frustrated and distraught as they helped him with his hand, and he demanded a cab to the airport.

Pat McKenna handled the defense investigation in Chicago. In his first report, which he filed on July 3, 1994, Pat wrote:

> Later that evening [Friday, June 17, five days after the murders of Nicole Brown Simpson and Ron Goldman], I was informed that the Chicago Police Department, following a request from the Los Angeles Police Department, had gone to the O'Hare Plaza Hotel... to conduct interviews and secure Room 915, O. J. Simpson's room...I learned that the crime scene personnel had taken photographs and drawn a plat of the suite, as well as processed fingerprints from a bathroom countertop and the telephone. They also found and processed broken glass from the bathroom

sink; the individual with whom I spoke would not tell me
if there was blood on the broken glass; But did say that
the sheets, pillowcases, washcloth and towel appeared to
them to be blood-stained... My source told me it was the
opinion of the Chicago Police Department that the blood
in the hotel room was probably fresh blood and probably
came from the broken glass in the sink. They didn't feel
that someone would be cleaning blood from themselves
in Chicago four hours after suffering a cut in Los Angeles.

On Monday, June, 20, McKenna interviewed key hotel personnel
at the O'Hare Plaza:

> I arrived at the hotel manager, Mr. Powers's office at 9:00
> a.m. on Monday morning, but was told he was in a meet-
> ing and could not see me. I stayed there and noticed that
> Mr. Powers was meeting with detective Bert Luper of the
> Los Angeles Police Department and another officer who
> was later introduced to me as Mike Fleming of the Chicago
> Police Department. When their business was concluded, I
> introduced myself, and Detective Luper asked to see me
> outside. I showed my identification to Detective Luper
> and explained that I was representing Robert Shapiro as
> an investigator and needed to conduct my investigation in
> a professional and timely manner. I asked Detective Luper
> if he was instructing hotel personnel not to speak to me,
> and he assured me this was not the case...
>
> I watched Detective Luper give numerous on-camera
> interviews during the week and I saw him becoming more
> and more animated with the press as he seemed to thor-
> oughly enjoy being in the limelight. For example, when
> he was questioned about the renewed efforts to search
> the field next to the hotel, he said that after returning to
> Los Angeles, he received information that gave him the
> impression that the murder weapon could be in Chicago,
> thus further fanning the flames of media hype against

O. J. Simpson. With respect to the cops' theory that O. J. Simpson left the hotel and buried the murder weapon in the field, an 'anonymous witness' surfaced in the news saying that he saw a man resembling O. J. Simpson leaving the field. Bert Luper indicated on camera that he wanted to interview that witness. It should be noted that just south of that field is the Cumberland Metro Office Center which houses dozens of companies that employ black males who routinely walk past the O'Hare Plaza to get to the Elevated train station in their commute to and from work.

Simpson's flight back to Los Angeles was on an American Airlines flight, in a coach seat on a plane that left Chicago at 9:15 a.m. He sat in the first row, aisle seat on the right-hand side. In front of him on the bulkhead was an air-to-ground telephone.

Seated next to Simpson was Mark Partridge, a Harvard-trained patent lawyer from Chicago. Partridge noticed that Simpson was frantic, and that he made a series of phone calls from the airplane. Because Partridge sensed that these calls involved something quite serious, he made handwritten notes, and then later wrote a letter outlining all of his observations in substantial detail, which he sent to both the prosecution and the defense.

In these calls, according to Partridge's notes, Simpson obviously did not know the details of what had happened to Nicole, and was calling a number of different people attempting to find out.

When the flight landed in Los Angeles, Simpson went immediately to his Rockingham home where he encountered Detective Philip Vannatter, who directed LAPD officer Donald Thompson to put handcuffs on Simpson and take him to the station for an interview. At about that time, Simpson's attorney Howard Weitzman arrived on the scene. After asking police if Simpson was charged with any crime and being told "Not yet," he demanded that the officers remove the cuffs, which they did. Weitzman agreed to accompany Simpson to police headquarters where the detectives could question him. But Vannatter and Detective Tom Lange told

Weitzman they would not interview Simpson in his presence, so Weitzman said the interview was cancelled. But Simpson insisted that he wanted to talk to the police with or without his attorney present to help the investigation, and said he thought he had a duty to do so. Weitzman had no choice but to watch his client go off to the station without him, against his advice.

At the station, for nearly three hours, Vannatter and Lange asked Simpson one very pointed question after another. About fifty minutes of the interrogation was committed to audiotape, and a copy was turned over to the defense early in the case. Most statements by even the most innocent suspects yield something police can use as incriminating, but Simpson's statement was all but flawless in this respect. The recorded fifty minutes of statement, which is very straightforward, sheds little light upon the question why or by whom Nicole had been so brutally murdered.[5] On one issue, O. J. was sheepish, and said he hoped the detectives would not make it public. He had once bought a set of earrings for Nicole and given them to her as a gift from him and their children. After they split up, she gave the earrings back to him, and he then gave them to Paula Barbieri, his girlfriend, a model from the Florida Panhandle. Beyond that one little secret, the resulting tape-recorded interview was to be a powerful weapon in the defense arsenal because Simpson seems to have the expected response of a shocked and grieving spouse. He's in no way defensive or wary. The tape would not be helpful to the prosecution. Like so many compelling pieces of the puzzle, however, it was one the jury never got to see. The defense repeatedly offered the statement in evidence, against the fierce objections of the prosecution. But, Judge Ito sided with the prosecutors each time.

After the statement was completed, Simpson was released. Later that day, Simpson's business lawyer, Leroy "Skip" Taft, and O. J.'s friend Robert Kardashian, decided that in permitting Simpson to talk to the police without counsel present, Weitzman had provided "ineffective service" and should be replaced. That evening, they interviewed and retained Robert Shapiro. (In fairness to Weitzman, he had tried his best to prevent the "no-lawyer" interview, but had been soundly overruled by his strong-willed client.)

Although Taft and Kardashian couldn't have known it at that moment—and were not competent to evaluate the statement even if they'd had it in hand—Simpson not only did not harm his case with this cooperation, but actually helped it in important ways.

* * *

Simpson was named by investigators as a prime suspect in the case, and was about to be arrested when Bob Shapiro agreed that Simpson would turn himself in to Parker Center, the LAPD head-quarters, at 11 a.m. on June 17. That morning, Simpson, several of his counsel, and a few friends gathered at the home of his friend Robert Kardashian. At some point that morning, an emotional Simpson slipped away with his friend, Al Cowlings, which would eventually lead to the sensational low-speed chase. Simpson had asked Cowlings to take him to the cemetery where Nicole had been buried. Simpson was carrying a gun, and Cowlings began to worry that Simpson was suicidal.

After a tense journey through the streets of Los Angeles, watched by an estimated 95 million people on television, Cowlings drove Simpson back to his residence at Rockingham where he was met by detectives, arrested, and taken to jail to await his following court proceedings. Now determined to be a flight risk, Simpson remained in jail throughout his nearly yearlong court proceedings, without the opportunity to make bail.

At a press conference the day of the arrest, memorably, Robert Kardashian read aloud the apparent suicide note that Simpson had left behind, which began, "First, everyone understand. I have nothing to do with Nicole's murder. I loved her; always have and always will."

Between Simpson's arrest and a preliminary hearing schedule to begin June 30, the defense team began its own investigation into what happened the night of the murders. Bill Pavelic, an investigator brought onboard by Shapiro, questioned a few witnesses, but his effort was generally superficial. (Bill had worked for the LAPD for nineteen years, and he retired as a detective a few days before he would have been eligible for a pension because of a dispute over policy with the department.)

I had recommended that Shapiro hire investigators Pat McKenna and John McNally, although they were just beginning to be involved prior to the preliminary hearing. Pat's initial focus was determining the events that occurred with Simpson in Chicago, and he spent time interviewing witnesses and hotel staff and police investigators.

CHAPTER 5
Pillars of Innocence

During the summer months, the investigators Pat McKenna and John McNally made good headway finding and producing support for the multiple defenses which had emerged in Simpson's case after their investigation.

These "pillars of innocence" represent the *affirmative defenses*, providing evidence that *contradicts* guilt. (This evidence stands quite apart from the defense case that criticizes the people's evidence, which we will review in detail later as it relates to the bloody glove and DNA findings.) In other words, these affirmative defenses—if accepted—show that the defendant *couldn't* have committed the crime and any evidence suggesting they did is erroneous.

The evidence arising from our investigation showed four totally independent principal lines of defense: the **timeline**, which would prove that there was no realistic opportunity for Simpson to commit the murders; the **demeanor evidence**, which presents the defendant's emotional response and affect as inconsistent with someone who could have committed the crimes; the **statement** made by O. J. immediately following his return home, which does not incriminate him; and the **lack of motive**.

I. The Timeline

The first, and by far the most significant, defense was that of the timeline. A timeline is a composite defense, meaning that when the testimony of *several witnesses* is linked, it provides evidence that it would have been impossible for the defendant to have committed the crime charged since he was in the company of others throughout the period of time when the crime occurred—even though no single person could account for the entire time span involved.

The single alibi defense, on the other hand, is one of the most conclusive and yet most risky in the weaponry of criminal law responses to accusations of crime. It simply relies on the principle that everybody's got to be somewhere all of the time and nobody can be in two places any of the time. If an alibi consists of records that show the suspect was in jail when the crime was committed elsewhere, or that he was paying a social visit to the Vatican, this would generally be considered airtight and would probably discourage the prosecution from going to trial. Alibis of this strength are rare, but I have had them happen.

However, the alibi defense is generally fraught with problems. Years ago, the Massachusetts Supreme Judicial Court permitted an instruction to juries which said, in effect, the defendant has raised the defense of alibi and if you accept his evidence in support of an alibi, then he must be acquitted. But you are cautioned that an alibi is frequently the product of subornation of perjury and is to be viewed with a jaundiced eye.

While the instruction was patently unfair, and has since been discontinued, it was grounded in the fact that too often a defendant asked to produce an alibi witness (especially for crimes committed in darkness) can only call upon family members, loved ones, and friends to establish his whereabouts at the time of the crime. This circumstance is the one which caused the court in Massachusetts to uphold such an instruction, because it is certainly true that loved ones and close friends may be persuaded to give false testimony, establishing an alibi which is fabricated. However, they are also capable of telling the truth.

So now imagine that the timeline is like a bridge over a chasm hundreds of feet deep. Most people would be skeptical of the notion that it would be safe to walk across a chasm of that sort supported by a single plank of wood. But many who would shy from this adventure would more readily accept a crossing on a bridge made up of many pieces of wood that had been carefully bound together so that no single failure of a component of the bridge could bring it down.

Compared to a straight alibi, a timeline defense is preferred by most defense lawyers, and we worked carefully to establish ours, "minute-by-minute." Our investigation provided this breakdown of the evening of June 12, 1994, in Brentwood, California, the night the murders occurred:

[10:00 p.m.] The 900 block of South Bundy Street
Tom Lang[1]—Lang is a witness who never testified[2] at the trial, but who may have been the only person who could have gotten a glimpse of the killer (or killers) that fateful evening. More important, this is the *first time* his name and witness account has ever been shared with the public, other than one short police report which was—alas!—falsified. Lang and his wife had just arrived home from a trip, and after a short debate as to whether they ought to unpack that evening or wait until morning, Tom decided to walk his dog. At 10 p.m., he stepped out the front door—a few doors south on Bundy from Nicole's condominium—and turned left on South Bundy Drive.

As he approached Dorothy Street, he heard the sounds of a "party." He said there were loud voices coming from the area near the intersection. Lang was approximately seventy-five feet from the intersection when he first heard the voices.

[Note: The sounds of the party were independently corroborated by witness Francesca Harman. She had been at a dinner party with at least four coworkers at 11908 Dorothy Street, Apt. 110.]

At the intersection, Lang noticed a Ford Model 350 pickup truck parked on the west side of South Bundy—a model he recognized because, as he told McKenna, who interviewed him on August 12, 1994, he was a contractor and he'd owned eleven Fords, and one of them had been a 350 truck. The truck's passenger door was open. Standing in the street next to the truck was a blonde woman dressed in dark clothing whom Lang thought was arguing with a passenger in the truck.

Lang also noticed a man standing directly in front of Nicole's gate, but he did not recognize any of the people involved, even though the man was well-lit with a street light above him. As Lang later said in the statement he gave to the LAPD, the man appeared to be about 5'11", and had his fists clenched, and standing in what Lang described as a "menacing" posture.

According to McKenna's August 23, 1994, memo, Lang described this man as "a male White or Hispanic standing on the sidewalk approximately fifty feet north of the vehicle, facing both the vehicle and Mr. Lang. The man was wearing a short sleeve shirt and long pants and had assumed an angry stance, slightly bent at the waist and with both fists clenched. Mr. Lang believed the man was possibly angry at him for walking his dog on the sidewalk without a leash. The man did not make any move toward him and Mr. Lang walked out of view, west on Dorothy Street. He did not see any of the persons or the vehicle again that evening.

"Concerned that his dog would volunteer to join the argument, Lang commanded a left turn west on Dorothy Street, and the dog obeyed. Lang neither saw nor heard any further commotion. According to Tom and Mrs. Lang, all of this took place at or about 10:00 p.m."

It is significant to note that Lang called the police on Monday, June 13, and was put on hold. When someone finally got to him, he said he had information about what he observed the night of the murders and provided his contact information. Lang was then interviewed by Detective Payne of the LAPD on June 20. Lang had made notes and offered them to Payne. When Pat McKenna interviewed Lang, they retraced Lang's steps up Bundy to Dorothy that evening and Lang provided McKenna with the same notes he'd shared with police.

After Lang provided his witness statement to police, Detective Payne, who interviewed him thereafter, *falsely reported* that Lang had said he'd seen a woman in a "white, flowing dress," thus eliminating the woman as Nicole, who was wearing a short, black halter dress when she was killed. But in fact, Lang had stated the woman was wearing dark clothing, which matched the dress Nicole was wearing that evening. Payne's change of a critical fact can hardly have been inadvertent. It took Lang down from a devastating defense witness to a contradictory one, a shabby but all too common police practice.

Unfortunately, Lang was one of the important defense witnesses who was prevented from testifying because of the ticking clock. We had a dwindling jury pool, which became an increasing dark cloud that hovered over this trial from the start, as you will learn.

[10:25 p.m.] A restaurant called Mezzaluna on San Vicente Boulevard

First-daters Danny Mandel and Ellen Aaronson had just finished dinner at Mezzaluna restaurant where Nicole Brown Simpson and her family had dined earlier that evening, and where Juditha Brown, Nicole's mother, had left her eyeglasses—the same glasses which Ron Goldman would bring to Nicole's condo as a courtesy, a fatally kind gesture on his part. The couple, Mandel and Aaronson, walked south by 875 South Bundy Drive (Nicole Brown Simpson's condo) at about 10:25 p.m. and didn't notice any commotion—no loose or barking dog on the sidewalk or the front walkway, no people anywhere in sight.

[Between 10:33 p.m. and 10:35 p.m.]
Denise Pilnak, who lived at 918 South Bundy, was with her friend, Judy Telander, who had been with her at her residence since 2 p.m. that afternoon. Between 10:20 and 10:24 p.m., Pilnak and Telander stood on Pilnak's front porch, discussing how unusually quiet it was on Bundy that evening. After Telander left, Pilnak called her mother. The call ended at 10:28. At 10:35, Pilnak heard a dog barking very loudly—a deep, throaty bark that lasted for a long time. Pilnak knew that the loud barking was clearly that of Kato, Nicole's Akita.

When Pilnak was questioned by Detective Philip Vannatter, of the LAPD Robbery-Homicide Division, he tried to get Denise to change the time to better match the prosecution's desired timeline, but she checked her telephone bill and reaffirmed it emphatically.

[10:35 p.m.]
Robert Heidstra, another neighbor, was walking *his* dogs at 10:35 p.m. and was in an alley parallel to and about 290 feet east of South Bundy Drive. Heidstra also heard the loud barking, and, fearing that his dogs might not fare well in a conflict with a dog with such a powerful bark, changed directions so that he would not be walking south on South Bundy Drive, as he had intended.

[10:40 p.m.]
While walking up the alley, Heidstra heard a male voice shout, "HEY, HEY, HEY!" and then the sound of a metal gate slamming. That was followed by loud arguing where he heard another male voice speaking rapidly and angrily about something, but it was drowned out by the barking dog. Heidstra walked away from the scene. (We believe that voice yelling, "Hey, hey, hey!" was Ron Goldman, who had unwittingly stumbled on the site of his own murder.) Continuing south to the end of the alley, Heidstra was

standing on the north side of the alley and Dorothy Street, where he could still hear dogs barking. He then observed a large white vehicle proceeding east on Dorothy, turning south on Bundy, away from the crime scene (and *away* from Simpson's Rockingham estate), at a high rate of speed. He estimates this time to be 10:50 p.m.

One must look at the next few minutes of elapsed time, if one is trying to show that Simpson had any opportunity to be the killer: The drive from the scene of the crime to Simpson's home covers 1.83 miles. Fuhrman testified that it took him and fellow LAPD Detective Ron Phillips, leading Detective Vannatter and his partner Detective Tom Lange, five to ten minutes to make the trip. Our investigator Pat McKenna drove the route on several occasions in O. J.'s girlfriend Paula Barbieri's Bronco, which was nearly identical to O. J.'s—between 10:30 and 11 p.m. on a Sunday night with little or no traffic. McKenna's best time was seven minutes. Assuming that seven-minute drive, if Simpson was stabbing Ron Goldman at 10:40 p.m., that would have left him all of about eight minutes to dispose of his clothing and the weapon, shower away the blood residue, meticulously clean his shower, get dressed, pack, and appear at his front door at 10:55 p.m. with bags, ready to get into a limo, which had been parked outside his gates for thirty minutes without seeing anyone arrive.

And there is an additional wrinkle here, bloody footprints that likely belonged to the killer left the crime scene and then returned, presumably to get or look for something that had been left behind. (The murder weapon or weapons or a glove?) We believe, based on expert (pathologist Dr. Irwin Golden's) testimony, that two different knives may have been used.[3] This backtracking by the killer would further reduce the already impossibly small window of time available to Simpson had he been the perpetrator. Added in for good measure, of course, is the fact that Simpson's face was well known—both internationally and certainly in the neighborhood where he frequently visited his young children. With the recent and ongoing commotion, from a barking dog to a shouting male voice, it seems improbable that—so great was the risk of recognition—he would return to the location of the bodies for any reason.

The showing we were prepared to make was that in that fifteen-minute span when a voice (almost surely Ron Goldman's) began to yell, "Hey, hey, hey"—at 10:40 p.m. and O. J.'s emergence from his home at 10:55 p.m., he would have had to have accomplished the following:

First, he'd have had to complete the murder of Ron Goldman, assuming that since no female voice was heard, Nicole was probably dead by the time Goldman's shouts were heard, and retreat to the vehicle, which clearly was parked on the backside of Nicole's condo in a roadway named Greta Green, based on the footprint evidence. Once at the vehicle, he would have doubled *back* to the scene, then returned again to leave.

Second, given the amount of blood that had hemorrhaged from Nicole (and in some locations, squirted from Goldman), the assailant would have been drenched in blood. He would have to effectively shed and conceal his outer clothing or risk getting the interior of his vehicle covered in blood, which would have necessitated an extensive clean-up operation.

Third, at least one knife, and perhaps two as the autopsy suggested,[4] were used in the course of the murders that would have to be discarded. No knife that came close to the specifications of the one which inflicted these wounds was ever discovered. This means that if Simpson had in fact been the killer, he would have had to get rid of the knife (or knives) in addition to the bloody clothes before, during, or after he traveled the approximately seven-minute drive from 875 South Bundy to 360 Rockingham.

Fourth, Simpson would then have had to dispose of his undergarments which inevitably would have suffered some transference of blood from the outer clothing to the inner.

The Brentwood area was repeatedly and intensively searched for bloody clothing and weapons, according to the police, and nothing has ever been found.

And last, within the same time frame, he would have had to take a *very* careful shower, making sure that no tiny flecks of blood remained anywhere on his person or in the drains, or anywhere else in the house where he was likely to have walked as he prepared for his trip to Chicago.

It seems extremely unlikely that a person inexperienced in the business of homicide would have pulled this off.

II. Demeanor Evidence

Prior to and during his trip to Chicago and then the subsequent ride to his hotel, Simpson was, by all accounts, affable and relaxed, completely inconsistent with the demeanor of one who had just butchered his children's mother and her friend who happened upon the scene.[5] Demeanor, when favorable, is a very strong defense in cases involving violent crime, particularly homicide. We felt that we had enough evidence on that issue alone to raise at least a reasonable doubt.

From the time he was first seen at 10:55 p.m. at his Rockingham home by limo driver Allan Park and Kato Kaelin until he was checked into his hotel in Chicago, O. J. was observed by all who saw and spoke to him to be relaxed and congenial. During his chance encounter on the plane with his acquaintance Howard Bingham and airline pilot Wayne Stansfield who had asked for an autograph, nothing about O. J.'s conduct indicated anything was amiss.

Furthermore, earlier in the evening, Simpson's behavior at his daughter's dance recital, his dinner with Kato Kaelin, and his attempts to spend time with his girlfriend before leaving for Chicago in no way suggests a person who has plans to carry out a brutal murder later in the evening.

In addition to interviewing employees of the O'Hare Plaza Hotel, McKenna also recorded interviews with several people who worked for Hertz and had observed Simpson's demeanor both *before* and *after* he got the news about Nicole. As mentioned, the first Hertz employee interviewed was James Merrill, who had been a sales representative for eight months, and had met Simpson's plane at 5:43 a.m. on the morning of June 13, the morning after the double homicide.

McKenna reported,

"Jim says that O. J. was either the first or second person off the plane. He approached O. J. and they shook hands and introduced each other and joked about each being up so early . . . Jim asked O. J. why a red eye flight, and O. J. responded that he had just done a pilot for a movie, had been involved in many events lately, including some for Hertz. He said he hadn't been spending much time with his family and his daughter had a dance recital on Sunday evening and this flight was the first one he could catch following the recital.

Jim stated that he never saw anything about O. J.'s behavior such as sweaty palms or appearance, no unusual thirst requests, no cuts, bruises, or injuries, only that he was a little tired.[6]

Upon arrival at the hotel, Jim helped O. J. check in. Jim drove home and remembers that a couple of hours later, O. J. called his home telephone number and stated, "Jim, I need you to pick me up, please come quickly." He said O. J. sounded very upset, anxious and distraught. Jim assured him that he would get there as soon as he could. Moments later, Jim received his second cellular call from O. J. Again O. J. was very upset, saying, "Where are you? Are you almost here?" It was only then that Jim explained that he was thirty minutes away from the hotel and he was coming as fast as he could.

Jim recalled a third cellular call from O. J. saying, "Where are you, Jim?" Jim responded that he was making good time but that he was still fifteen to twenty minutes away. He recalls saying, 'O. J., you sound very upset, what's wrong?' He thought O. J. was crying, and he heard O. J. put the phone down. O. J. then picked up the phone and said 'Jim, I can't talk about it but please hurry.'"

McKenna also interviewed other Hertz employees who met Simpson after he got the news about Nicole.

On June 23, 1994, I interviewed Dave Kilduff at the Hertz Corporation offices in Des Plaines, Illinois. Mr. Kilduff is a Division Vice President of Sales for the Hertz Corporation. On June 13, 1994, Dave Kilduff picked up John Johnson of Hertz, Jack Reyneart and Jim Hoey from three different flights at the airport and drove them to the O'Hare Plaza Hotel, arriving at approximately 8:45 a.m. As they drove up, he recalls seeing O. J. sitting outside on a bench, and Dave thought that was unusual. Dave parked the car, got out and shook O. J.'s hand, saying "Remember me? Dave Kilduff of Hertz?"...O. J. responded, "You've got to get me to the airport." John Johnson then said "Juice, what's going on?" O. J. responded, "Something really bad has happened, and I need to get to the airport." O. J. got in the car with Dave. O. J.'s hands were at his face and he was visibly upset, saying, "Oh my God, oh my God, this is bad." Dave said O. J. was visibly shaken and on the verge of tears. Dave said he noticed a cut on his left hand which was bandaged and showing some blood on it.

O. J. was fishing in his bag, looking for his ticket. Dave asked, "When is your flight?" O. J. responded, "9:15, we've got to get going, please." Dave said they took off for O'Hare and O. J. kept saying, "Oh my God, this is bad. You're going to hear about this on the news."

III. Simpson's Statement to Police

The third line of defense was the near bulletproof statement that Simpson had given to police. This was, frankly, an extraordinary accomplishment for a layman with no prior police experience who did not have the comfort or the skill of a seasoned defense lawyer by his side. With no chance to have dovetailed his account with those of Park and Kaelin, there is a near-perfect fit between the three statements. O. J. answered every question and volunteered a blood sample and generally agreed to all police requests.

There has been much confusion over the years with whatever happened to the detailed statement O. J. gave to police shortly after he arrived back in Los Angeles from Chicago. Because this is another of the terribly bizarre twists in the Simpson case, it is worth a moment of explanation for its cardinal significance to be properly understood.

In most criminal cases, police detectives get to question a suspect long before he has a lawyer, or even realizes that he needs one. To afford those being questioned some level of protection against unwittingly implicating themselves, the US Supreme Court requires that when the cops are zeroing in on someone they believe to have guilty knowledge of the crime, and if he is in custody at the time, those cops must advise the suspect of his Miranda Rights: That is, that anything he says will be used against him; that he has a right to the advice of a lawyer and if he is indigent, a court will appoint one for him, and that he can stop answering questions at any time during the interrogation. Most criminal cases are disposed of by pleas of guilty, many of them because the defendant made a confession (admitting to the whole crime) or admissions (significant concessions of the truth of facts pointing to guilt). It is not uncommon for skilled investigators to compromise a naïve suspect by framing questions in an unfair manner, so that almost any answer will pour fuel on the embers of suspected guilt and light a fire.

The Simpson interrogation circumstances were almost completely contrary to the usual scenario when a suspect is "taken downtown for questioning." He was at his home at 360 Rockingham when he first met Detectives Lange and Vannatter upon his arrival from the airport. They wanted him to go to Parker Center robbery-homicide headquarters to give him the third degree. Simpson already had a highly qualified lawyer in Howard Weitzman, who was present, but Weitzman had had little chance to confer with his client and thus little concept of the dimension of the case he was undertaking.

The police demanded that they be allowed to exclude Simpson's lawyer from any interrogations that might ensue. Weitzman said that if he were not allowed to sit in, he would not permit Simpson to be interviewed. No thinking lawyer would have done otherwise. His client had different ideas, which a guilty man would have likely considered very risky; but it was risky either way. Police have been known to lie and attribute statements to suspects that were never made. With no witness to join him in contradicting the liar, one can be convicted on that fabricated testimony alone. O. J.'s position was simple: "I'm told my former wife has been brutally murdered, and the cops are asking that I help them. How could I refuse, no matter what my lawyer wanted?"

Seems logical enough, but Simpson had unwittingly cut his legal protection off at the knees. If a client says he wants to talk to the police—even if alone—there is not much a lawyer can do to overrule him. That happened to me only once that I can recall in an unrelated, but significant, case. My client was not very bright, and an arrogant detective had seduced him into having a private talk which I could not attend. The detective smirked as he started to leave the room.

"Officer, you might want to stay with me and enjoy the fireworks. You'll find not much is happening if you just talk to him."

The detective began to pay attention. "What fireworks?"

"Just imagine," I said, "I call for a conference of these nice press people hanging around us like flies, and announce that you have illegally detained my client, and barred him from his constitutional right to a lawyer. I will be seeking sanctions and discipline. You, mister detective, are interrogating my client without his lawyer. I would think we'd have a colorful dustup here within minutes."

The officer looked at me with daggers in his eyes but wouldn't call my bluff. "You can be present," he said.

In his case, Simpson spent nearly three hours alone with Vannatter and Lange, two of the senior detectives in the department. Between them, they had thousands of hours of experience interrogating witnesses and people suspected of crimes. In a session of that length, with two wizened professionals looking for any scrap of an admission or piece of information that might tie O. J. to the crimes, they came up totally empty. They recorded about forty-five minutes of the interview, and we were given a copy, which we transcribed.

From a defense point of view, it was flawless. Simpson was convincing in maintaining that he knew nothing about the crimes. It is more than infuriating to have a client reject his lawyer's advice and seemingly cozy up to the police because such a move by a layman unsophisticated in criminal law almost always produces disastrous results. However, there are times when it can be a brilliant decision. If the suspect-client is factually innocent, and has, say, a valid alibi for the time of the crime, it is best to get it on the table as soon as possible. The most common attack on a defendant's alibi is that it was fabricated after the crime occurred. By offering it to detectives early on, one can show that there was no opportunity to make up a story; therefore, if the account given by the suspect checks out as true, the cops pretty well know that prosecuting this person is going to lead to a dead end, and they will begin to look elsewhere.

People with guilty knowledge of the crime under investigation will often try to feed the cops a story protesting their innocence. Almost inevitably, those folks will make unwitting admissions which are later used against them at trial, simply because they are no match for seasoned cops when it comes to interrogation. But when one is truly ignorant of the facts surrounding the perpetration of a crime, there are no places to trip up, and a suspect's story becomes unwavering. Had Howard Weitzman listened in—as passenger Mark Partridge did on Simpson's Airfone conversations on the trip back from Chicago—he would have been greatly comforted. O. J. clearly had no knowledge of the murders and was desperately trying to find out what had happened to his former wife. Therefore, there were no admissions for the cops to get. When that became clear after more than an hour of questioning,

Lange and Vannatter turned on the tape recorder and took what they could get, including O. J.'s repeated complaint: "You guys aren't telling me anything."

At trial, this transcribed statement became a hot potato. The defense desperately wanted the jury to hear it because it showed a still-bewildered ex-husband whose answers to police questions were completely nonincriminating. At the end of the day, the defense wanted to argue that no guilty man could have survived the intense, experienced questioning of detectives of this caliber. The defense argued repeatedly and forcefully that the document should be received in evidence. We felt sure that O. J.'s performance during this interrogation would go a long way to support a reasonable doubt.[7]

However, the statement was turned away by Judge Ito, who ruled that basically the account was fundamental hearsay—a statement made out of court, not under oath, and not subject to cross-examination—and absent the application of an exception to the rule it would not be admitted. O. J. was alive, well, and present in court, able to tell the jury his story (as set forth in his statement) from the witness stand. Judge Ito did indicate that he might allow the statement in the event Simpson testified. Because we never reached that point in the trial, the chance for the jury to hear the statement died with the verdict.

IV. Lack of Motive

The fourth pillar of the defense was a lack of motive. While it is often said that motive is not a necessary element in the proof of a crime, juries expect to see a motive somewhere in the fabric of the evidence presented. We knew that the prosecution would try to present Simpson as an ex-husband with a murderous rage toward his ex-wife. But we found, in our investigation, no evidence whatever of this or any other motive.

At the recital that evening and during the time O. J. spent with Kaelin up to 9:37 p.m., just one hour before the murders occurred, he evinced no sour mood toward anyone. There was no evidence that anything had happened that would make him suddenly become enraged at Nicole and slaughter the mother of the two small children he adored. To fit the prosecution's theory, O. J. would have to have attempted (unsuccessfully) to arrange a date that evening with his girlfriend, Paula Barbieri, then subsequently have gone to McDonald's with Kaelin as a second resort, *then* work himself into an unprovoked, white-hot rage, searing enough to cause him to murder two people. He would have had to travel to Nicole's house with a knife with the intent to murder her, knowing that his limo ride to the airport was scheduled to arrive at his Rockingham house at 10:45 p.m. where O. J. would be expected to let the driver inside the gate, just before leaving for Chicago.

The only motive ever really put forth during the entire trial was grounded in an incident that occurred in 1989 wherein Nicole and O. J. had gotten into a physical fight in the home. Bruised, she filed a complaint against him. He apologized, pleaded no contest (the equivalent of guilty in the circumstances), and received a sentence of community service, which he completed.

Although several of Simpson's wannabe friends offered some speculation as to the source of his anger with Nicole, two different events pointed in exactly the opposite direction.

In the first situation, Nicole, post-divorce, had acquired a boyfriend named Keith Zlomsowitch, who was in the restaurant service business. He had managed the Mezzaluna in Brentwood and also the one in Aspen, Colorado, which is where, several years earlier, he'd first seen Nicole on a ski site, and told his friend, "That's the most beautiful woman I've ever seen."

One evening, O. J. stood at the front door of Nicole's condominium and, having a plain view of the living room, observed Zlomsowitch sitting on the couch, with Nicole kneeling in front of him and apparently performing fellatio. O. J. took no action other than pressing the front door buzzer and walking away.

The next morning, however, when Simpson came over to visit, he remonstrated with both Nicole and Zlomsowitch for their lack of discretion: Anyone could have walked in on them, including the children. He expressed no anger toward Zlomsowitch, and in no way challenged Nicole's right to have boyfriends. His only concern, he said, was the welfare of the children. Before the grand jury, Zlomsowitch testified to the truth of all of this, adding that Simpson was cordial, unruffled, and "a gentleman" throughout, and mentioned that Simpson offered his hand to him as he was leaving.

The second contradiction of the "angry lover" theory involved O. J.'s protégé, Marcus Allen, who, like Simpson more than a decade earlier, had been a star running back at the University of Southern California.

The year following the Simpson divorce, Allen and his fiancée were married at O. J.'s house with Simpson as the host. Shortly before the wedding, however, Allen had had sexual intercourse with Nicole. While one might easily expect a more fragile man to come unhinged upon learning that one of his best friends and his former wife were "getting it on," O. J.'s only reaction was merely to caution Allen, saying that Nicole could do whatever she wanted with anyone she wanted, but Allen was about to be married and shouldn't be fooling around.[8]

Simpson's behavior repeatedly was inconsistent with the "jealous murderous rage" motive that the prosecution would need to present in order to convince a jury beyond a reasonable doubt. And finally, we have the fifth pillar of innocence . . .

V. The "Shadow" Pillar

There are two conventional ways to prove the occurrence of an event after—sometimes long after—it has taken place. The first is by use of "direct evidence." This would usually consist of testimony by one or more eyewitnesses who claimed to have been on the scene when things were happening and saw or heard the events occurring when they did. These witnesses may be attacked on numerous grounds by the defense and frequently are, since when available they tend to be the backbone of the prosecution's case.

But there are many cases where the crime is concealed, per-formed under stealthy conditions where no eyewitnesses are pres-ent. No one can claim to have seen anything as it happened. The case therefore must wholly depend on "circumstantial evidence" to show guilt.

Criminal prosecutions often depend heavily on circumstan-tial evidence. Some lawyers prefer circumstantial evidence over that which is direct because the human foibles which often infect observation, memory, and oral descriptions can often be badly wobbled by a clever cross-examination. Circumstantial evidence is present when proof of one fact gives rise to a solid *inference* that a consequent fact must be true.

As an example, assume that you heard a loud noise from an adjacent room that sounded like a gunshot. You quickly open the connecting door and see two men near the center of the room. One is on the floor, gasping his life away while blood runs from his chest. The other is standing a few feet away with a gun in his left hand. Turns out that the defendant and the victim bitterly disliked one another over a money dispute.

The survivor is charged with murdering the gunshot victim, who died minutes after you opened the door. You are the only witness other than the defendant, who told the first policeman to arrive on the scene that the victim owned the gun and was trying to kill him; he grabbed the victim's gun hand, and as they strug-gled, it went off, putting a bullet in his chest from close range.

The defense admits that your testimony is accurate. And while one can infer that the defendant shot the victim in anger, is the evidence sufficient to support the requirement of "proof beyond a reasonable doubt?"

The prosecution has established *opportunity*, which is essen-tial, and a *motive* which is not, but is shown in most criminal trials. But has it established an *intentional act*, which is also essential to support a conviction? With nothing more than what is described above in the way of proof, the defendant should be acquitted. Because where the evidence establishes that this could have been intentional and malicious, it leaves lots of room for other theories.

If the defendant's story is to be believed, the shooting was caused by an unlawful assault by the victim, followed by the shooter's efforts to defend himself and disarm his assailant. This would be—in this fictitious example—a reasonable hypothesis of innocence. It is a hypothesis which the prosecutor was unable to contradict. If his case relies only on circumstantial evidence, where inferences must be drawn from what is shown but no direct (eyewitness) proof has been offered, the rule is:

The prosecutor must eliminate every reasonable hypothesis of innocence which could be fitted to the known facts.

Nothing described so far in our fictious scenario would have satisfied that requirement. If the jury had been instructed accordingly, it would have been required to acquit.

While more innocent people are convicted through erroneous eyewitness identifications of suspects, incorrect inferences by judges and jurors have landed far too many hapless defendants behind bars, sometimes for extended periods.

To protect against mistakes of this sort, in cases where circumstantial evidence is relied upon exclusively to support a criminal conviction, this supervening rule is applied—applicable in most US courts, state and federal criminal and civil, as well as military. Where there is no *direct* evidence, but only *circumstantial* evidence, it seeks to protect against one of the great dangers in dealing with purely circumstantial evidence, and that is ambiguity.

Now in the real world, there would have been more—much more—evidence received. This would have included the track of the bullet in the body, from which the angle of the weapon when fired can be determined. The presence or absence of a "stippling" of burnt gunpowder around the entrance wound on the victim's clothing or skin would have enabled an expert to calculate the distance from the weapon's muzzle to the victim's body when it was fired. The manner in which the defendant was holding the weapon when first seen by the witness, together with the location and ownership of any fingerprints found on its surface, could have provided powerful support for, or a sharp contradiction to, the defendant's story.

To review the rule, in purely circumstantial cases, when the evidence is closed, the judge must instruct the jury:

"If a proven fact supports two different inferences, one of which points toward guilt and one of which does not, you must vote not guilty. In other words, the circumstantial evidence you accept if you convict must be such as to *rule out every reasonable hypothesis of innocence*. If not, the defendant is entitled to an acquittal."

Consider the sweep of that rule! Now consider the glove "discovered" at Simpson's home.

It didn't walk there. It was dropped or put there by a human being. Yes, if Simpson had the opportunity to have inadvertently dropped it, that would be one inference which could be drawn if one assumes it was actually discovered there, as Detective Mark Fuhrman claims. Or, one could infer that the killer left it there, trying to cast suspicion on O. J., and at least deflect it away from himself. Or, one could infer that Fuhrman put it there during his suspicious visit to that remote area soon after gaining access to the premises to anchor his role in the case and get his name in the papers because he resented being left at the altar in his first big case.

We thought a jury would have found it impossible to totally accept the first theorem and, at the same time, would have accepted one of the other two. So even if the first four pillars had been toppled, the prosecutors still had an enormous hurdle to confront with this "shadow" pillar.

CHAPTER 6
Case Preparation

In the late fall, by agreement of all the other lawyers by then involved in the case, our already voluminous files had been packed in boxes and shipped to my office in West Palm Beach. For those charged with the final preparation of the case, there would be no holiday respite. Investigators Pat McKenna, John McNally, Howard Harris, and I worked in my conference room on every day but Christmas, organizing documents, photographs, and other exhibits in an orderly fashion so that each could be readily brought to hand when the trial was in progress.

Joining us during this holiday work session was Dr. Bernard Yudowitz, probably the most accomplished criminal homicide psychiatrist in the United States.

By virtue of the official position he held for some years in Massachusetts, Dr. Yudowitz was required to examine any person who'd been arrested in the state for homicide. It was his responsibility to determine whether the accused had the capacity to understand court proceedings, and thus whether they fit to enter the legal system. In this capacity, Dr. Yudowitz had examined more than *five hundred* people who had caused the death of another human being. When I had practiced out of Boston, my law office had used his services on several occasions, both as an examining psychiatrist and thereafter as an expert witness, and always with more than satisfactory results. If any one person in the United

States had the ability to discern, after a lengthy examination, whether an accused killer had any complicity in the crimes, Dr. Bernard Yudowitz was that person.

In the Simpson case, I had hired him to conduct a thorough evaluation of O. J. for a couple of reasons. Although there was no longer a doubt in the defense camp about whether Simpson had participated in the murders of Nicole Brown Simpson and Ron Goldman, I wanted Dr. Yudowitz's assessment of his personality on two important issues.

First, I was puzzled as to what had prompted Simpson to evade arrest in the famous low-speed chase and threaten to take his own life, to become so despondent that he willingly shouldered the very real risk of being shot or killed as a fugitive while he visited Nicole's grave in the midst of that car "chase." Secondly, I wanted Dr. Yudowitz's impression on how Simpson might stand up to a grueling cross-examination, should the prosecution manage to surface a lawyer talented enough to conduct an effective attack on his credibility.

Although it was generally assumed in the defense camp that Simpson would probably have to testify, the team was looking to me to superintend the substantial undertaking of helping a client/defendant with little courtroom experience, i.e., Simpson, to become effective in the witness box.

Those who have little appreciation of—or contact with—courtroom proceedings don't realize the enormous weight which juries usually give to testimony by an accused. Once a defendant elects to offer up his side of the story personally, the jury's focus tends to home in on an evaluation of whether they find the story to be believable, and whether they personally like the defendant. If he is seen in a positive light on both counts, an acquittal is all but assured.

On the other hand, should the jury conclude—after a defendant has been fully tested on cross-examination—that his story has been undermined by inconsistencies in what he has said or by his unpalatable demeanor—or both—jurors tend to look for ways to return a guilty verdict.

This is always the enormous risk faced by a criminal defendant and his counsel who must carefully weigh the decision as to whether the defendant should testify. While it is true that if he remains silent he will have the benefit of instruction from the bench that he had no obligation to take the witness stand, and that the jurors are prohibited from drawing any inference from his silence, history has taught that this rule is almost impossible to follow. (However, an exception applies to military jurors, who are better educated than the average civilian panel, and who are highly disciplined to follow orders whether they agree with them or not.)

Compounding the risk of calling a defendant to the witness stand is a phenomenon I call the appellate aftershock. When the defendant does not testify, supervisory courts of appeal must cobble together from the pieces of information which were admitted in evidence enough of that evidence to support a reasonable doubt. But when the defendant does contribute to that evidentiary matrix, especially where the other evidence is skimpy, appellate courts often fall back upon a line of reasoning that all defense lawyers hate and fear:

Although phrased somewhat differently from case to case, the litany usually follows this avenue of twisted logic: *The jury saw and heard the defendant's testimony and did not find it to be credible as evidenced by their verdict. These circumstances, coupled with the other evidence introduced in this case, are sufficient to sustain the verdict of guilty.*

Dr. Yudowitz spent eight hours in the Los Angeles County jail interviewing Simpson. He then arranged to meet with those members of the defense team who were in South Florida during the Christmas holidays. He certainly had our attention when he entered our conference room that day because he opened with remarks that would warm the cockles of the heart of any defense lawyer. In tones that hinted at exasperation, despite his professional demeanor, he said, "I don't know why they have this guy in jail. He hasn't killed anyone, and there is little or no likelihood that he ever will."

He also went on to explain that, like many athletes and rock stars, Simpson had come from a hardscrabble life and thought subconsciously that his hold on fame was a fragile one. When his former wife was slaughtered, it rattled his persona to the core. Then, when hard on the heels of this tragedy he was accused of killing her, he felt that all had been lost, and lacked the grit to face the situation. This, Dr. Yudowitz said, drove O. J. to flee his home on June 17 as part of the infamous low-speed chase.

Because I expected the prosecution's case to be supported by a very weak link between Simpson and the murders—that is, the testimony of Mark Fuhrman—and because it was clear that Fuhrman's testimony would be sufficient all by itself to prevent a directed verdict of acquittal by the judge, putting Simpson on the witness stand loomed as a critical decision. Had he been an ordinary defendant, I might have been inclined to counsel him to avoid testifying. However, such a decision always belongs to the defendant, and Simpson had made it plain when I first met him in the Los Angeles County jail that he was living for the day when he could face the jury and explain to them his grief for both victims *and* his lack of involvement in the crimes.

As I saw little chance that this attitude would change, it was the clear obligation of the defense lawyers to prepare him as a witness in meticulous fashion.

It is important to note, here, that the average decent citizen is unlikely to turn in a stellar performance on the witness stand unless they have been given some training. Turning claimed recollections into answers that are both responsive and believable is a feat not accomplished easily, and this is especially true when it comes to cross-examination, where the questions are intended to upset the witness and put them in a bad light. A common objective among experienced cross-examiners is to so antagonize the witness as to cause them to get angry. Losing one's temper on the witness stand is almost as deadly as playing Russian roulette with all cylinders of the revolver loaded.

The simple fact is that people with healthy, pleasant personalities tend to make good witnesses, while those whom most of us would prefer to avoid do not fare as well. In all of the many thousands of lectures I have given in the past fifty-five years, by far the most popular topic is "How to Be a Good Witness."

I have given this speech to doctors, lawyers, and law enforcement officers of every kind and at every level including students at the FBI Academy in Quantico. Even those who are not strangers to the courtroom by virtue of their calling—expert witnesses, or experienced investigators—seldom have a deep appreciation of how much weight demeanor and responsive answers carry with those in the jury box.

I offer this detail to throw some light on two aspects of the realities of the trial process to which ordinary citizens have little access. First, and especially in criminal cases, it is common to find that 95 percent of the disputed evidence is the oral testimony of witnesses. Second, because it appeared to be a foregone conclusion in the Simpson case that he would choose to testify, it was critical that the jury see what kind of man he really was. Although I thought—from the outset of the case—that an acquittal was likely, I believe that there is an additional responsibility laid in the lap of counsel who is defending a public figure.

There is an unfortunate tendency among members of the general citizenry to say, when someone is acquitted by a jury, that they "beat the rap." This result is especially unbearable for someone who needs public admiration to be effective in their chosen field. In Simpson's case, as it was clear that most of his accumulated property would be dissipated in paying the costs of a very expensive trial, and if he had any hope of regaining the income he made from being a rental car pitchman and a sports commentator, he would need to be seen, once again, in a favorable light.

For this to occur, his testimony would not only need to raise serious doubts in the minds of the jurors, but also to persuade the public that he was in fact innocent and was wrongly accused at the outset of the case by irresponsible law enforcement officers who—as Johnnie Cochran said more than once during the trial—rushed to judgment. If that seems a lofty goal it is nonetheless attainable if the defendant's testimony is sufficiently persuasive.

Although ultimately the public never got a look at Simpson since we were forced to terminate the trial without calling our most important witnesses—including the defendant himself—the picture that was being painted by the press was extremely degrading with no basis in truth except the old allegations surrounding his one court appearance for domestic violence.

During the trial itself, I was usually the first member of the defense team to arrive at the courthouse on the days I attended. Many of the others on both sides were chronically late, something Judge Ito tolerated without rancor and which I would have put a stop to immediately if I were on the bench. Because my adult life had been spent as a pilot and a lawyer, the importance of being on time has been ingrained in me. So, between 8:00 a.m. and 9:30 a.m., I had a lot of time to review with Simpson the evidence that had already come in; what we anticipated would be available when our turn rolled around to counter that evidence; and what additional evidence we had to show the further unlikelihood of Simpson's having had any participation in the murders.

I found O. J. to be a delightfully consistent human being, without mood swings or depressed moments, which under his circumstances showed a remarkable degree of resiliency.

I spent a good part of my time talking strategy with him and explaining to him what I expected to happen and when, and listening to his ideas as to how that scenario might be changed one way or another.

I also concentrated on gradually turning Simpson into a good witness. It is important to note that in a criminal case, if the jurors like the defendant, they are very apt to believe him or at least try to believe him. If they believe his story, and he has a positive defense such as a timeline, he will almost surely be acquitted. If they *don't* like the defendant a whole lot but are enamored with the skill and charm of his counsel, there is *still* a strong chance that the result will be an acquittal. On the flipside, if the jury dislikes defense counsel for any of several reasons, the defendant's chance of being successful begin to decline sharply. Worst of all, if the jury dislikes the defendant, they will do their best to convict him.

With this in mind, I spent many hours attempting to educate O. J.—who for all his courtesy and collegiality was a talkative man. I explained to him the importance of short but complete and responsive answers to any questions, and to understand a little bit about the techniques of cross-examination so that he could stand up to the cross examiner without appearing to be flippant or dismissive.

Because I knew I would not have the time to do a thorough job of preparing the defendant for his venture to the witness stand, I arranged to bring in one of the partners from my Boston firm, Daniel Patrick Leonard, who was skilled at educating ordinary people to be good witnesses. I had been impressed that during the initial interrogation of O. J. at the LAPD, he'd said nothing damaging to himself despite the best efforts of two of the top Robbery-Homicide Division (RHD) detectives on the force, who tried every trick in their bag to trip him up. But I was even more impressed by his responses to my questions when we were talking alone. If anyone has a criminal defendant at a disadvantage, it is his own lawyer. There are no Miranda or other rules that keep tension between the interrogator and the suspect. One's own lawyer can ask him anything under the sun, and if he knows the answer, the client is expected to give it truthfully.

There are two unfortunate and opposite avenues defense lawyers can take that lead down a dangerous path. One group would seek to represent a guilty person as if they are innocent. They will avoid, if possible, any admissions by the defendant that curtails the parameters of his defense. For instance, if a defendant says, "Yes, I killed her, I didn't mean to, but I did shoot her in the head," it is no longer open to an ethical defense lawyer to raise any positive defense other than entrapment or insanity.

Insanity is, in reality, not a defense at all—but it confesses to the charge and avoids responsibility by showing lack of mental capacity to formulate intent to commit the crime. Nevertheless, many lawyers think that by not burdening themselves with the client's statement that he is guilty, they have a license to put on all kinds of affirmative defenses including self-defense, alibi, and a denial by the client under oath that he committed the crime. The sad fact is that the first group is badly deluded in thinking they have a license to studiously ignore the truth, and thereafter play fast and loose with it. Not only is this grievously unethical conduct, but it is also a fairly dependable route to conviction.

A lawyer who defends a guilty person as if he were innocent is almost sure to get ugly surprises along the way and perhaps be embarrassed before both judge and jury. This is not a formula for acquittal.

On the flip side of that coin is the lawyer who defends an innocent man as if he were guilty, simply because he has made that assumption without seriously investigating the likelihood that it is so. The history of criminal litigation is littered with examples of this disastrous approach. One of the best examples in history is that of Dr. Sam Sheppard, whom I defended in his second trial in 1966.

Sheppard is known to most people today as the basis for the protagonist in *The Fugitive*, of both television and movie fame. Sheppard's original lawyer, who was not a criminal lawyer but a labor specialist, plainly thought he was guilty of murdering his wife and defended him as if he were guilty, contributing unfortunately to the fact that Sheppard was wrongfully convicted in 1954 and spent ten years of his life in prison as a penalty for his lawyer's ineptitude.

In the Simpson case, right up until the day that we had to acknowledge "game over" because we dared not take a chance on losing additional jurors (as will be explained in context later), I never doubted the feeling that with a little bit of training, Simpson would be a powerful and probably a definitive witness in his own case, assuming that the jury had not already decided—as I expected they would—right after the prosecution had rested that there was little evidentiary support for the Simpson indictment.

Early on, Bob Shapiro—in one of his best pretrial moves—had hired two lawyers, Barry Scheck and Peter Neufeld, assistant professors at the Benjamin Cardozo Law School in Manhattan, who had made names for themselves as forerunners in the brand new field of DNA testing. Since it was claimed that blood evidence was to be a significant factor in this case, Shapiro thought it would be wise to have on board a couple of lawyers who knew the territory.

I asked for a meeting with them in New York to get their read on what the blood evidence showed thus far and compare it to the results of our investigation of other factors.

When we met for lunch, Scheck said, "You don't remember me, do you?" I had to confess that his face did not bring up an immediate recollection. He said, "When you were trying the [Carl] Coppolino case in Freehold, New Jersey, I was the editor of the high school newspaper. My dad prevailed upon you to grant me a profile-type interview, which you did. We had an appointment for four o'clock on a Saturday afternoon at the Warwick Hotel in Manhattan. As I entered your suite, a man named Nat Hentoff was coming out the door, and you explained that he had just completed taping an interview which would appear in the next month or so in *Playboy*. I was sixteen at the time and thought it would almost be more fun to interview Nat Hentoff than you, but that was not the assignment I had given myself."

After this cordial introduction, the faces of the two men seemed a little glum. Neufeld, who hadn't at that point thoroughly done all the required homework surrounding the blood evidence, felt certain aspects could be difficult to manage.

Perhaps impatiently, I brought them both up short. I said, "Gentlemen, we are now four months into this investigation, and we have a pretty good handle on the factual circumstances surrounding the homicides—who was where and when, and how different kinds of blood evidence might be contradicted or explained. I will simply tell you that the evidence is clear that Simpson could not have committed this crime and had no reason to commit the crime, so your job—if you wish to stick with it—is to explain whatever blood evidence is out there in terms totally consistent with Simpson's nonparticipation in this crime."

Bob called me that evening and I gave him a report of our exchange concerning DNA. Shapiro asked if I would be capable of taking over the handling of the DNA evidence if he were unable to reach a satisfactory fee arrangement with the boys from New York for a long trial. I replied no, but as a quick study, felt that I could be adequately prepared prior to trial if I had to be.

To buttress this proposed effort, we brought in another lawyer, Robert Blasier from Sacramento, who was well-schooled in DNA evidence. Bob joined the team, brought a fresh perspective to the case, and turned out to be an excellent lawyer. Throughout the trial, when I was preparing for the various witnesses assigned to me prior to their being called, I was grateful for Bob Blasier's ideas and preparation. He was an asset that clearly belonged in the "dream" column of a team that had started to morph into a bit of a "dream/nightmare."

* * *

Regarding DNA, there was a dustup prior to the beginning of the trial itself: A decision had been made that there would be no effort by the defense to keep DNA evidence out of the case as unreliable. This is important because we felt we had strong evidence that the methods of testing and collection posed problems with accuracy.

In the mid-nineties, DNA had been shown to be capable of identifying individual human beings by their bodily excretions, including blood, urine, and hair. There were two types of DNA analysis used. The first was RFLP, restriction fragment length polymorphism, a molecular method of genetic analysis that allows individuals to be identified based on unique patterns of restriction enzyme cutting in specific regions of DNA. The tests in this case—of blood evidence found in drops or larger—had been conducted by a reputable company in Maryland called Cellmark Diagnostics.

The other technique, known as PCR—polymerase chain reaction, makes many copies of a specific DNA region in vitro, meaning in a test tube rather than an organism. It was invented by Dr. Kary Mullis of La Jolla, California, for which he was awarded the Nobel Prize in 1993.

In simple terms, the application of this second technique begins with a speck of human DNA which by itself is too small to be tested for its individual characteristics. But, by in effect cloning the substandard sample over and over, it becomes large enough to submit to conventional RFLP testing. Thanks to this invention, many crime scene findings that would have been worthless prior to the time PCR began to become viable.

During this stage of the pretrial, when both sides were submitting evidence to Judge Ito for his decision as to what to accept as evidence, DNA became an area of intense disagreement.

Our defense team agreed that RFLP testing met the necessary scientific criteria to be admitted into evidence, but we hotly contested the samples which had been developed through the PCR process.

The first of these objections was that if the original speck is even slightly contaminated, the cloning of the speck also clones the contamination and the sample becomes worthless for further use. We already had plenty of evidence of people playing fast and loose at the crime scene and intended to show that all the PCR evidence ought to be either excluded or—if it did reach the jury—rejected by them as untrustworthy.

To establish our position, we expected to have the testimony of Dr. Mullis himself, who was prepared to say that from his review of the police laboratory reports, none of the PCR-created evidence should be received. As scientific and forensic evidence goes, it had little if any value because of sloppy collection and handling methods by the LAPD crime lab.

Early in January, Johnnie Cochran began to have misgivings about using Dr. Mullis as an expert witness. These arose because he had been told—through the rumor mill—that he had been a chum of the well-known Dr. Timothy Leary, the Harvard psychologist who had strongly promoted the use of LSD—lysergic acid diethylamide—a potent hallucinogenic drug used for recreational purposes. There had been some articles that said Dr. Mullis had joined him in this effort, and that Dr. Mullis was quite a free spirit.

Johnnie had picked up some chatter from the prosecution that they planned to bring in a heavyweight cross-examiner named Rocky Harmon to beat up on Dr. Mullis and make him look like a self-indulgent anarchist. Johnnie asked me to go personally to interview the good doctor and give my impression as to how he might hold up on the witness stand. I drove down to Dr. Mullis's oceanfront home in La Jolla.

When I arrived at his house, a young man greeted me by handing me a glass of red wine, which he said Dr. Mullis had ordered because he'd read somewhere that I liked red wine.

"That's dandy," I said, "But where is Dr. Mullis?" The young man pointed out at the ocean where, about three hundred yards out, somebody was surfing, and said, "He'll be in in a few minutes, but he wanted to make sure you were comfortable since he's a little bit late."

While I waited, I became fascinated with the doctor's refrigerator, which had at least forty magnetic photo cutouts of nude women on its door. I was standing directly in front of that door when a wet hand landed on my shoulder. It was Dr. Mullis, still dripping, his tousled gray hair soaked with saltwater.

"Do you find any of those interesting?" he asked.

"Some," I replied. "But by the way, doctor, what do you do if one of your photographic subjects finds herself here in your array and makes a complaint because of her exposure?"

"I just take it down," he said. "I have a number of others to replace it with."

He opened the drawer under a counter adjacent to the display to reveal dozens more of these racy magnets.

The business phase of my visit with Dr. Mullis lasted more than an hour, and I left confident that he would be a knowledgeable and blockbuster witness, perhaps capable of making Rocky Harmon wish he had stayed away from the courthouse.

CHAPTER 7
Jury Selection

The California courts, which can turn any brief trial into an odyssey, used—in my view wasted—a great deal of time in *The People vs. Simpson*. Although the murder occurred in Santa Monica, a very prosperous, mostly white community, District Attorney Gil Garcetti and his colleagues decided to move the trial to downtown Los Angeles—a place whose cultural dimensions are almost the reverse of Santa Monica's. Why that happened is still the subject of debate. Garcetti's explanation was that because the state trial of the offending officers in the Rodney King case had been moved to Simi Valley, a sterile, all-white community outside the metropolitan area, he felt that leaving the Simpson case in a heavily white community would cause more unrest among those who still felt that the state's handling of the Rodney King case was nothing less than fraudulent.

I also suspect that Garcetti knew his evidence was weak. The fact that any jury selected from downtown would be heavily minority and, presumably, anti-law enforcement, would give him a handy excuse should the case result in an acquittal.

Although I am confident that a Santa Monica jury would have acquitted Simpson just as the one in Los Angeles ultimately did, I had to wonder if the case was transferred downtown for the convenience of the prosecutors who lived and worked there and the inconvenience of the defense lawyers, most of whom came from points west of the downtown area.

As is usually the case, jury selection, which in this case took *eleven weeks*, was drudgery. A group of citizens is called in, by subpoena, to the courthouse, where the judge either questions them orally or by way of a written questionnaire as to whether or not they believe they can view the evidence and listen to the testimony and arguments presented and then decide the case impartially, without bias or prejudice toward either side. The trial judge then certifies the pool of potential jurors.

The next step in the process is for the prosecution and the defense to pick, based on answers given to direct questions (called *voir dire*), which members of the pool are acceptable to them. If a person is not rejected for cause (knowing the accused, being related to someone in the case, etc.) or by way of a peremptory challenge where no cause need be given, then that person is deemed acceptable and becomes a juror in the case.

In the modern era, both sides in major cases often use jury consultants to help pick the jurors. In the Simpson case, each side had a consultant well-known in their field. We used Jo-Ellan Dimitrius and the government used Don Vinson, often called the father of jury consulting.

One media outlet reported that "Dimitrius is involved in everything from picking the jury, to coaching witnesses, to fine-tuning arguments. 'I almost act as a 13th juror,' she said.

"I hear a case for the first time. I want to know what the good is. I want to know what the bad is, so that we can figure out a way to desensitize or neutralize the negative components.

"With a PhD. in criminology, Dimitrius has never spent a day in law school. Rather, she's hired for her 'intuition.' She says she gets a sense of a person from their body language."

While scientists tell us that certain animals appear to have intuition, or a sixth sense, human beings do not.

We had Jo-Ellan sit with us at the defense table in full view of the jury pool, but the government put Vinson in the back of the room among the public spectators, almost as if they didn't want the pool to see they were using a consultant.

Vinson did not last long as part of the prosecution team. He was dismissed on the second day of jury selection—because he was apparently telling the prosecutors exactly what they didn't want to hear.

According to one news account:

> Don Vinson, head of Litigation Sciences, assisted the prosecution team, led by Marcia Clark... The advice he gave was ignored, the prosecution had their own ideas of a pro-prosecution juror. Vinson felt African American Women would be strong Simpson supporters, Clark thought otherwise.
>
> Based upon his reading of the voir dire transcript, Vinson compiled the following profile of the jury: One African American Male; One Hispanic Male; 8 African American Females; And two Caucasian Females. Only two were college graduates. No juror regularly read a newspaper. Two were supervisors. Eight watched tabloid news shows like "Hard Copy." Five had a family member who ran afoul of the law. Five thought using physical force on a family member was sometimes acceptable. Nine thought O. J. was unlikely to have committed murder because he was such a great football player...
>
> Prosecutor Marcia Clark thought that African American females would be: More likely to have experienced domestic violence in the past, and therefore would judge Simpson more harshly than males. She was guided by her own "Implicit Personality Theory."

One of the many tasks Dimitrius performed for the defense was to compile opinion surveys of what the public, the man or woman on the street, thought about the defendant and the issues in his case. We were heartened to learn that almost half—46 percent—of the people surveyed said they would "like to believe that O. J. didn't do it." As Johnnie Cochran later wrote, "That is an extraordinary reservoir of goodwill in a society in which little more than lip service is paid to the presumption of innocence." At least equally heartening was Dimitrius's finding that 66 percent—two-thirds—didn't think O. J. had enough time to commit the murders based on what they'd learned in the news. This was arguably the strongest of our four main lines of defense.

Marcia Clark's dogged insistence that the seven middle-aged black women on O. J.'s jury were sure votes for conviction, proved to be a fatal error for her team.

But then, the defense made errors as well in jury selection. One day, during the weeks of this ordeal, while Bob and Johnnie were working as ostensible equals, a sixtyish white woman came to the box to be examined. She had a rather stern look about her, and Cochran thought she would not make a very sympathetic juror. However, Shapiro informed the defense crowd that he knew of this juror and that she was extraordinary and liberal. He said that one time, she had taken on a jury of twelve in which she was the sole vote for acquittal and with her persuasion turned the jury around so that all voted for acquittal.

It turned out that Bob was completely wrong and that her role had been the exact opposite in the earlier case, wherein she had turned eleven jurors from acquittal to conviction. That revelation did not emerge until it was too late to remove her from the jury, and she remained the only white person on the panel who participated in the verdict.

Jury selection, which had begun September 16 and ended October 3, ultimately produced what Johnnie Cochran said was the best jury he'd ever selected. The principal jury, the first twelve picked, included eight black women, one Latino man, one black male, and two white women. In the next several weeks, twelve alternate jurors were selected.

After their selection, the jurors and the alternates had been allowed to return home until they were called for trial, on January 25, 1995. Now reassembled, they were told that they would be in custody, sequestered, until the end of the trial. Had they at that point been warned that due to the antics of some counsel and the great lassitude shown by the trial judge, they would be in custody for nearly nine months, I think that many of them might have jumped ship. But they were given no clue. In my wildest dreams I could not imagine that this trial—even in California—would take ten times as long as it should have.

Over the next one year and one week—fifty-three weeks—the jurors would sit through 253 days of trial, be sequestered for 266 days, and hear testimony from 126 witnesses.

Testimony by the prosecution would take ninety-nine days, by the defense fifty-four, and the jury would hear 126 witnesses, seventy-two for the prosecution and fifty-four for the defense.

The prosecution would show them 488 exhibits, the defense 369, and the jury would see twenty different lawyers put on evidence, eleven for the defense and nine for the government. By the end of the trial, ten jurors would be dismissed, leaving just two alternates.

Jurors would listen to four days of opening statements, four days of closing arguments, and deliberate for less than three hours.

CHAPTER 8

The "Dream Team" Becomes a Nightmare

W ith the trial date drawing near and case preparation in full swing, the defense team, dubbed in the media as the "Dream Team," was working around the clock. However, during this time, tensions within the group began to mount as Bob Shapiro grappled for control, despite his lack of experience in capital murder cases.

Quite apart from the questions we planned to raise about the origin and development of the PCR-tested blood evidence, there was also perfectly credible evidence of corrupted blood samples—not only because of faulty handling by the technicians, but also because the evidence was deliberately planted by police officers working the case. The best, but not only, example of this was a certain sock which was recovered from Simpson's bedroom carpet, and those blood samples found to contain EDTA (a stabilizing preservative chemical added by crime lab personnel to human blood).

Before the trial began, CNN, which was very actively covering the trial both on the scene and from its home offices in Atlanta, broke a story saying the defense was going to concede a good part of the DNA evidence. Since this was scheduled to become a public announcement within a matter of a few days, it seemed to me that little harm was done by the leak, whatever or whoever its source.

Nonetheless, Shapiro immediately accused me of having spoken clandestinely with the CNN reporter and given him a scoop, and therefore I could no longer be trusted on the defense team. This was not true, and merely reflected Bob's growing paranoia. His complaint was given short shrift by the rest of the team and the matter did not arise again.

Initially, I agreed to be chief spokesman for the defense, and after the failure of the defense team at the preliminary hearing, to undertake the trial cross-examination of Mark Fuhrman. I later agreed to take responsibility for the overall preparation of the defense, using my investigators and staff to erect the counterattack structure. Up to this point, there had been no discussion with Shapiro regarding fees.

Then, in October 1994, it came to light that Bob had not only planned to take over the Fuhrman cross examination (which we knew would be pivotal in the case), but that he also arranged to sop up whatever money he could glean for himself, surreptitiously orchestrating a contract whereby I would be part of the case as a *volunteer*.

I received this information in an indirect yet most fortunate way. Bob Shapiro had a secretary who did not feel well-treated, and as a result, let's say, didn't like him a lot. But from the start, she did like my "guys from the East," Pat McKenna, John McNally, and Howard Harris. On Friday nights, they would occasionally have a beer or two together. On more than one occasion, she made the mistake of thinking that she could match the group, beer for beer, and when her imbibing hit a certain level, she would begin to chat.

On one such occasion late in the fall of 1994, she told McKenna and Harris that Shapiro secretly intended to keep me involved up to and until the cross-examination of Mark Fuhrman, which was, at that point, my principal reason for remaining in the case. She explained that Shapiro intended to announce at the last minute that as chief counsel, he was taking over the cross-examination of Fuhrman.

I shouldn't have been surprised, but I'll admit that I was. I'd anticipated Bob would realize that his cross-examination skills were sparse, and that he couldn't sacrifice his client to his ego with the only critical witness in the entire case.

At about the same time, Harris, the computer expert who had been imported from my Florida office, discovered a document in the outgoing fax machine tray in Bob's office that had been sent to a reporter to prove that Shapiro was the lead guy. It was Shapiro's contract with Simpson for $1 million for defense services.

In the body of the letter of agreement, it stated that Shapiro would provide my services throughout the case. As I had been paid absolutely nothing up to this point, and had shouldered my own expenses, I was more than a little taken aback by this revelation.

It was then I was made to realize that having one's name in the "of counsel" slot on a legal letterhead enables any of the firm's principals to bind that person to render services in a given case, even without that person's knowledge. In short, I was committed to the defense of the Simpson case with no allocation of any fees and no share of the fee charged Simpson by Shapiro, who was being paid at the rate of $100,000 a month. I also had no real desire to trek back and forth from West Palm Beach, Florida, to Los Angeles like a commuter when I had important and much more valuable work to do in other cases, which extended across the US, Canada, and Europe.

Based on these circumstances, and upon learning that Johnnie Cochran and I were both to be in New York at about the same time, I asked Johnnie to meet me for lunch.

As I contemplated the meeting with Johnnie, my inner voices were telling me that as Simpson was now in his good hands and blessed with the services of an experienced and talented lawyer, it would be a good time to contract the range of the contribution I had been preparing to make, and to remain as an advisor to the defense from whatever remote location I might happen to be in when questions arose. This was particularly appropriate because I had an active schedule going to and from France, trying to liquidate the assets of a client, Claude Duboc, as the official representative requested by federal government attorneys to accomplish that purpose. In retrospect, it is clear that I would have benefited greatly from taking exactly that position and backing off the Simpson case.

Nonetheless, and mindful of my admiration for O. J. and my belief in his innocence, I badly underestimated the charisma and magnetism of Johnnie Cochran, my acquaintance of four months at that point. His experience as a capable and successful trial lawyer, including numerous homicide cases, was well established. In addition, Johnnie was as handsome as any man I have ever known and had a personality to match. When he smiled, a special kind of light danced in his eyes. He was a marvelous speaker—a skill that I especially value—and would have been a renowned preacher, like his father, had he chosen that path.

In all of the many cases I had handled during my forty years in courtrooms (as of that time), I had always been lead counsel or co-lead counsel when the defense required separate lawyers for separate clients. Even in those circumstances, I was usually chosen as the lead cross-examiner of critical prosecution witnesses. I had never before acted as "second chair" in any civil or criminal case. Although in the Marine Corps I had been trained both to obey orders and to give them, my persona as an experienced pilot of sophisticated aircraft had led me to rely extensively on my own ability to make quick and correct decisions.

But whatever reservations I had about being at the end of a tether controlled by some other lawyer dissipated rather quickly as I got to know Johnnie. He had an infectious habit of painting that sunshine smile across his face each time he greeted me and saying, "Hello, my brother, I'm okay—you okay?"

At our lunch in New York, I explained to Johnnie that I had entered the case principally to help Shapiro get a day in the sun and get credit for winning what I saw as a slam dunk acquittal in the Simpson case, despite its many warts. I also told Johnnie that I felt that as the case was now in his capable hands, if he didn't require my services any further, I would approach Simpson to see if he would allow me to withdraw. Once an attorney has filed an official "appearance" in a federal criminal case, counsel cannot be withdrawn without the consent of the client, the court, and in some instances, the prosecution.

"Johnnie," I said, "O. J. has made it clear to me that he expects me to stay. I'm not talking to Shapiro anymore but, clearly, he shouldn't be trying this case. O. J. doesn't want him to, and he is indicating to me that he wants me to do at least some of the work with you in charge. I'm not happy about being in California, but I have a chance to make a pretty good deal on an apartment and have to decide quickly."

Johnnie quickly answered, "I would like you to stay."

He then explained that he anticipated the examination of Mark Fuhrman would be a bloodbath in several respects, and that inevitably Fuhrman would be labeled a racist of the worst kind by the defense. He thought to the extent that such a confrontation was inevitable, it had best be carried out by a white person rather than an African American.

When he asked—in tones that did not invite a "no" answer —that I remain on board specifically to cross-examine Mark Fuhrman, and to handle some other witnesses thought to be key to the prosecution's case, my reservations wilted like a tulip in the Phoenix heat. There was simply too much to like about the man— and the prospect of working with him in this most challenging case—to refuse to go further.

While there are a great many things that I regret about the entirety of the Simpson case, being shoulder-to-shoulder with Johnnie offset much of the pain. His evenhanded leadership of the defense team was as consistent as the sunrise.

* * *

With the trial set to open on January 24, 1995, Judge Ito declared a two-week Christmas-New Year hiatus to enable all parties to have a holiday breather, and get ready for war. Bob Shapiro decided to take his family on a two-week vacation in Hawaii over the holiday break. And he did so under an assumed name—"Tony DeMilo"—apparently so the family could have some privacy. Meanwhile, the rest of the team was working every day but Christmas to get the defense case in order. I had still not been paid a dime.

To compound matters, Bob had fired investigator John McNally, whom he felt had not shown him enough respect. When McNally learned of Bob's Hawaii caper, he tipped off a reporter friend with the *New York Daily News*. This produced a scathing article, damning Shapiro for frolicking in the surf while his client was facing Armageddon.

Bob's reaction to the publication of this information was to go ballistic. And that reaction intensified when, at the end of 1994, I had written a comprehensive memo called "Cut One" outlining the defense and how it should be presented, and sent it to all counsel. The last sentence called upon Johnnie to mesmerize the jury with a searing opening statement. Bob called me, obviously flustered. "I had planned to give the opening statement," he said. "Looks like you're handing it to Johnnie!"

"I'm not handing anything to anyone," I replied. "O. J. has made that decision with great finality on his own, which he declared at a recent meeting. You must have been at the beach.

"By the way, Bob," I asked, unctuously, "I have heard a report about a contract you signed obligating me to try the case, a contract that pays you a million dollars for *our* services. Since you have received half of that already, I am wondering what part of it you have set aside as my share?"

Shapiro responded in a heartbeat, "You get nothing. You are a mere volunteer in this case."

The minute Bob returned to Los Angeles, Simpson called a meeting in his prison cell, attended by Shapiro, Cochran, and me. Simpson began in very calm and measured tones, reminding Bob that at the time he was hired, it was strictly for the purpose of trying to avoid an oncoming indictment—and with the clear understanding that if that failed, someone else would be hired to be the lead trial lawyer in the case.

Therefore, said O. J., Bob was effectively benched and his role changed into that of coach, rather than player. Shapiro's reaction to this suggestion was immediate and strident. "I will not accept that," he said. "And if you do that to me, I will resign immediately and tell the public what I really think of your case. If the bar wants to come after me, I don't give a shit. I've got plenty of money."

Had the decision been mine to make, I would have called a guard and had Shapiro escorted out of the building. But O. J., a man of measured judgment, could see that this kind of trouble in an already unfriendly community could win him nothing, and so he fashioned an alternative which still strikes me as quite clever.

Before football became a burgeoning national favorite sport, teams often ran plays from what was then called the "single-wing" formation. In that configuration, the running and passing was done by the halfbacks and the fullback. The quarterback was simply used for blocking, and seldom got to handle the ball. All of this was changed by the arrival of the T-formation, which quickly became the favorite strategy.

Simpson looked at Shapiro and said, "Okay, Bob, you can stay on the team as a player. You can be the quarterback, but we will use a single-wing system and, bear in mind, Bob, no passing."

That seemed to quiet Bob down some, and Shapiro's threats of resignation were not heard again. The meeting ended, but we were not quite done with the who's-in-charge issue. The next morning Shapiro, attempting to get his coveted number one position back, tried—to extend the football analogy another couple of yards—an end-around play.

When he showed up at Johnnie's office, along with Alan Dershowitz who had just flown into town, Shapiro took the chair at the head of the conference room table and announced, "I've just had a meeting with O. J. I am in charge. There is no question about it."

"Goddamn it, Bob," I roared, "you've been down there threatening the client. I don't believe it."

At that point Alan said, "I was there. I heard O. J. say it."

I snapped at my friend, "Alan, I don't care what you heard O. J. say—he certainly was forced into any statement supposedly putting Bob Shapiro back in charge. He told me personally he didn't want that."

The tension hung in the air like a San Francisco fog until Johnnie Cochran, in a calm and measured voice filled with authority, said simply, "Tell the truth, Bob. O. J. called me right after you guys left the jail. He was beside himself at your behavior. He's going to call here in a minute, and I am going to put him on the speakerphone and let him tell everybody who's in charge."

"As if on cue, the phone rang," Johnnie later wrote in his book, *Journey to Justice.* "O. J. spoke quietly, but firmly, for a few minutes and then concluded: I want Johnnie to be my lead attorney, and I want the rest of you to do what he says."

On the way back to Cochran's office for a team meeting, I began to put together a list of witnesses that Shapiro could be entrusted to handle even with his limited trial experience and promised to help him along the way. It was important to keep this mess contained in the defense camp.

At about the time Cochran became chief counsel, an article appeared in the *New York Post* saying, "Black Takes Over Lead in Simpson Case." Not long thereafter, my friend Roy Black from Miami, then recently in the national news because of his defense of William Kennedy Smith, called me and asked, "Lee, have I been hired without being consulted?"

* * *

While I might ordinarily have been very unhappy with the non-division of fees in the Simpson case, I was not, because I believed I had an ace up my sleeve...

In March 1994, a few months before the murders of Nicole Brown Simpson and Ron Goldman, I was finishing up the trial of a first-degree murder case in Boston when I got a call from Bob Shapiro. He said that he had signed up a very wealthy client named Claude Duboc, who had been seriously—and very successfully—in the business of importing marijuana and hashish into Canada. He was successful, that is, until he tried to bring a freighter with thirty-seven thousand tons of the stuff into San Francisco Bay and got caught.

One of the crew members had already pleaded guilty to a federal indictment that had been lodged in the Northern District of Florida. That district claimed it had jurisdiction and venue because a part of the conspiracy that resulted in the major seizure in San Francisco had been hatched along the northwest coast of Florida.

Bob wanted me to handle the Florida aspects of the trial, wherever they might lead, and to travel to England as soon as possible to meet with Robin Duboc, Claude's ex-wife. Mrs. Duboc lived mainly in Switzerland, but also had a home in Aspen, Colorado, where she became acquainted with Bob. When she and Claude divorced, he had given her $10 million as a settlement, along with some real estate. She and her lawyers were desperate to hear my opinion as to whether the government could come in and seize that money and property as having been drug proceeds.

I flew to London, and had the meeting in which I explained that the United States government does very much as it pleases, particularly in drug cases, and that there was a genuine risk that someone would try to have her settlement forfeited as drug profits.

I recommended to Bob, and to Mrs. Duboc and her lawyers, that the first order of business in the Duboc case, which looked as though it would be stuck in Tallahassee, Florida, would be to try to secure an agreement from the government prosecutors that in exchange for concessions of some kind from Duboc, the divorce settlement would remain untouched.

Prior to the trip, I had met with the prosecutors in the Duboc case, Gregory Miller and Thomas Kirwin, in their offices in Gainesville, Florida, to learn their views, and to find out what they were willing to share with me as to the strength of their case, and what negotiating room they had to consider a deal of some sort. I was informed that one of the crew members, a Norwegian tough guy named Nic Grenhagen, was ready to become a government witness if Duboc insisted on going to trial. I left the meeting convinced that Duboc's case could not withstand courtroom scrutiny by either a judge or a jury.

I also learned that Duboc had a partner named John Knock, who probably had profited as much as Duboc had—more than $100 million dollars—and that Claude's participation in helping them locate Knock, a fugitive at the time, would enable prosecutors to recommend a lenient sentence, because sentencing in criminal cases involving drugs is keyed to the amount of the shipment seized. Duboc, who was way over the top of all described limits, was facing a life sentence for the importation and twenty additional years for money laundering.

I arranged with Bob to visit Duboc, who at the time was still reposed in the Los Angeles County jail. He had been arrested in Hong Kong on an extradition warrant and was waiting for authorities to decide whether his case would proceed in Northern California or Northern Florida.

The DEA agents in California were keen to get credit for the conviction of such a large villain and were trying to persuade federal authorities to hold the case there because Duboc was already in California. It was determined that he change plans and continue to Tallahassee.

Shapiro and I spent two hours with Claude in the jail. I suggested that the ploy of the California agents was doomed to be rejected because Tallahassee having initiated the extradition warrant meant that their priority in time would most likely prevail.

I also suggested that going to trial on the facts known to me up to that point would border on the suicidal, and I thought that Claude ought to face up to that fact. Because if he expected me to win a drug case that was in this configuration, he was going to be disappointed for a very, very long time. After some reflection, he agreed, and we arranged to have him continue on to Tallahassee several days later.

So when it came to the Simpson case, Shapiro had apparently forgotten that I controlled the fees in the Duboc case, the substantial fees set aside for defense counsel by the government. So, I could simply deduct what was ultimately determined to be my share of the Simpson case fee from Shapiro's share of the Duboc fee.

In other words, we had each other by the short hairs.

Or so we thought.

* * *

That seminal meeting in Johnnie Cochran's office was the end of Shapiro's grapple for control, except for one isolated incident when Shapiro told the defense team that I had—"without question"—been responsible for the article in the New York paper describing him as ill prepared and enjoying the Hawaiian surf when most lawyers would have their noses to the grindstone on the eve of trial. As punishment for that transgression, Shapiro asked that I be removed from the defense team.

As I had had nothing to do with that incident, I got John McNally to call into Cochran's office and explain that providing the columnist with that story was solely *his* work because he thought Shapiro's conduct was outrageous, and that he had not forewarned me that his interview was about to take place.

Things became sufficiently tumultuous so that Roosevelt Grier, an All-Pro lineman in the National Football League—and later an actor and preacher who happened to be standing right next to Bobby Kennedy when he was gunned down in Los Angeles in 1968—served as a mediator in the wrangling among counsel which was taking entirely too much time as the trial drew near.

While the rest of the defense team was still unaware that it was John McNally and not Lee Bailey who had ratted out Shapiro to the columnist, no one had acted on Shapiro's demand that I be excommunicated. And Carl Douglas, Cochran's associate who was acting as case manager, informed me I was scheduled to cross-examine one of the prosecution's witnesses at a pretrial hearing—and that that performance would factor into a decision as to whether I would be invited to stay or expelled. It is a conversation which should have included Johnnie; much as I liked him, I thought he was ducking.

The witness was a Canadian doctor who offered an opinion that Simpson had an innate hostile attitude toward Nicole, and that even though he plied her with gifts, including a Mercedes convertible, he was simply trying to appease her by appearing to be generous. On cross-examination, most of the doctor's claimed opinions got peeled back, and when we came to a point in the cross-examination (which was before Judge Ito; there was no jury) when I thought we had accomplished our purpose, I said to him, "Doctor, isn't it possible that Mr. Simpson gave Nicole gifts not to appease her, but because he still had a great deal of affection for her?" The doctor seemed surprised by the question and answered without hesitation. "Yes, that could well be."

The state's motion was denied, and Douglas came over to me and said, "Welcome aboard. Probation period over." It was a bit humiliating, but this is a business of hard knocks.

CHAPTER 9
The Prosecution Begins

On the eve of trial, I sat down and wrote the following personal memo to all the lawyers involved in what would be an historic trial:

The PEOPLE vs. O. J. SIMPSON

From: Lee Bailey
To: My advocate colleagues on both sides
Copy: Hon. Lance A. Ito, Presiding
Date: January 23, 1995
Subj: The trial, the public, and our profession

Dear Marcia:

Suffice it to say that the jury trial we are about to commence will be scrutinized and critically reviewed throughout its progress more thoroughly and by more viewers than any other trial in American history. A large and variegated array of lawyer-commentators is at the ready, each aspiring to be the John Madden of the Simpson case. I suspect that because trials of this magnitude are extremely rare, what we say and do in the weeks and months to come is going to leave an indelible and unalterable impression—worldwide—of American trials and trial lawyers that will last for many years. Simply put, we are about to make important history and set some significant landmarks.

All of you—each and every one—are trial lawyers of quality and skill. Some are stars already. The rest likely will be before this trial ends, if each will but "stay the course" of living within the parameters of high professionalism, and the boundaries of human decency. And while each of you has a paramount duty to represent our respective interests with vigor, determination, and resolution, it seems to me after more than forty years of living in courtrooms that the "high road" is as likely to produce victory as any combination of less desirable measures. In the heat of battle, and while honestly pursuing their objectives, lawyers in court often appear to be too acerbic, self-righteous, pompous and snarling. I think we owe a duty to everyone—the parties we represent, the public, our country and the profession we revere—to try more deliberately than have any lawyers in history to stand tall. We have the supervision of an able and patient trial judge who allows lawyers wide latitude to try their cases according to their own designs. We have every chance to make an exemplary mark in the yearbooks, and to add luster to American jurisprudence.

Hopefully, when a conclusion is reached and a verdict has been returned, what millions have seen will leave them convinced that we did our jobs well, and the result was a just one. Each of you has my admiration and respect as we begin. Hopefully, when we have finished this trial, the vast majority of those who have followed this "Trial of the Century," will share my views.

* * *

The People of the State of California v. Orenthal James Simpson creaked to a start on January 24, 1995, almost six months after our preparation began. But before the opening statements, we, the defense, wanted the jury to see something; we wanted the jury to see O. J. Simpson's knees, which bore the scars of several operations and no longer operated as the knees of a man his age should function. Our point, of course, was that a man with such scarred, beat-up knees could hardly have managed the physical feat of a brutal murder that involved the struggle of a very strong young man, who had clearly fought back in a valiant but doomed effort to save his life.

Fearing that Simpson's still-considerable "star power" would bedazzle the jurors, the prosecution, of course, wanted no such showing to occur. But first, there was a lot of back and forth with Judge Ito (without the jury present) about the physical route that Simpson would have to walk to the jury box. The best route, obviously, was the one that would take him right past the table where Marcia Clark, Chris Darden, and William Hodgman, the three prosecutors who were in court for the State that day were sitting. They objected, apparently worried that Simpson (who would not be handcuffed) in a sudden crazed fit, would lunge across the table and with his large hands, somehow choke the three of them simultaneously.

As far as letting the jury see O. J.'s scarred knees, Marcia Clark was having none of it. She responded to our request for the showing by labelling it "simply an attempt to capitalize on whatever defendant's star appeal currently is with the jury and to get him to have close proximity with them to impress them. What is the probative value of a scar?" She said we should make our point through testimony so the prosecution could then cross-examine O. J. on his physical condition and ability.

Judge Ito made his decision quickly, ruling that O. J. could display his battered knees to the jury. A small victory for us, but whatever hope this might have engendered that Judge Ito would continue to favor the defense in his rulings soon dimmed.

Opening statements, which began on Tuesday, January 25, were predictable and unremarkable. Christopher Darden went first, laying out for the jury what he and his fellow prosecutors had settled on as the motive for the killings:

We're here today, obviously, to resolve an issue, to settle a question, a question that has been on the minds of people throughout the country these last seven months. . . .Did O. J. Simpson really kill Nicole Brown and Ronald Goldman? . . .

Well, finally, ladies and gentlemen, I am here in front of you this morning to answer that question. And we will answer that question from the witness stand, and from the exhibits you'll see in this case, and from the evidence. And when you see the evidence, and when you hear the witnesses, and when you put it all together and consider the totality of circumstances in this case, the answer will be clear to you as well.

For years, I have said—and especially when speaking to groups of lawyers—that the opening statement is a promissory note to the jury. You can't tell them "the evidence will show" and then not put on actual evidence that does in fact "show" what you are talking about. Yet that's just what Chris Darden and Marcia Clark did in their opening statements to the Simpson case jury. They promised evidence, but what they delivered was something different: grand, formless concepts.

Darden:

Why? Why would he do it? Why would he do it? Not O. J. Simpson. Not the O. J. Simpson we think we know, not the O. J. Simpson we think we've seen over the years. We've seen him play football for USC, we watched him play against UCLA, play in the Rose Bowl, we watched him win the Heisman Trophy. He may be the best running back in the history of the NFL.

We watched him leap turnstiles and chairs and run to the airplane in Hertz commercials...We watched him with a 50-inch Afro in Naked Gun 33 1/3. We've seen him time and time again. We came to think that we know him.

What we've been seeing, ladies and gentlemen, is just a public face, a public persona, a face of the athlete, a face of the actor. It is not the actor who is on trial here today, ladies and gentlemen. It is not that public face. . . .

There is that other face. Like many men in public, there is a public image, a public side, a public life. He may also have a private side, a private face. And that is the face we will expose to you in this trial, the other side of O. J. Simpson. . . .

He killed for a reason almost as old as mankind itself. He killed her out of jealousy. He killed her because he couldn't have her. And if he couldn't have her, he didn't want anybody else to have her. He killed her to control her. Control was a continuing thing, the central focus of the entire relationship. By killing Nicole, the defendant assumed total control of her. By killing her, nobody could have her.

Chris Darden, like O. J. an African American, was tall, thin, and well dressed. He sported a shaved head and looked to be calm and collected. His presentation, however, had been anything but calm and collected. The jury had listened to him attentively, but I couldn't get a read on what they made of it, or him.

Next came Marcia Clark, the lead prosecutor. Forceful, reasonably articulate, and in command, she picked up where Christopher Darden had left off:

Now you've heard the *why* . . . . Why would Orenthal James Simpson, a man who seemingly had it all, commit such heinous crimes, throw it all away? The one simple truth about the evidence described to you by Mr. Darden is that it shows that Mr. Simpson is a man—not a stereotype but flesh and blood who can do both good and evil.

Being wealthy, being famous cannot change one simple truth: He's a person and people have good sides and bad sides. Whether you see both sides or not, both sides are always there.

Now we will show you the other side of the smiling face you saw in the Hertz commercial. Remember that in *voir dire*, we asked you if you could use your common sense and reason to fairly and to objectively evaluate this evidence as neutral impartial judges of the facts. You all promised that you could and you would and we believe that you will.

We have every faith and belief in the fact that you will all keep that promise, but it will not be easy. You will be tested and tempted throughout this case to accept the unreasonable and be distracted by the irrelevant.

You are going to have to be ever vigilant in acting as the judges in this case. Each one of you is a judge. Each one of you is a trier of fact. You have to examine all the evidence very carefully and ask yourselves, 'Is this reasonable? Is this logical? Does this make sense? Would I look at this evidence the same way . . . you would for any other case?'

Now, winning is not what this is about. This is not a game. This is about justice and seeing that justice is done. Two people have been brutally murdered and the evidence consistently will point to the guilt of only one person as the murderer . . . My job is to seek justice. I've had cases before this one, there will be cases after it. This case is not about the lawyers, myself, Mr. Hodgman, Mr. Darden, or Mr. Cochran.

We have to remember what this case is about. And justice for all. Ladies and gentlemen, if those words are to mean anything, we must all be equal in the eyes of the law and we cannot use a sliding scale to judge guilt or innocence based on a defendant or a victim's popularity. . .

On behalf of all of us for putting up with the rigors of sequestration, we all know it's difficult, and we appreciate all of your dedication to duty and service in this case. Thank you very much.

Marcia Clark went on to paint a picture of Simpson as an ogre who would murder at the drop of a hat if you as much as disagreed with him; the opening remarks were heavy on personalities and emotional appeals, but described very little in the way of evidence as a good opening statement should.

The prosecution's case began on the last day of January 1995. The Brooklyn Bridge that the prosecution wished to sell the jury had two spans: The first was that O. J. had killed his former wife because he wanted to control her; the second span was that Simpson was a wife-beater and the killing was the final act of a marital drama marked by frequent and continual abuse.

To establish that second level, Darden opened the prosecution's case by putting several witnesses on the stand who could testify about the single well-known, on-the-record example of domestic abuse in the seven-year marriage of O. J. and Nicole: the 1989 New Year's morning incident.

"I heard a female screaming, and then I heard what I thought was a slap," testified prosecution witness number one, Sharyn Gilbert, the 911 operator who took the New Year's Day call in 1989. To buttress her testimony, Darden played a recording of the tape, and it was easy to detect Nicole's trembling voice, but the other background sounds were not clear.

We, the defense, weren't particularly worried about the facts of the incident because the details had been well-publicized at the time. Simpson had admitted guilt for striking her and performed his public service "sentence." But we knew that after hearing the desperate voice of the late Nicole Brown Simpson, the jury might view our client in a less than favorable light.

The next day, prosecutors had O. J. Simpson's longtime friend Ron Shipp take the stand. Shipp was an ex-cop who sometimes helped O. J. with security. He viewed himself as a member of O. J.'s inner circle. But in their book *American Tragedy*, Lawrence Schiller and James Willwerth described Shipp as a "Rockingham hanger-on."

The prosecution was high on Shipp—in her book, Marcia Clark called him "a man of integrity and courage"—but his testimony presented some problems for the government. For one thing, his claimed closeness with Simpson was exaggerated, and he'd been suspended from the LAPD because of a drinking problem. The prosecution claimed that he'd conquered that problem years ago, but we knew he had been drinking on the night of June 13 and planned to introduce that fact.

Shipp testified that when he learned of the murders, he went to Simpson's Rockingham residence, joining "maybe ten to fifteen" people who had gathered there. He then retreated to Simpson's bedroom, alone with O. J., where he said Simpson told him he had dreams of killing Nicole.

Carl Douglas, one of Johnnie Cochran's associates, did the cross-examination. By this point, no one was playing softball, and Carl beat up on Shipp to the extent that Carl later expressed regret. But we certainly did not want the jury to think that Shipp had been telling the truth about what he claimed O. J. had said to him in his bedroom on the night after the murders.

On cross examination, Douglas got Shipp to admit that he didn't initially tell investigators, prosecutors, *or* the defense team about the "dreams" conversation, and that Shipp had first mentioned it to author Sheila Weller, who wrote the February 1995 book, *Raging Heart: The Intimate Story of the Tragic Marriage of O. J. and Nicole Brown Simpson*, one of the very first books on the trial.

Douglas portrayed Shipp as an opportunist, piggybacking off the tragedy. He got Shipp to say that, despite knowing Simpson for twenty-six years, they were not close friends. They never went to dinner together or football games or golfed or even once played tennis together on Simpson's court. Douglas also told the court that Shipp had been admonished by Simpson's assistant, Cathy Randa, for frequently dropping by the house unannounced. On the stand, Shipp agreed that he "used to have" a drinking problem, and that he did stop by Simpson's home several times after the murders, unannounced and impaired, much to the displeasure and concern of Randa.

In fairly short order, Douglas accomplished his goal of discrediting Shipp's testimony about the "dreams" and called into question whether, given such a loose friendship, Simpson would have confided in him at all.

After Shipp's testimony, prosecutors called LAPD investigator Mike Stevens to the stand. He testified that via a search warrant, they drilled into a safe deposit box that Nicole Brown had opened. It contained items that documented the 1989 domestic violence incident with Simpson, with three photos of her injuries, newspaper clippings, and letters from Simpson. It also contained her will.

"It appears to us that what Nicole Brown was doing was leaving a trail for us of what happened in 1989," Darden said.

The next day, on Friday, February 3, 1995, the government put Denise Brown on the witness stand. It wasn't long before Denise, Nicole's sister, became very emotional. When she could not control her crying, Judge Ito adjourned the trial for the day in mid-afternoon. The defense was not pleased that the image the jurors would take into the weekend break was such a sad and emotional one, but there was nothing we could do about it.

When court reconvened the following Monday, Darden changed the subject, asking Denise how Simpson had reacted on an occasion she described when she told him he took Nicole for granted.

She replied, "His whole facial structure changed" and then added more details in her attempt to paint a Jekyll and Hyde portrait of O. J.

Denise's testimony got to Simpson, who from the outset had been in the habit of scribbling notes—orders, sometimes—to the lawyers, or even speaking directly to them with instructions, often almost loud enough for the jury to hear. This time he was rather subdued as he whispered something to Bob Shapiro, who was slated to cross Denise.

Shapiro, who'd been paying attention to what the witness was saying, lost his cool:

"I'm the lawyer. This is what you're paying me for. If you want to run things, you don't need me."

Nevertheless, during Shapiro's cross-examination, he did begin gently and got Denise to admit that she'd been drinking on the night in question. When Bob had finished, the defendant had a request. He wanted Shapiro to replay part of the video introduced by Chris Darden taken after the dance recital, specifically the part where Simpson lifts up Justin, his young son. O. J. felt it demonstrated that he had to strain to do so, and would illustrate to the jury that if it was hard from him to pick up a child, how could he have had sufficient strength to kill two healthy young adults just hours later?

When Shapiro balked, calling the idea "foolish," Johnnie Cochran intervened, telling Shapiro to do what the client wanted. Shapiro did, but in such a manner that produced the opposite of what Simpson wanted him to accomplish. In *American Tragedy*, Shapiro's compliance was described as "the loudest fuck-you [Johnnie Cochran] had heard in years."

* * *

After Denise Brown had come and gone, the prosecution put on a long string of witnesses, the first group to establish its version of the timeline, and the second to give the jury a vivid, and purposely gruesome, picture of the murder scene. Of the first group, the most key—in the prosecution's view—was Pablo Fenjves.

A neighbor of Nicole's, Fenjves was a transplanted New York writer who'd written for a time for the *National Enquirer* and subsequently found limited success in Hollywood. (Oddly enough, Fenjves eventually went on to ghost write the controversial *If I Did It* book, published in 2007, the bizarre, fictionalized version of Simpson's "hypothetical" confession to the murders of Nicole Brown Simpson and Ronald Goldman. Although it was pulled from circulation almost immediately, and its editor fired, the book hurt Simpson badly in the public eye.)

During the preliminary hearing, Fenjves testified that as he and his wife were watching the ten o'clock news on television, and at about ten or fifteen minutes into the show, he heard the loud barking of a dog in distress. Fenjves described it as a "plaintive wail," a phrase which stuck in the minds of almost anyone who heard it.

What made his testimony so important is that he established the government's version of the timeline—beginning almost a half hour earlier than would the accounts of the defense witnesses.

If the jury believed Pablo Fenjves, then there *might* have been enough time for Simpson to commit the murders, drive home, clean up, and greet the limo driver at 10:55 p.m.

When he cross-examined Fenjves, Johnnie Cochran tried his best to shake his testimony as to the time he heard the dog's cry, but Fenjves stuck to his account. And the *New York Times* reported the next day that "in a case without a weapon, Mr. Fenjves's recollection may be the single most important bit of evidence besides some drops of blood."

In the *Times* article, David Margolick reported that at the preliminary hearing on June 30,

> Mr. Fenjves put a name to what he had heard. His interrogator was Marcia Clark, the chief prosecutor in the case. "At some point, while you were watching the 10 o'clock news on Channel 5, did something distract you?" she asked him.
>
> "I heard a dog barking," he replied. "Sort of a plaintive wail."
>
> The phrase resonated. "People have asked me if I thought about it for days, when the truth is that I didn't think about it at all," Fenjves recalled recently as he walked [his dog]... 'It's not exactly brilliantly eloquent, but the minute I said the line, Marcia Clark's eyes lit up."
>
> When Mr. Fenjves prepared to testify last month, he decided not to repeat it, even though it has become as inextricably linked with Simpson as the "grassy knoll" has with John F. Kennedy. After all, no writer likes recycling his material. But one of Marcia Clark's subordinates, Cheri Lewis, would hear none of it. "She said: 'Oh, no, please. That's a very important phrase.'" So, he used it again.

The next day, Johnnie Cochran heard from Michael Schneider, an associate of Alan Dershowitz, who said they'd received an "interesting tip" that the prosecution was based on two Perry Mason stories, "The Case of the Howling Dog" and "The Case of the Buried Clock."

CHAPTER 10
Planning "Fuhrman's Funeral"

In March 1995, it was time for the fireworks: the testimony of the government's most crucial, even indispensable, witness, LAPD Detective Mark Fuhrman.

Bob Shapiro had asked early on if I would be willing to take on the cross-examination of Fuhrman at trial. I agreed to do so—and with a certain amount of zeal—because I saw Fuhrman as a juicy target. This was not an assignment that could be taken lightly. From my perspective, Fuhrman, by "finding" the glove, was the only meaningful link between the homicides, which took place two miles away from Simpson's home and Simpson himself. The proposed attack on Fuhrman was a moment I had been waiting for with great anticipation.

Up to that point, my contributions to the defense team had been principally behind the scenes. I'd only cross-examined two witnesses, and the media had taken what seemed to me undue pleasure in pointing out that the "once-legendary" F. Lee Bailey had "lost his fastball" or whatever sports analogy was in vogue at that moment. Frankly, I didn't care what they wrote, but I'd be lying if I said I didn't look forward to proving them wrong. I even had a name for the ceremony I had in mind for the former Marine: I thought of my preparation as "Planning Fuhrman's Funeral."

The fundamental strategy overarching all the planning for Fuhrman's cross-examination was to catch him in an important lie, and then to prove to the jury that he deliberately lied for the purpose of deceiving them. He knew what he was doing, and it proved none of his testimony was sufficiently trustworthy to support a conviction for murder. The obvious target, of course, was his deeply ingrained hatred of anyone with black skin.

During and since the Simpson trial, there has been a pervasive claim by many that the "race card" was unconscionably used, dealt from the bottom of the deck. To the extent that race became a major issue, the provocation rested entirely on the moral cavern brought to the table by Mark Fuhrman. The Rodney King debacle that divided Los Angeles along racial lines had no direct relationship to the murder trial except in the shared sense of outrage experienced by African Americans as they watched repeated videos of King being beaten with sticks by police, only to then be confronted with an acquittal of those same police in a trial that took place in a heavily white community in Simi Valley, California. Simpson had many friends among law enforcement officers, and was generally quite popular with them. There was no claim or even hint that he had been mistreated by the police. But race was the elephant in the room.

By all accounts, Mark Fuhrman was a racist. According to witnesses, he repeatedly asserted that it made his blood boil to see a black man with a white woman. He must not have been pleased to find that exact situation when he answered a distress call from Nicole in 1985 and confronted the two at their home. But I did not feel that in the circumstances of this case, Simpson's race was an important factor in the decision of Fuhrman to place himself at its center. After all, he had no way of knowing where Simpson was during that fateful evening or whether he might have an unassailable alibi that would totally exclude him as a possible suspect in the perpetration of the crime. I think his manipulation of the glove evidence was done for entirely different reasons: He was simply desperate to cling to some part of this hugely important murder case and in some role. Since he had been rejected as the detective in charge, he contrived to cement himself into the foundation of the case as a singular and necessary witness. Indeed, in a recording made about a month after the murders occurred, he said as much in his own words. (More on that to come…)

In my experience in the Marine Corps and with both law enforcement and the court system, I have met people like Fuhrman—although in much less virulent colors—from time to time. One of the attributes that turned a man into a fearsome fighter was a deep and abiding hatred for the enemy as a class, race, or breed. I believe that this embedded hostility was in large part responsible for the ugly manner that American soldiers executed women, children, infants, and elderly people in the Mai Lai Massacre during the Vietnam War in 1968.

From all that we could learn, Fuhrman's disdain for black people had unfortunately been tolerated during his service as a Marine. Indeed, he attempted to reenlist at the Marine recruitment center, possibly inspired to do so by his frustration with the youthful gangs of minorities in Los Angeles with whom he was forced to contend as a policeman.

Another attribute impressed upon Marines from boot camp and thereafter is the need to have a resolve parallel to that which carried Great Britain through the darkest hours of the Nazi assault upon its homeland, uplifted by the immortal words of its leader, Winston Churchill, who said, "Never, never, never give in." An attitude of determination to succeed in combat is one of the core elements of a good fighting man. In my view at the time, as Fuhrman saw the brass ring about to slip out of his hands, he decided to take a severe risk and plant evidence in a murder case which had almost immediately exploded into a notoriety that encircled the planet and captivated the attention of all who had access to news reports.

Once he had been notified by his commanding authority that he and his partner, Ronald Phillips, were simply to babysit the case until the grizzled senior detectives could arrive to take over,

I believe that Fuhrman began to explore the means by which he might be able to avoid being dumped out of the boat, as Phillips was almost immediately. Fuhrman's experience had certainly taught him that once a prosecutor had identified and gotten the cooperation of a critical witness, that person had to be protected, nurtured, and cajoled until his evidence was complete and his cross-examination was over.

Remember, at the preliminary hearing, Fuhrman testified to the glove found at the Bundy crime scene as "them"—not a single glove, when he had observed the area around the bodies. They were quite obviously implements of the murders that had taken place and had thereafter been discarded by the killer that wore them. The killer was necessarily not sufficiently sophisticated to realize that evidence on the glove—both exterior and within its lining—might yield enough DNA to establish the identity of the person who had last worn them.

It seemed likely to me that anyone who contemplated that he might possibly become a suspect in the case would not leave any personal items at the scene which might in some fashion be traced to him, unless that were the safest course available. It would be much more damning if the killer tried to carry the instruments of murder away from the scene and was apprehended with them in his possession.

I doubt that this troubled Fuhrman. The fact that a glove quite clearly used during the murder was found on Simpson's property would be sufficient to lock Fuhrman into his role as a witness no matter which direction the investigation took following its discovery.

My theory about Mark Fuhrman's deliberate interference with the evidence was informed by the bold civil suit that he had filed against the LAPD in 1981.

Fuhrman began his career at the LAPD in 1975. Six years later, in September 1981, he concluded that the daily stress of his job had caused him permanent injury that left him impaired both physically and psychologically, to the point where he no longer felt able to discharge his duties as a police officer. He hired a lawyer and applied for a disability pension. As a result, he was examined by a number of doctors—including some selected by either Fuhrman or his counsel—who reported their findings to the board reviewing his application. The Board of Pension Commissioners adopted them *in toto* to deny Fuhrman's claim, a ruling that was later upheld in the Superior Court of California.

According to the official record of the 1981 claim, Fuhrman, who'd been a Los Angeles police officer for only six years, applied for a disability pension alleging his "psychiatric, hypertension and gastrointestinal problems were caused by his police duties."

Following standard LA city charter procedure, Fuhrman was examined by three psychiatrists, Drs. Robert McCauley, Augustus S. Rose, and Sarkis Arevian. In addition, as part of the workers' compensation claim, Fuhrman was examined by several other doctors, including Drs. John Hochman and Ronald Koegler. Fuhrman could not have been happy with, or proud of, the professionals' evaluations.

All the medical men laid it on the line, bluntly.

According to Dr. McCauley, Fuhrman's hypertension "need not represent an uncontrollable risk factor" or "an impediment to work full duty within the Los Angeles Police Department." Paragraph 5 in the report's *Findings of Fact* stated, "The applicant's December 28, 1982 MMPI [Minnesota Multiphasic Personality Inventory] Clinical Profile indicated that he may be consciously exaggerating problems or malingering in an attempt to achieve some goal."

The two other psychiatrists, Drs. Rose and Arevian, were equally unimpressed with Fuhrman's claims. The former found that the applicant's mild reactive blood pressures were of "no significant consequence to his health, either at this time or in the future," and the latter "did not feel that the applicant gave him a reasonably accurate picture."

The two doctors who evaluated Fuhrman's claim for workers' compensation also did not find in his favor.

Dr. John Hochman reported: "There is some suggestion here that the patient was trying to feign the presence of severe psychopathology. This suggests a conscious attempt to look bad and an exaggeration of problems which could be a cry for help and/or [an] over dramatization by a *narcissistic, self-indulgent emotionally unstable person who expects immediate attention and pity*. However, from behavioral observations and from an overall pattern in the tests, the presence of severe psychopathy is doubtful to say the least."

An equally dismissive Dr. Ronald Koegler commented that "in observing and talking to this man, it is hard to conceive that he is being considered for total disability and is applying for a pension from the police force. ...This man is not significantly psychiatrically disabled ... It appears to me during the evaluation that he was deliberately exaggerating his preoccupation with violence in order to make himself appear unsuitable for police work."

Dr. Koegler's next statement struck the Simpson defense team as being right on the mark: "This man has become tired of police work just as he became bored with life as a Marine. He does not want to quit and lose his benefits, so he is attempting to get pension and compensation benefits." The report concluded by stating that there were a variety of "light duty, low stress" jobs that Fuhrman could do in which "gun, uniform and public contact would not be required."

In the unsuccessful appeal of the no-pension, no-disability decision, Fuhrman's lawyer complained that none of these jobs had ever been offered to his client. I suspect that the LAPD recognized that Fuhrman would never take a job in which he could not wear a badge, carry a weapon, and harass, mistreat, and beat up minorities. In effect, the police department report denying the application for pension, disability, and early retirement said that Officer Mark Fuhrman was fit to serve the public, a classic irony if ever there was one.

And the report, which ran for close to two hundred pages, also contained a copy of the fitness summary done in 1977, when Fuhrman had been on the force for less than two years. It contained a statement with which the Simpson defense team totally agreed: "Officer Fuhrman has made a fair transition into the Hollenbeck area. He is enthusiastic and demonstrates a lot of initiative in making arrests. However, his overall production is unbalanced at this point because of the greater portion of time spent in trying to make the *'big arrest.'*"

To test my theories about the conduct of the man who was indeed to become *the* linchpin witness in the case, I consulted my expert forensic psychiatrist, Dr. Yudowitz. He studied the reports and Fuhrman's history in the police force and agreed that in all probability Fuhrman was a driven man of sociopathic tendencies, who would reach far beyond the bounds of propriety to get something he wanted, if he wanted it badly enough.

* * *

When Mark Fuhrman had testified on July 5, 1994, as the star witness at the preliminary hearing, I was watching him on television. Fuhrman was only partway through his direct examination—conducted by Marcia Clark—when I realized that the witness was giving off a noticeable stench.

One cannot practice law on the criminal side of the court for many decades without encountering police officers from all points on the personality spectrum. Some are honest, outstanding—even heroic—people who are absolutely essential to any well-managed society and who are never unpleasant to encounter even when their evidence is anything but helpful to the defense. I have had the good fortune to know many and sometimes even hire this kind of cop.

I have also come to know police officers from the dark side, cops who think that falsifying their reports and lying in court are all part of the game. And I have learned that their "co-conspirators," ambitious prosecutors who, when they are parading the lies of a sociopathic badge-bearer, pretend not to know that vouching for such tainted testimony could put an innocent defendant behind bars or at the business end of an execution device. These prosecutors are far-right disciples of the Vincent Lombardi philosophy of competitive sports: *Winning isn't everything; it is the **only** thing!*

At first glance, Fuhrman at the preliminary hearing appeared to be clean-cut, fit, and reasonably well spoken—your model of a former Marine. But as he went on, little flaws in both the manner and the content of his testimony began to pop up and fester. Without a proper cross examination by the defense, Fuhrman's credibility went unchallenged. It came as no surprise that Judge Kennedy-Powell not only found the warrantless search of Simpson's premises to be within acceptable legal bounds, but also found that there was sufficient evidence to hold O. J. over for trial.

Vince Lombardi would not have applauded us: We had lost the preliminary hearing.

More conscientious law enforcement and prosecutors would have confronted the many contradictions in their case, and perhaps kept looking for those who in fact had committed these awful homicides, culprits who are now, of course, totally insulated from any comeuppance for their foul deeds because innocent people have been accused.

But the justification for our adversary system is that well-trained advocates will test the evidence in what the legendary defense attorney Edward Bennett Williams once called "the crucible of cross-examination," and in the process burn away the slag and allow only the pure truth to remain on the scales of justice. Of course, in the reality of criminal litigation this ambitious plan is too seldom achieved. But any hope that it may be effective is grounded in the availability of someone who is adept—and, one hopes, highly skilled—in what has been described by titans of the courtroom as "a bulwark of liberty," and "the greatest engine of truth known to man."

Once the preliminary hearing had been concluded, it was pretty clear to all concerned—the prosecutors as well as the defense—that come verdict time, the prosecution would have most if not all of its cards riding on Mark Fuhrman. I have no doubt that as the "Fuhrman Saga" continued to unfold, the prosecutors must have greeted each upcoming odiferous disclosure with an ugly sense of foreboding.

Assuming they already knew what the defense was learning in clumps and pieces, they must have been well aware they had a monster witness on their hands, and as bad news followed bad news with respect to the probable performance of this witness on the stand, I believe that the prosecutors and senior police began to sink into that quicksand known as the "ostrich syndrome." When confronting bad news, they stick their heads in the sand like an ostrich in a sandstorm, hoping that by the time they pull it out, the trouble will have blown away. This was not to be.

In any organization as large as the Los Angeles Police Department, there will be someone who has or develops a deep-seated dislike bordering on hatred for one or more of their fellow officers. Fuhrman's frequently expressed contempt for those he considered to be genetically inferior—African Americans and Jews—had been widely noticed among his discomfited associates, and more than one of them, ignoring the old World War II maxim that "loose lips sink ships," talked derisively about his frequent rancid epithets.

However, as is often the case, many people were willing to give information only if assured that their names would not be used, and that they would not be given a subpoena to testify in open court or be seen on television. Like most seasoned investigators, Pat McKenna and John McNally knew that if they promised witnesses there would be no attribution but later made their names public, people would stop talking to them. In this business, investigators on both sides of the fence often must take what they can get and use it as effectively as they can without breaching their promises of confidentiality.

CHAPTER 11

Getting Fuhrman in the Crosshairs

O n March 9, 1995, Fuhrman took the stand in front of a packed courtroom. The air crackled with the electricity of tension and expectation. At first impression, Fuhrman could be called handsome, fit, alert, and reasonably articulate. But any favorable impression was greatly dimmed by the opening battery of questions and answers. With them, Marcia Clark used a letter from a woman named Kathleen Bell to introduce Fuhrman to the jury. Bell had said she heard Fuhrman openly disparage African Americans, and he didn't care who knew it.

The technique, in courtroom jargon, is called "stealing your thunder." When your opponent has a piece of evidence or testimony, which is particularly devastating to your witness, get it out on the table before the opponent's cross-examination, and try to defuse it and explain it. But the letter from Bell described attitudes so offensive that it is doubtful that it could have been much palliated by any lawyer's technique. In the letter she states that Fuhrman advocated putting all "niggers" in a pile and burning them. Fuhrman denied having made any such statements, but a majority of the jurors – interviewed after the verdict was in—said that they thought he was lying from the outset. Clark asked Fuhrman if he was nervous because of the public attention that had been brought to bear on him from publicity that had preceded the trial. He indicated that these media reports made him uneasy.

Clark first led Fuhrman through a 1985 visit to the Simpson home where he had been called for a family dispute. The call didn't result in any arrests or reports as Nicole declined to file any charges.

Then Clark turned his focus to the murders at hand, and Fuhrman testified to his observations at the Bundy crime scene when he arrived at 2:10 a.m. He and Detective Phillips decided to enter the scene via the back alleyway so as not to disturb evidence. He went on to describe seeing a glove and a cap, footprints, an envelope with glasses, blood drops by the footprints leading away from the bodies. He also testified that Officer Riske noted a blood "smudge" on the rear gate at Bundy.

After the observations concluded at Bundy, Fuhrman testified that Detective Phillips asked if he knew the way to O. J. Simpson's Rockingham home. He stated it was not his idea to go to Simpson's residence, but the commander in charge that morning wanted an in-person notification so Fuhrman and Dets. Phillips, Lange, and Vannatter went to the property at around 5 a.m. As the other three investigators stayed at the gate, ringing the buzzer, Fuhrman walked alone around the house outside of the fence and noticed a white Ford Bronco parked on the street "a little askew."

Fuhrman said he noted a "small spot" above the driver's side door handle and pointed it out to Lange and Vannatter. When unable to reach anyone inside the property, Fuhrman suggested to Vannatter that he could jump the wall, and Vannatter agreed. Marcia Clark felt it was important to underline that Fuhrman was being directed by other, more senior detectives and that he was not acting of his own volition.

The investigators met Kato Kaelin and Simpson's daughter Arnelle. Fuhrman took the lead to question Kaelin, alone in his room. When Fuhrman asked if he noticed anything unusual the evening before, Kaelin mentioned the thumps he heard at about 10:45 p.m. on the side of his guest house. Fuhrman walked Kaelin to the main house and after telling Vannatter to talk to Kaelin at the bar, Fuhrman said he left to investigate the thumps, wondering if there could be another victim who collapsed in the narrow walkway. This is when Fuhrman said he found the bloody glove, describing it as "moist or sticky." Fuhrman left the glove and brought out each of the detectives, one by one, to show them this evidence.

Fuhrman testified that after the discovery, Vannatter told him and Phillips at about 7 a.m. to return to the Bundy crime scene to see if the glove there appeared to be a match to the newly found glove at Rockingham. Fuhrman returned to Bundy and directed a crime scene photographer, Rolf Rokahr, to take pictures of the Bundy glove. Fuhrman said the glove appeared to be a match and he returned to Rockingham to tell investigators. Rokahr followed Fuhrman so he could photograph the Rockingham glove as well.

Upon hearing this news, Vannatter determined that Rockingham was now a crime scene and requested the property be secured and a search warrant be issued. Fuhrman remained at the Rockingham estate until about 6 p.m., keeping media outlets at bay and waiting for the warrant.

* * *

After his direct examination, I had the opportunity to cross-examine him. But I was hampered in my ability to put the screws to him. Holding true to this trial's litany of twists and surprises, Judge Ito issued a ruling that was, at the time, a major blow to the defense. He stated that I could not, on cross-examination, inquire about Fuhrman's use of the "N-word" going back more than ten years. By doing this, he neatly covered up the damning contents of the bizarre lawsuit that Fuhrman had filed against the City of Los Angeles after being denied a disability pension. More importantly, his ruling effectively barred mention of the numerous medical reports we have described.

These findings relating to Fuhrman's character would have been much more than mere cannon fodder in the armory of the cross-examiner: They would have been the equivalent of tank-obliterating rockets, so blazingly did they spotlight Fuhrman's scheming, severe psychiatric deficiencies, and—from all those who examined him—pure and simple malingering. It seems more than coincidental that Fuhrman's case to sue for disability pension terminated just over the ten-year line before the Simpson murder trial. By imposing a "ten-year" door-slammer on inquiries, Judge Ito did the prosecution an enormous favor, in a way that had no legal support in the case law, the statutes, and the court rules. Judge Ito's ruling was fashioned out of his own head and narrowly tailored to benefit the prosecution.

Had these findings been presented to the jury in the form of questions to Fuhrman, he would have lost all credibility as a witness.

However, just as cunning lurks in the minds of men after Judge Ito's decision, Johnnie and I created a plan for the reemergence of Fuhrman's pension application report.

I was barely into the area of my cross-examination of Fuhrman, about to raise the specter of his use of racially obnoxious language, when Judge Ito imposed the surprise ruling—apparently to cut me off, at least temporarily, at the pass—by saying that until I produced the witnesses who claimed to have heard Fuhrman use the N-word, I could not question him about racially loaded statements he allegedly made in their presence. This, like the ten-year rule, was suspected of having its origins in the judge's desire to avoid the divisive racial debacle which was threatening to unfold in his courtroom at any moment, ushered in by a group of aggressive defense lawyers.

* * *

Our preparation of materials affecting Fuhrman became more and more voluminous. For those who have never been tasked with the job of slicing into a narrative description of a series of events—such as Fuhrman's story—there is generally little appreciation of the great amount of work that is involved in a thorough battle plan. In homicide cases, with the penalties at the end of an unsuccessful trial ranging from *true* life imprisonment to execution, the stakes are enormous. There is never an excuse, among real professionals, for leaving any stone unturned in defense of a client.

It has always been my practice to study the wisdom of the lawyers who have influenced me over the course of my life—both living and deceased—advice imparted in lectures, books, articles, and of course transcripts of their work. The technique I adopted as a non-lawyer trial counsel in the Marine Corps is still viable today: begin by arguing within your own mind the case for each side, in turn, looking for strengths, weaknesses, evidence in need of meticulous scrutiny, and holes in the evidence which badly need to be filled if possible.

Such was the mantra of the man I considered to be my principal mentor, Edward Bennett Williams. Another luminary of the trial bar, Louis B. Nizer, author of *My Life in Court*, emphasized the notion that trial lawyers, as they analyze the available evidence, should give much weight to what he called the "probabilities." This has proven to be a useful technique, and I found myself applying it constantly as I groped my way through the labyrinth of case preparation. In the matter of The People vs. Orenthal James Simpson, I attempted to evaluate the "probabilities" both as to the prosecution's theory of the case, and the "evidence" of Mark Fuhrman, which from all I could assimilate was in need of punctilious examination.

The theory adopted by the prosecution seemed to be that Simpson had suddenly become a homicidal monster who risked everything he had accomplished in life by butchering the mother of his two young children in their own front yard.

It seemed to me that this Jekyll-to-Hyde transformation would have required a monumental triggering event at its threshold, but the file we had assembled contained not even a suggestion that such an occurrence had taken place.

Both sides, prosecution and defense, agreed that when Simpson attended his youngest daughter's dance recital on that

Sunday afternoon—an event populated principally by his former wife's friends and family—he was in a cordial frame of mind. After leaving this group, he made an unsuccessful attempt to find some female companionship by calling his girlfriend, Paula Barbieri. Having no success in reaching her, Simpson went to a fast-food restaurant with his house guest-tenant, Kato Kaelin, and had a quick burger. Simpson and Kaelin parted back at the house at 9:37 p.m. Phone records show that Simpson called Barbieri again at 10:03. From the time Simpson returned from dinner with Kaelin, no third person could attest to his whereabouts until Kaelin and the limo driver, Allen Park, saw him near his front door at about the same time, just prior to his departure for the airport at 10:55 p.m.

Therefore, assuming—as did both the police and the prosecution—that something caused Simpson to morph into a homicidal monster, and assuming that he then drove his white Bronco to Nicole's home, and at some point after 10:30 p.m. attacked her with a knife, nearly severing her head, with full knowledge that his young children might be observing the incident through a window in the home. Then assuming further that he was surprised by the arrival of Ron Goldman as Nicole was rapidly bleeding out, he proceeded to dispose of Goldman with some seventeen stab wounds. Then he left the murder site and then returned—apparently to retrieve something thought to be of importance (perhaps a weapon)—and drove six miles to his residence, where he effectively concealed all of the evidence, and then cleaned himself up so that he could present himself packed, dressed, and ready for travel by 10:55 p.m. The question presented was not the time at which the homicides had begun, but the time at which they had ended. The prosecution team was acutely aware from the outset that it had a serious problem with the clock.

As I looked at the totally uncontradicted statements of the string of timeline witnesses beginning with Tom Lang and ending with Robert Heidstra, it became clear to me that a guilty Simpson could not have left the scene before 10:40 p.m. *at the earliest*. And fifteen minutes was simply nowhere near the minimum amount of time it would have taken him to leave the bloody carnage of the slaughter and accomplish all that would have been necessary for him to make his appearance, relaxed and affable, before Kaelin and Park at 10:55.

Ignoring for the moment the lack of motive sticking out from the case file like a large sore thumb, the scenario which the prosecution had married was not only incredible, it was not even close to plausible. At that point, it seemed clear to me that if Simpson were called upon to present a defense, he had a veritable cornucopia of evidentiary weapons with which to shred the prosecution.

Flipping the coin, I then examined—with a jaundiced eye—what I perceived to be the prosecution's case. It appeared to be held together not just by spit and baling wire, but by the uncorroborated testimony of Mark Fuhrman, who had asserted that he had happened upon smoking gun evidence that tied the accused directly to the killings at South Bundy.

* * *

In preparation, I obtained a transcript of the entire preliminary hearing, video tape recordings of the live action in the courtroom during the hearing, and all of the investigative reports I could gather from every source, including that which had been turned over to the defense by the prosecution.

At this point, it should be helpful to provide some insights into the world of cross-examination:

Most people whose lives are not intertwined with the court system get distorted views of what the technique is all about. Occasionally, a book or a movie will describe or depict the cross-examination of an important witness the way it actually happens in real life. However, for many reasons, this is rare.

In the first place, readers and viewers would probably become impatient if they were required to sit through the often-plodding phases necessary to a properly executed cross-examination. A well-trained lawyer does not simply "jump for the prize" and begin their cross by skewering the witness right out of the gate. This is especially true when cross-examining experienced witnesses who testify frequently, such as law enforcement officers and experts.

When properly done, cross-examination is a very complex technique. The stream of variables confronting the cross-examiner—as answers are given to their questions—requires rapid-fire decisions with as few mistakes as possible. Perhaps this is why many say that flight training is an excellent background for learning cross-examination. Why? Because once aloft, lots of decisions must be made without hesitating or flinching—decisions that, if wrong, could result in catastrophe.

Many a good case has been lost because of faulty cross-examination. Those examples portrayed in the dramatic arts bear little similarity to the hurly-burly of live testimony in a real courtroom. The cross-examination itself is the tip of the iceberg—perhaps seven-eighths of the total effort involved is below the surface, seldom glimpsed by the public. During a well-prepared cross, every stone under which some possibly relevant fact could be hidden has to be upturned, a drudgery that frequently reveals little except the fact that this particular stone can be discarded as unimportant. However, to assume such irrelevance without looking closely can be a very grave mistake.

In anticipating what may become important in the ever-shifting sands of a cross-examination, an accomplished cross-examiner must simply stuff his head with every detail and scrap of minutiae that can be discovered about the witness: their beliefs, proclivities, habits, preferences, aberrations, weaknesses, prior history, and predictability. These are all part of the matrix which must be assembled to do the job properly—and not only is the collection of this data from every possible source essential, but so is the ability of the cross-examiner to absorb the information and keep it literally at their fingertips, at least until the case is over.

If this seems to be an insurmountable task, beyond the reaches of human memory, it is not. Expanding one's memory and causing it to function like a machine gun in rapid-fire mode is akin in some respects to bodybuilding with strength machines. Onlookers marvel every year at the performance of professional weightlifters who can bench press five hundred pounds or more. The feat is the result of intense workouts over time. So, too, is training memory. Anyone who has ever sat for an examination—written or oral—has accomplished to some extent the exercise I described. Those who pass the most complex exams, such as the bar exam in most states of the United States, have learned to cram at a higher level. The problem is, like the weightlifter who decreases his training, over time muscle will be replaced by flab.

The advent of the smartphone has proven to be a toxic enemy to the exercise of developing and keeping an agile and active long-term memory. Many people now have some difficulty in remembering their own telephone numbers, simply because they don't have to. The advantage of having instant access to much more information than you could ever remember is offset by the fact that the human memory tends to shrink from lack of use. To a top-shelf cross-examiner, this is anathema.

An expert in cross-examination comes to the podium with no notes or other documents, and keeps his eyes constantly in use: watching the witness, primarily, but also the judge and jury, and from time to time (from the corner of the eye) the opposing counsel. Are notes being taken? Does the other lawyer look apprehensive as you change subjects and begin to home in on some new phase of the case?

This critical and essential use of the cross-examiner's eyes would be hampered if, from time to time, he had to glance at notes, outlines, cue cards, or other memory "crutches." If the witness feels that he is being drawn into troubled waters, the first indication of the onset of a wobbly self-confidence can be seen in the eyes. What may have been a steady gaze from the witness stand, will suddenly degenerate into shifty looks (left, right, and down), accompanied by nervous body movements in the hands, shoulders, and facial features. At the same time, the structure of the witness's responses become hedged (e.g. "I would have..." instead of "I did..."). Most telling of all, when it happens, is the witness looking for help of some kind from the lawyer who called him to the stand. Jurors are sometimes inclined to think that the witness is seeking signals and hints that will guide him toward the answer the lawyer would like to hear. When this happens, it is often appropriate to challenge the witness directly and forcefully by demanding to know why he is looking at your opponent when a question is pending. This is easily accomplished by one skilled in the business of questioning witnesses in the heat of the trial.

It is unfortunate that, unlike the medical profession which abounds in training for specialists of many different kinds, American law schools don't provide specific training for trial lawyers. Although some programs claim to offer expertise in trial advocacy, there are few that have been shown to generate trial lawyers who have rapidly ascended to the top of the profession. Many of us who have spent years in the courtroom dealing with cases of every sort and stripe believe that we should emulate the British system, which gives special training to those law school graduates who wish to practice as courtroom trial lawyers, called barristers in the U.K. Our system of trial-lawyer training is not a formalized method, but essentially an apprentice system.

Perhaps the greatest benefit of the development of barristers in the United Kingdom and many of its sister countries is that good cross-examiners are easier to find—and predict—than in the United States.

I seem to have been training to be a trial lawyer my whole life. At a very young age I became fascinated with the ability to remember things and did exercises in my head that others would most often do on paper. Indeed, I was expelled from grammar school on two occasions for "cheating" because my "answer sheet" on arithmetic tests disclosed no written calculations. Two different teachers assumed that I had copied the answers from one of the students sitting nearby. On both occasions my mother—herself a respected educator—had to come to the school and demanded to see the answer sheets of those other students who had been sitting within my view to challenge the accusations. When it turned out that none of the "abutters" had gotten a score nearly as high as my own, the accusers wilted and—unhappily, I am sure—reinstated me.

In truth, I must admit that this habit of doing calculations in my head was in part because my handwriting was so atrocious—and still is. Indeed, after my first semester grades at Boston University Law School were not up to my own standards, I petitioned the school to allow me to type my exams. The school agreed, and I was first in my class every semester after that.

From my very first contact with the Simpson case, I began to memorize facts and circumstances which I thought might be useful in the cross-examination of Mark Fuhrman. First and foremost was the item which generally tops the list of assets that all cross-examiners crave, prior statements by the witness. In this case, the prior statements were contained in the transcript of the preliminary hearing and they were in many respects precise. However, that transcript would have been more valuable had Fuhrman been effectively cross-examined during that proceeding. He should have been sharply challenged as a racist and a man of constricted moral dimensions with an innate desire to be the star of "a big arrest," as well as one who had—for a brief moment—seen himself as the star in what he termed the "biggest case of the century" only to find that he was unceremoniously dumped as one of the lead detectives. If so, Judge Kathleen Kennedy-Powell might have been much more hesitant to accept him as the only linchpin connecting the suspect Simpson to the murders most foul.

Unfortunately, defense lawyer Gerry Uelmen was neither adequately prepared nor sufficiently experienced to hog-tie his witness. A first-rate cross-examiner might well have made clear—as hindsight has clearly shown—that the prospective trial of O. J. Simpson was an adventure in futility and a guarantee of effective immunity for those who had actually perpetrated the killings. Nonetheless, I do not wish to appear before my colleagues as one who is willing to denigrate them. In murder cases such as this, the defense is rarely afforded a preliminary hearing and no opportunity is given to pin down—even partially—rogue witnesses such as Mark Fuhrman.

Like most prior statements, this one had value in part not because of what Fuhrman did say, but because of what he *did not* say or explain when he had the opportunity. Time after time after time, I pored over that transcript until eventually I knew it almost word-for-word.

At the same time, I attempted to assimilate the statements offered by several witnesses who would be prepared to describe the racial slurs and white supremacist beliefs that had emanated on a regular basis from the mouth of Mark Fuhrman. Heading this list—which turned out to be extensive—was a woman named Kathleen Bell.

Bell had encountered Fuhrman at a Marine recruiting station on more than one occasion because she worked in a real estate office in the same building. Fuhrman was apparently exploring the possibility of reenlisting in the Marine Corps.

Bell wrote the following letter to Johnnie Cochran when she recognized Fuhrman on television:

Dear Mr. Cochran:

I'm writing to you in regards to a story I saw on the news last night. I thought it ridiculous that the Simpson defense team would even suggest that there might be racial motivation involved in the trial against Mr. Simpson. I then glanced up at the television and was quite shocked to see that officer Ferrman [sic] was a man that I had the misfortune of meeting.

You may have received a message from your answering service last night that I called to say that Mr. Ferman may be more of a racist than you could even imagine. Between 1985 and 1986 I worked as a real estate agent in Redondo Beach for Century 21 Bob Maher Realty, now out of business. At that time, my office was located above a Marine recruiting center off the Pacific Coast Highway. On occasion I would stop in to say hello to the two Marines working there. I saw Mr. Ferman there a couple of times. I remember him distinctly because of his height and build. While speaking to the man I learned that Mr. Ferman was a police officer in Westwood, and I don't know if he was telling the truth, but he said that he had been in the special division of the Marines. I don't know how the subject was raised, but officer Ferman said that when he sees a "Nigger" (as he called it) driving with a white woman, he would pull them over. I asked would [he] if he didn't have a reason, and he said that he would find one. I looked at the two Marines to see if they knew he was joking, but it became obvious to me that he was very serious.

Officer Ferman went on to say that he would like nothing more than to see all "Nigger's" (sic) gathered together and killed. He said something about burning them or bombing them, I was too shaken to remember the exact words he used. However I do remember that what he said was probably the most horrible thing I had ever heard someone say. What frightened me even more was that he was a police officer.

I am almost certain that I called the LAPD to complain about officer Mark Ferman, yet I did not know his last name at the time. I would think that the LAPD has some record of this. Now that I know Mr. Ferman was the investigating officer, I must suggest that you check into his background further. I am certainly not a fan of Mr. Simpson, but I would hate to see anyone harmed by an officer's extreme hatred.

If you have any questions, you may contact me at work (310-519-xxxx, or at home, 310-987-xxxx.)

Sincerely,
Kathleen Bell

As a result of this letter, Pat McKenna went to the recruiting station to interview the Marines who had been on duty at the time of Fuhrman's visit, and he also talked to Kathleen Bell. At the same time, other witnesses came forward—some with considerable hesitation—to relate similar experiences with Mark Fuhrman.

Before Fuhrman took the stand in the government's case, I was able to summarize the testimony which we had already documented, as well as that which we felt we could produce once we had the power to subpoena reluctant witnesses. In what I termed "Fuhrman's Funeral," I set forth where I thought we were, and where I thought we could go. It was becoming increasingly clear that unless the prosecution could pack the jury box with rabid racists, Mark Fuhrman would kill their case because of his loose and filthy tongue.

Below is a copy of that summary of witnesses who could testify to Fuhrman's character:

Kathleen Bell: This 32-year-old Caucasian woman worked in 1985-86 for the Century 21 real estate chain in Redondo Beach. Her office was located near (and above) the Marine Recruiting Station where Fuhrman inquired—on several occasions—about renewing his affiliation with the Marine Corps. Believing him to be an attractive man when she was introduced to him, and noting that he was 6'3", she inquired as to whether he would be interested in meeting a friend of hers named Andrea Terry, who was attractive and quite tall. Bell mentioned that Terry was a fan of (pro footballer and O. J. Simpson friend) Marcus Allen, whereupon Fuhrman exploded into a racially based tirade.

Andrea Terry: Kathleen Bell's friend, who is now married to a former BYU football star. She was in Hennesey's Tavern in Redondo Beach with Bell a few days later, when Fuhrman walked in. She introduced herself to him. She heard substantially the same stream of racial epithets as had been visited upon Bell.

Max Cordoba: Max is African American, in his early forties, retired recently after serving 20 years in the Marine Corps. His last assignment was in the recruiting office at Redondo Beach. He had seen Fuhrman there before, handling some paperwork with Sgt. Ron Rohrer. In the spring of 1986, Fuhrman came to the office with some papers; Rohrer had stepped out for a few minutes. Cordoba was about to explain this to Fuhrman when he spotted Rohrer walking back toward the office. He called to him: "Hey, Rohrer, your boy is here!" Fuhrman turned on Cordoba and snarled: "Let's get something straight—the only 'boy' around here is you, nigger!" Max stood and walked out to the parking lot to defuse the situation. Fuhrman followed him, and repeated the insult.

Carol Hannack: Carol is Caucasian, 34, and comes from a small town in Eastern Pennsylvania. When she was 17, she was one of two high school students picked to go to Washington to work for the FBI. She eventually came to LA, and presently works for a music entertainment manager. In 1987, Carol was living in West LA Carol met Fuhrman's then partner, Tom Vettraino, on August 24, 1987, while her roommate—Natalie Singer—was admitted to a hospital with a kidney stone. The officers were at the hospital on another matter at the time. Carol had dated Vettraino a few times, and Fuhrman would come with him to their apartment. Fuhrman was always drawing attention to himself. He explicated his hatred for "niggers" on several occasions. Eventually, Singer refused to let Fuhrman in the house, because of his vocal racial attitudes. Carol stopped seeing Vettraino in the middle fall of 1987; about a month later, Fuhrman bumped into her on the street and called her a "dirty cunt" for "breaking Tom's heart." Carol reported this fact to Natalie. Carol is attractive, articulate, and will make a good witness. She is apprehensive, and has been harassed by Anthony Pellicano, the well-known Hollywood private investigator who wound up in federal prison. She met with Pellicano in the presence of her lawyer, Howard Levy, whom Pat and I are to interview soon.

Natalie Singer: Natalie is 38, of Jewish-Italian descent, and grew up in New York's upper west side. She has many friends who are minorities and is offended by racial slurs of any kind. She says she was repelled by Fuhrman when she first met him; At that time she was working in the film industry here in West LA, Fuhrman came to the apartment she shared with Carol Hannack on three occasions that she remembers, in the fall of 1987. Each time he tried to be the center of attention and expressed his hatred for "niggers." On the third visit, Natalie was in the upstairs bathroom when Fuhrman and Vettraino came walking up the front walk of the apartment. Fuhrman was cursing loudly. Natalie called down: "I don't want Mark to come into this house!" Vettraino came in alone and visited with Carol while Fuhrman waited outside. Pellicano has called Natalie and has admitted that Fuhrman used the word "nigger" a lot; Pellicano says he has heard that Natalie may testify that Fuhrman admitted to her that he dropped the right-handed glove at Rockingham. Natalie has refused to talk to Pellicano, and has referred him to her attorney, James Neal of Nashville, for any further communications.

Judge Tracy Houston: Mid-thirties Caucasian woman lives in Fort Bend, Texas. She graduated SMU law school in the spring of 1987, and took a trip to Los Angeles to visit her brother, whom she describes as a musician "whose name we would recognize." She presently adjudicates unemployment claims, largely through hearings held over the phone, using an interpreter where necessary. One evening she was driving her brother's car, looking for an address of someone that she planned to visit. While she was driving slowly near the curb, Mark Fuhrman—who was in LAPD uniform—pulled her over to challenge her sobriety. While she was explaining who she was and what she was doing, a car pulled up next to Fuhrman to ask directions; the driver was black, and the lady in the passenger's seat was white. Fuhrman said something to them, and then turned back to Tracy, to whom he expressed his disgust with "niggers." Tracy was struck by the fact that a uniformed officer would use that word so casually to a total stranger and remembers the event vividly.

Roderic Hodge: Hodge, African American around thirty-five—a Marine from 1983-1989. He first encountered Fuhrman when Fuhrman arrested him. Fuhrman used to arrest Hodge several times, take him downtown and force him to post bail (costing $300.00). The third time Fuhrman arrested Hodge, on January 10, 1987, the latter was charged with "sale or transportation of a controlled substance." While driving to the police station, Hodge was sitting in the rear seat of the cruiser; Vettraino was driving, and Fuhrman was sitting in the front passenger seat. Fuhrman turned to Hodge and said, "I told you we'd get you, nigger!" Hodge was tried and acquitted—with co-defendant Earl Thompson—in LA Superior Court in 1987. While Fuhrman was strip-searching Hodge and his co-arrestees, he made them bend over and stood behind them. While doing so, he said: "You assholes all look alike to me . . . " or words to that effect. Mr. Hodge is tall, very handsome, and should be an excellent witness.

Joseph Britton: An African American man shot and arrested by Fuhrman or his partner for robbery. Britton was shot, it was claimed, because he was brandishing a knife. Britton claimed in a civil suit filed later that he was the victim of "planted evidence."

We proposed Britton's situation to Judge Ito as a basis for cross-examination, but were turned down because Britton described his assailant as having "red hair and a red moustache." One would think that the slugs removed from Britton's body might have been traced to the gun of one officer or another, and between the two Britton arresting officers, he could select one of them as the one who placed the knife at his feet. Significantly, the city settled Britton's civil suit—for $100,000—shortly before Fuhrman was to take the stand. On August 18, 1995, CBS News quoted Robert Deutsch, Britton's lawyer, as saying, "My theory is that the city didn't want to have Fuhrman exposed to the cross-examination in our case, in which we had a lot more damaging evidence on him than the 'Dream Team.'"

Apart from the history of racial bias, there were quite a number of items described in Mark Fuhrman's own narrative which were decidedly atypical conduct for a detective, especially in a murder case that was sure to capture and even dominate public curiosity. For example, the primary instance of aberrant conduct which centered upon the number of times wherein Fuhrman had contrived to be somewhere or do something without any other witnesses present. First, in ordinary practice, detectives operate in pairs for a number of sound reasons. Fuhrman had consistently pursued the role of the "lone wolf" in circumstances where a vicious killer might have been working in the area and had every reason to make sure that his partner or one of the other detectives was at his side constantly.

The second strange factor in the Fuhrman equation was that he seemed to be the instigator of most of the significant steps taken that night by him and the other detectives.

It was Fuhrman who first suggested that a trip to Simpson's home might be a good idea, to determine whether any mayhem or other murders had been carried out there. When the senior detectives agreed with him, Fuhrman offered to lead the way because he knew the location of the Simpson home from his 1985 encounter with O. J. and Nicole in the driveway.

Once the detectives arrived and were confronted by a locked gate and got no response from pushing the call button, it seems highly probable that Fuhrman jumped the fence on his own initiative on the grounds that the detectives were presented with an emergency situation, and although Vannatter claimed otherwise, it appeared to be quite likely that he actually ratified this conduct after the fact, but did not approve it beforehand.

What Mark Fuhrman did gives rise to a strong inference that he was desperate to gain access to the Simpson home.

The security company, Westec, maintained twenty-four-hour service and could have opened it either with a remote electronic signal or by sending a representative to the location within a few minutes. There were no external signs or sounds coming from the premises at the time which validated the assumption that the detectives were confronting an emergency.

In retrospect, Fuhrman's frantic efforts to have access to the home and fenced-in surroundings strongly suggest an ulterior motive rather than a genuine concern for possible victims.

Next—and this is a curious twist in Fuhrman's overall conduct at the Simpson home in the early Monday morning hours—with no clear direction from either of the two senior detectives nor his partner, Ron Phillips, Fuhrman wound up talking *alone* to Kato Kaelin. Kaelin described to him that sometime after 10:40 p.m. the previous evening he was talking with his friend Rachel Ferrara on the phone when he heard some loud "thumps" which appeared to have originated on the outside of the wall in his bedroom through which an air conditioner had been mounted.

This incident, further reported by Kaelin to Simpson just before the latter boarded his limousine, remains unexplained to this day. No set of circumstances supported by logic would seem to link the "thumping" to any other fact or set of facts related directly or indirectly to the murders.

Kaelin speculated with his girlfriend whether the thumps were related to a minor local earthquake.

If Simpson had committed the crimes and carried with him from the scene of the murders an item of evidence which—if later linked to him could be terribly damning—is even more incomprehensible that he would bring evidence onto the premises of his own home. And even assuming he did that, why in the world would he then bang upon the wall next to Kaelin's air conditioner, inviting someone to come out and take a look at the source of the sound? And—another good question—why would Simpson take *that* route, the least logical, if he were planning to enter his house?

By the same token, it makes very little sense to hypothesize that the true killer or killers would successfully escape from a rather public murder scene undetected, and then spit in the face of fate by going to O. J. Simpson's home to plant evidence which might distract those who would otherwise be searching for them, the killer(s). Since it was conceded by the prosecution that the shrubbery growing along the fence which defined the property line between Simpson's home and that of his abutting neighbor did not show any signs of damage from being pushed aside, it is fair to assume that the culprit would have had to gain access to Simpson's property to accomplish his purpose in the same manner in which Mark Fuhrman did.

CHAPTER 12
Fuhrman Takes the Stand

Faced with cleaning up Mark Fuhrman's image, which had been severely damaged by the racist information that had come out about him in the media, Marcia Clark, as lead prosecutor, had a tough job on her hands. She had to somehow convince the jury that while he was, yes, probably a "bad guy," his story was still good. I certainly wouldn't have wanted to be in her place.

At this point in the trial, it was no secret that the defense suspected Fuhrman of carrying the bloody glove from Bundy to O. J.'s house. However, we had not offered any evidence that he had done so (because it wasn't yet our "turn"; the prosecution was still putting on its case.) But the charge was in the air. The previous summer, an anonymous defense lawyer had told *The New Yorker* magazine just that.

According to the magazine:

> In a series of conversations last week, leading members of Simpson's defense team floated this new and provocative theory...Those conversations revealed that they plan to portray the detective as a rogue cop who, rather than solving the crime, framed an innocent man. "Just picture

it," one of the attorneys told me. "Here's a guy who's one of the cops coming on the scene early in the morning. They have the biggest case of their lives. But an hour later you're told you're not in charge of the case. How's that going to make that guy feel? So now he's one of four detectives heading over to O. J.'s house. Suppose he's actually found two gloves at the murder scene. He transports one of them over to the house and then 'finds' it back in that little alleyway where no one can see him." That would make him "the hero of the case," the attorney said.

At one level, it is a brilliant theory. It's what some defense lawyers call a "judo defense," in that it turns the strength of the prosecution's case against the prosecution. The fact that the blood on the glove is consistent with the victims' blood goes from being strong evidence of Simpson's guilt—who else but Simpson could have been at both Nicole's house and his own that night?—to being evidence of a police conspiracy. If it was Fuhrman who transported the glove, then the bloody gloves become, for the defense, harmless at worst and exculpatory at best. That the Simpson defense team is advancing this theory shows just what kind of hardball it plans to play at the trial. For the theory, while ingenious, is also monstrous. It means that the defense will attempt to persuade a jury of Los Angeles citizens that one of their own police officers planted evidence to see an innocent man convicted of murder and, potentially, sent to the gas chamber.

In fact, the defense's theory is even more monstrous. The defense will assert that Mark Fuhrman's motivation for framing O. J. Simpson is racism. "This is a bad cop," one defense lawyer told me. "This is a racist cop. . . ." If race does become a significant factor in this case—if the case becomes transformed from a mere soap opera to a civil-rights melodrama; that is, from the Menendez brothers writ large to Rodney King redux—then the stakes will change dramatically. Simpson's attorneys understand the implications of a racially tinged strategy, and there appear to be subtle but real differences of opinion within the defense camp about how hard to push the race angle. One Simpson attorney asserts that, while his client does appear to be the victim of a racist cop, the team will not claim that he was framed unless it truly believes he was. Another says that the Fuhrman defense is a done deal. Still, it appears that the case is about to enter a new phase—one with the potential to affect the city of Los Angeles as a whole, and not just one of its most famous residents.

Nonetheless, skepticism bloomed everywhere. "The charge that Fuhrman planted evidence does not seem credible and to this point there has not been a shred of evidence offered that he did so," reported the *New York Times*, quoting Erwin Chemerinsky, a professor of law at the University of Southern California. "The reason we pay attention isn't because it's believable, but because if the jury believes it that could decide the case."

The *Times* reported further,

> Key to that accusation of racism is Kathleen Bell, a real estate agent who has told the defense that at a Marine recruiting station a decade ago, she heard Mr. Fuhrman launch into a racist diatribe. She described those experiences in a letter to Mr. Simpson's chief trial lawyer, Johnnie L. Cochran Jr., a letter Judge Lance A. Ito had said he would let the defense introduce....[Ms. Bell wrote, in part], "Officer Ferman [sic] said that when he sees a 'nigger,' (as he called it) driving with a white woman, he would pull them over," she wrote. "I asked what if he didn't have a reason, and he said he would find one. Officer Ferman went on to say that he would like nothing more than to see all 'niggers' gathered together and killed. He said something about burning them or bombing them."
>
> Eight of the twelve jurors in the case are black. There were no winces, pursed lips or other facial expressions as

they read the letter; only one of them appeared to move, and it was simply to rock back and scratch his head.

The reporter also wrote,

> But throughout Ms. Clark's examination, Mr. Bailey did not make any objections, nor did he take any notes—because, he said, afterward, Ms. Clark had been doing his work for him.
>
> "They knew they couldn't block it, so they decided to do what's called stealing the thunder of the opponent," he said. "I seriously doubt that if I'd been prosecuting, I would have put those words up. Any African Americans looking at those phrases—put them all in a pile and burn them—have got to have an impression that's going to be hard to get rid of."
>
> Of Mr. Fuhrman, Mr. Bailey said: "He's articulate, presents himself well, and would appear at first blush to be a credible witness."

Referring to Ms. Clark, I told the reporter that I thought she'd done well, considering the challenge. It's a difficult thing to do to start out trashing your own witness. But her examination would open the door to other potentially explosive racial episodes in Fuhrman's past that Judge Ito had previously ruled off-limits.

The prosecution knew they had a live grenade on their hands with Mark Fuhrman and wanted desperately to put the pin back in. Like the defense, they knew Fuhrman had sought early retirement, and had he been successful, he would have been pensioned out after a relatively short six-year career. His claims were grounded on the notion that because of the severity of the circumstances he had to endure in dealing with these troublemakers—whom the report said he persisted in calling "assholes"—he was no longer able to perform the duties required of him. In other words, he was no longer fit to be a cop.

Despite Fuhrman's claims of being unfit to serve those he was hired to protect, the management of the Los Angeles Police Department, in its wisdom, not only kept him in service but then *promoted* him to detective. Fuhrman's lawsuit generated sensational stories by reporters from the *New Yorker* magazine and *Newsweek* and led to speculation that Fuhrman's role in the forthcoming trial would either be greatly diminished or eliminated entirely.

Before the end of the year, defense investigators Pat McKenna and John McNally had developed information sources from a couple of "moles" on the other side of the fence. Our information was that the prosecutors were heartsick to learn how terribly vulnerable their only true nexus to the crime was in the area of racial bias, in part because of his own admissions in formal legal pleadings in the California Superior Court.

Indeed, we learned that the lawyers on the other side—including District Attorney Gil Garcetti himself—had explored every conceivable way that they might put in a case against Simpson without putting Mark Fuhrman on the stand and in the line of fire. Some of their proposed schemes, we were told, were so off the wall they verged on the hilarious.

When push came to shove, no workable routes to prosecution without "the witness Fuhrman" were discovered or developed, and the prosecutorial strategy was reduced to two prongs. One, they would try desperately to convince Judge Ito to completely exclude from cross-examination any mention of Fuhrman's disdain for African Americans. And two, they hoped to coach Fuhrman into being a reliable witness.

As to the issue of keeping Fuhrman's racist history out of evidence, Judge Ito was too tightly shackled by existing law to do so. Not long before the Simpson case arose, the United States Supreme Court had ruled in clear language that when relevant, racial bias on the part of the witness was a legitimate ground for exploration. To put frosting on the cake, the California intermediate appellate court, whose rulings controlled all of the superior court judges in Los Angeles County, had specifically echoed the ruling of the "Supremes" in Washington. In deference to these two cases, Judge Ito ruled that racial bias was fair ground.

As a second—and really the *only* remaining option—prosecutors attempted to literally "brainwash" Fuhrman into being a "nice guy." Toward this end, we learned in delicious detail of the efforts of Assistant District Attorney Alan Yockelson and several of his colleagues to reform the personality of their witness by putting him on the stand in the grand jury room (thus ensuring minimal intrusion) and trying in several ways to school him in how to be a good witness. To assist them, they hired a psychologist named Mark Goulston to monitor the proceedings and give advice as to how they might improve their endeavors. In short, and although none of the "instructors" was a skilled or experienced cross examiner, we understood that their main objective was to convince Fuhrman that he was going to be pummeled heavily for his use of racial epithets, and that he had better admit to using offensive language and apologize for it rather than trying to claim his vocabulary was pristine.

We planned our strategy for when it was our turn to cross-examine Fuhrman, and my path was clear: by picking the right moment when it appeared that he did not have the will to own up to his transgressions and hitting him squarely with questions about the use of the word *nigger*, we would pin him to an emphatic denial from which any retreat would be impossible.

Judge Ito's order barring any reference to racially derisive rhetoric from Fuhrman from more than ten years ago meant I could not mention the contents of the pleadings filed in his lawsuit or the circumstances and conditions which motivated him to attest to them. But I felt that the chances were better than even that, using techniques found in the arsenals of most seasoned cross-examiners, I would find a moment when he would let his guard down and be unable to resist denying that which we were prepared to prove thoroughly and extensively was a poisonous racial attitude against blacks. We had done our homework and had statements from a dozen different people who'd heard him use the N-word in the past decade.

Photo by Vinnie Zuffante/Archive Photos/Getty images

O.J. Simpson and his ex-wife, Nicole Brown Simpson, on March 14, 1994, at the premiere of the movie, *Naked Gun 33 ⅓*.

Photo by Lee Celano/WireImage

A family photo of Ronald Goldman, who was murdered with O. J. Simpson's ex-wife on June 12, 1994.

Photo by Lee Celano/WireImage

Attorney F. Lee Bailey at a pre-trial hearing, January 12, 1995.

Defense attorney Johnnie Cochran in discussion with prosecutors Marcia Clark and Christopher Darden, Feb. 9, 1995.

Defense attorney F. Lee Bailey cross-examines LAPD Detective
Mark Fuhrman, March 14, 1995.

Defense attorneys F. Lee Bailey and Johnnie Cochran hold a press conference outside the courthouse in Los Angeles, March 15, 1995.

Defense Attorney Barry Scheck, June 1, 1995.

Defense attorney Carl Douglas (center) confers with defense team members Johnnie Cochran (left) and Robert Shapiro during testimony, June 1, 1995.

Defense attorney Johnnie Cochran (left) speaks with deputy district attorney Christopher Darden, June 15, 1995.

In front of the jury, defendant O. J. Simpson tries on the gloves found at the murder scene and his estate, June 15, 1995.

Superior Court Judge Lance Ito presides over the court in the Simpson trial, July 5, 1995.

Defense attorneys F. Lee Bailey and Johnnie Cochran confer with Assistant District Attorney Marcia Clark, July 5, 1995.

During the hair and fiber cross-examination, defense attorney F. Lee Bailey (right) shows a physical evidence book to FBI agent Douglas Deedrick (left), July 5, 1995.

Media gather for the decision of the O. J. Simpson verdict at the Los Angeles Courthouse, October 3, 1995.

Myung J. Chun/AFP via Getty Images

"The camera affixed to the wall of the court enabled the world to share an historic moment, and the resulting photograph was published within minutes in every country that had electricity. We show it here because without it, my description of its contents could not sufficiently resurrect that occasion. In the forefront, I am seen wearing the slight smile of a Cheshire cat, calculating that this minute in history will be a proper 'I told you so' to those who had so badly misled the public with their inaccurate analyses of the strength of the prosecution's case. Behind me is Simpson, not surprised but thumpingly vindicated by the jury's swift decision. Next Johnnie Cochran, still not sure he could believe his ears, but knowing the man I knew him to be, he was uttering thanks to the Almighty that his monumental effort had been properly rewarded." —Defense attorney F. Lee Bailey

Los Angeles District Attorney Gil Garcetti, along with prosecutors Marcia Clark and Christopher Darden, speaks with reporters at a press conference after O. J. Simpson was acquitted of double homicide, Oct. 3, 1995.

Even if he were to admit occasional past slips of the tongue and express his "regrets," I was reasonably confident that at some point he would start denying the more disgusting statements from his past that we could establish with these solid witnesses, and at least wind up with his credibility, if not destroyed, then seriously undermined.

His chronic racist misconduct was not his only area of vulnerability.

Once again, one sees the wisdom in the venerable advice of famed trial lawyer Louis B. Nizer: "Always examine and analyze the probabilities involved and look for the anomalies that appear to be present." We did, repeatedly and in detail, go over, on a moment-to-moment basis, Fuhrman's statement at the preliminary hearing about what he had been doing from the time he got a phone call early Monday morning until the time he left the premises at 360 Rockingham Avenue, sometime after 7 a.m. His statement had contained enough detail that he would not have a great deal of wiggle room as he proceeded through cross-examination.

By the time Fuhrman took the stand on March 13, 1995, for the first day of my three-day cross-examination, my initial negative impression of him (both as a liar and a dirty cop) had been strengthened by additional information the defense—principally Pat McKenna—had dug up since the preliminary hearing back in July. And at this point we did not know about the silver bullet: the Laura Hart McKinny bombshell tapes (more on these shortly) that definitively proved Fuhrman to be a perjurer and a bigot. Even so, when Marcia Clark turned Mark Fuhrman over to me for cross-examination, I was ready for him.

* * *

In my 1992 book, *To Be a Trial Lawyer*, I wrote that witnesses, having seen many movies and television shows, expect the cross-examining lawyer to "come at them with a snarling attack." But my practice is to the contrary; I want the witness to relax and be thinking to himself: "This isn't so bad, after all." I also follow my own advice that the cross-examiner's hands must be empty most of the time, and his eyes must be riveted on the witness. If he needs constantly to refer to notes and other written materials, he will sacrifice something essential: *speed.*

I began my interrogation of "Bloody Glove Fuhrman" as if he and I were two former Marines having a casual chat. Of course, we were definitely not. We were in fact, a hungry cat and a nervous mouse that had to keep both his lies and his lines straight. I suspected that Mark Fuhrman had played this scene many times before and was perhaps good at it.

When I began to cross-examine Detective Fuhrman, there was no doubt in my mind that I would eventually ask him about his use of the so-called N-word. The defense team had discussed it, and I knew that some of the other team members didn't want me to use it too often, but I would have to play that by ear. It was clearly not a term I liked to use, even in the context of asking a witness if they had used the ugly epithet. But, fortunately or otherwise, I had been down this road before.

In 1972, in a mail fraud trial in Florida, one of the prosecution's chief witnesses was a disgruntled former employee named Jimmie James who'd been passed over for a top job and eventually let go. He testified on direct examination that he'd been fired because he was unwilling to go along with the scheme the government said was fraudulent. But, thanks to our investigators, we knew that wasn't at all true—and we also knew he had another problem: James, *a la* Mark Fuhrman, didn't like black people. We would see what he had to say about that when I cross-examined him. I described the exchange in my 1975 book, *For the Defense:*[1]

> *Q. Did you also say ... "He's right about one thing, I hate niggers."*
>
> *A. No, sir.*
>
> *Q. Did you make that statement or didn't you?*
>
> *A. Absolutely not. And you heard me correctly, sir. I absolutely did not say that.*

Mr. James made the answer sound as emphatic as he could, but he was clearly nervous. And the atmosphere in the courtroom was equally tense, for it had changed noticeably when I said "niggers." I had barked out the word, trying to give it as much meanness and venom as I could: It hung in the air, an all but palpable accusation. Within seconds the witness was showing signs of strain. He sat motionless, but he was biting his lip frequently now, and the jury was staring at him.

My pace had been very fast, so I slowed it a bit by pausing, and then picked up the speed again. My voice was firm and loud.

Q. You say that you did not. You do not use that word at all, do you?

I knew if James denied using the word, I could put the investigator on the stand to refute him, thereby impeaching that statement and casting doubt on the rest of his testimony as well. The witness must have had similar thoughts.

A. I'm sure I've used it, yes, sir, because I'm from the South.

Several jurors who'd been watching me returned their gaze to the witness. As soon as [he] said he had used the word, I had what I needed to ask the next two questions without objection from the prosecutor. I almost shouted them.

Q. As recently as last week, perhaps, in Greenville?

James went literally pale. His hand gripped the top of the witness box.

A. I may have.

Q. Describing your own employee, LEE GRIMES, whom you call a nigger on a daily basis?

Jimmie James must have known we had checked him out, but he never expected it had been that thorough a job. His answer startled the entire courtroom. Even I was not prepared for it.

A. He enjoys it.

...One black juror, a woman who had betrayed absolutely no emotion up to that point, appeared stunned. She stared at the witness...and continued to stare at James through the prosecutor's less-than-enthusiastic re-direct examination. The juror next to her, another woman, kept patting her on the knee the whole time, saying what even an amateur lip reader could recognize as "Calm down now, calm down."

I did not expect anything nearly so dramatic—and damning—to come from the mouth of Mark Fuhrman. All I needed from him was a denial, preferably a blanket denial, that *nigger* was a word he used. It took me several hours to get there, but it was more than worth the wait.

I began my session with Fuhrman by going over the sequence of events that led up to his claim that he had found—on O. J. Simpson's property on Rockingham, a few feet from the outside wall of Simpson's home—the left-hand glove used at South Bundy by the killer. Fuhrman explained why it was that he was chosen to lead the other detectives to Rockingham, because he'd visited that same residence nine years earlier in answering a 911 call. I took him over his initial conversation with Kato Kaelin in Kato's room, and that he had then brought Kaelin to the kitchen of the main house where he, Fuhrman, all but directed his senior detective Phil Vannatter to talk with the young man.

*A. I couldn't [begin a formal interrogation of Mr. Kaelin]
at that point unless I'm directed to by Detective Vannatter.*

Q. Okay. But instead you directed him, it sounds like.

*A. I didn't direct him. I just said, "You might want to
talk to this guy at the bar or talk to this guy at the bar,"
something along that—*

I cut off Fuhrman's answer and moved on to what he had done
next, which was, after making sure that all three other detectives
were busy inside the house, to go out alone alongside the edge of
O. J.'s property, ostensibly to see if he could determine what made
the thumping noises Kato Kaelin had told him he had heard.
Fuhrman testified that indeed he was alone outside for almost fifteen minutes.

Q. Now, you then walked out the front door?

A. Yes.

*Q. You had no direction from anyone to do that, did
you?*

A. No, I didn't.

*Q. This again was Detective Fuhrman on his own, was
it not?*

A. Yes.

I considered this answer a crucial juncture in the cross-examination because having said yes to my Fuhrman-on-his-own question,
he could no longer claim that he had been directed by a superior
to go out alone in the dark to investigate Kaelin's "thump-thump"
report.

The examination continued:

*Q. You had an idea that you would like to check out
Kato's claim that some unusual noise had occurred.*

A. That's correct.

Q. All right, did Kato tell you, by the way, that O. J. had left for the airport in the limo he had seen when he came out that night after hearing the noise at around 11:00 p. m.?[2]

A. No.

Q. Did you ever ask him what a limo was doing there at 11:00 p.m.?

A. No. I cut his conversation off and brought him into the house.

Once again, Fuhrman had defied standard detective procedure in favor of some other—unusual—purpose. The words *I cut him off* are a giveaway, because interrupting a witness who is talking freely flies in the face of every principle of interrogation. Unless Fuhrman had had his own agenda that morning and was anxious to get on with it.

I used the next series of questions and answers to establish that Fuhrman did not tell any of the three other officers that he was leaving to investigate "thumps," which to me, strongly suggested that he went out to the isolated chain linked fence area specifically—and alone—to plant the glove. Then I went on to have Fuhrman, who had testified earlier that he believed there might have been suspects on Simpson's property that night, to admit he could not remember whether or not, as he went out alone to check a remote area of the property, he had drawn his service pistol.

As to why he couldn't remember, he testified: "After twenty years, you draw that weapon, you lay it down to the side of your leg, you walk, you don't even know you are doing it."

Given that this was the biggest investigative night of his life, I found Mark Fuhrman's answer to be simply preposterous. At one point during Fuhrman's first day on the stand, I asked him bluntly, "Did you wipe a glove in the Bronco, Detective Fuhrman?" He of course immediately said no. But sometimes you have to ask that type of question anyway to let the jury know what you contend did in fact happen.

Another reason for doing it is that if you can show, later, that the witness has testified falsely, then the jury may well apply the old Latin maxim, *Falsus in Uno, Falsus in Omnibus,* which means "false in one thing, then false in everything." In law, it's a principle that holds that a witness who testifies falsely about one matter is not credible to testify about *any* matter.

I'm sure Officer Fuhrman thought he was doing just fine in avoiding my little linguistic traps, but I noticed that after a while he would sometimes answer, "I would have," rather than "I did," or "I did not." That can be a clear signal that a witness is prevaricating. If, in addition to using this conditional answer, they also appear to be rattled, I might ask that the answer be stricken and the witness be directed (by the judge) to give an appropriate reply to the question as it was put. If the witness does not appear to be rattled, I might observe in my final argument that the witness was "bobbing and weaving," a description that may well have occurred to more than one attentive juror in the Simpson case.

On Thursday, March 16, 1995, I was set to conclude my cross-examination of Mark Fuhrman. I felt confident that I had given the jurors something to think about when they retired to deliberate. I had shown that Fuhrman, while not the superior officer on the scene at O. J.'s house on Rockingham Avenue, had done a number of things on his own, as if he were in charge: He had brought Kato Kaelin into the main house, told him where to sit, and then told Detective Vannatter, his superior, to "talk to him"; I also got him to admit that he went out *alone* to the area alongside the chain link fence where he found the bloody glove; He further testified that the glove was still shiny with blood that had not dried despite the fact that at least six hours had passed since the killings on Bundy; Fuhrman then brought each of the three other detectives, separately, out to the area to show them where he had found the glove. I suggested that when Fuhrman went out alone, he did not take the kind of precautions that a seasoned police officer would take to protect himself in case he found a killer hiding there. I'm sure that not all the jurors bought Fuhrman's many glib explanations of why he had done these things, several of which were definitely not "by the book."

My main purpose on that final day of my cross-examination was to ask the witness if he had ever used the infamous N-word:

> Q. *You say under oath that you have not addressed any black person as a nigger or spoken about black people as niggers in the past 10 years, Detective Fuhrman?*
> A. *That's what I'm saying, sir.*
> Q. *So that anyone who comes to this court and quotes you as using that word in dealing with African Americans would be a liar, would they not, Detective Fuhrman?*
> A. *Yes, they would.*
> Q. *All of them?*
> A. *All of them.*

I felt that with that string of answers, Fuhrman had lied himself into a corner, and there is nothing easier to impeach than "never." Why Fuhrman, who is not a stupid man, had chosen to answer with such an absolute, all-encompassing denial still eludes me. Even Jimmie Jones, back in my 1972 case, was wise enough to say, "I'm sure I've used it, yes, sir."

Johnnie Cochran, who had seen more than his share of lying, racist cops, put it down to Fuhrman's arrogance. He was probably right.

* * *

I find it interesting that my cross-examination of Fuhrman, while generally praised by experienced criminal defense lawyers who saw the testimony, did not impress my critics in the media.

But I wasn't working for the media. I was working for the defense.

In *Journey to Justice*, Johnnie Cochran's 1996 memoir, he included his account of the Simpson case. In it, he had this to say:

> Bailey's cross-examination of Fuhrman was almost as widely panned as it was misunderstood ... on this occasion

he knew exactly what he had to accomplish. It is also worth noting, by the way, that while the commentators scoffed at Bailey's performance that day, the jurors subsequently told us they loved it. "He was just like a lawyer in the movies," one of them later said with obvious pleasure.

More important, he did just what Simpson's defense required him to do. Playing on Fuhrman's arrogance and obvious disdain for blacks and rules, Bailey danced him around until he stated two things without qualification: he had "never" spoken the word "nigger" in the past ten years, and he had "never" planted evidence. ...

"Are you therefore saying you have not used that word in the past ten years, Detective Fuhrman?" Bailey said.

"That's what I'm saying, sir," responded Fuhrman, his voice firming.

"So that anyone who comes to this court and quotes you as using that word in dealing with African Americans would be a liar, would they not, Detective Fuhrman?" said Bailey.

"Yes, they would," the detective replied.

"All of them, correct?" wondered Bailey, who could hear what others could not, *the sound of a very large door opening* [my italics].

"All of them," Fuhrman said.

It would be months before we would discover screen-writer Laura Hart McKinny's tape-recorded conversations with Fuhrman, and even longer before the jurors would hear the detective impeach himself in his own voice. But, the truth was, it did not really matter. Lee Bailey had accomplished what our client required of him, and if the pundits missed it, the jurors did not.

"I could tell by the way [Fuhrman] twisted around in his seat and clenched his hands in his lap, that he was lying," Armanda Cooley, the forewoman, would tell us. From her vantage point in the first seat of the jury box's front row, she had seen all she needed to see.

It was Lee's finest moment in the trial.

Lawrence Schiller and James Willwerth, in *American Tragedy*, wrote, "In the twelfth floor pressroom, the consensus was that F. Lee Bailey had, in fact, lost his fastball. The reporters had no way of appreciating the groundwork he had laid for the defense attack on the LAPD."

The dynamics of my final exchange with Fuhrman were fascinating. We had interviewed several witnesses who, in the past, had plainly been repulsed by Fuhrman's epithets, but declined to become involved for fear that if they testified any skeletons in their own closets would become public. Many of them were clearly torn between a feeling, on one hand, that such lying should not go unchecked, and, on the other, a fear of the spotlight. The defense team—well, most of its members—felt that a flat lie on Fuhrman's part would stiffen the backbones of our potential witnesses, causing them to come forward and testify.

The moment Fuhrman's position was frozen in stone by his use of the word *never*, the look on his face told me that he was anxious, fearful that he'd made exactly the mistake he'd been warned by the prosecutors not to make. When it was suggested to him that there were a lot of people who would call him a liar, he did not flinch, but instead hung even more tightly to his position. He had to have known that we had a large group of folks who could—if they would—attest to his racist arrogance. But I sincerely doubt that on March 16, 1995, he realized that one of those folks would be Mark Fuhrman himself, first on Laura Hart McKinny's tapes, and then by his own "no contest" plea to perjury.

Although it would have better served the public—and justice itself—if, right after my cross of Fuhrman ended, we could have put on our witnesses to impeach him and show him to the world as the racist bigot he was and is, we were not allowed to do so. Judge Ito ruled that before Fuhrman could be cross-examined further about statements he'd made to other people, we, the defense, would have to put our witnesses on the stand. This meant, in essence, that any further cross-examination of Mark Fuhrman would be suspended until all of those accusations had been put on the record, which couldn't happen until we were in the defense phase of the trial, then at least two months away. It was a rather awkward situation, but I comforted myself by visualizing Mark Fuhrman having to deny, one after another, the statements of our many potential witnesses.

But that moment—delicious as it was to contemplate—was never to be. Before we reached the stage of the defense case where he could be recalled, the infamous Fuhrman tapes surfaced and he was boxed in. He took the Fifth Amendment, and thus, Fuhrman's cross was never completed.

Although the prosecutors were loath to admit it, their case was over, and they began desperately looking for a mistrial.

CHAPTER 13
The "Fuhrman Tapes"

I'm the key witness in the biggest case of the century. If I go down, they lose the case. The glove is everything. Without the glove—bye, bye.

—Mark Fuhrman on tape with Laura Hart McKinny, July 28, 1994

No one could have predicted the bombshell hurtling toward us that would explode that coming July. Following Mark Fuhrman's denial of using racist language in his March 1995 testimony, we were hip-deep with credible witnesses to prove him to be both a liar and a bigot. When it was our turn to call people to the stand, we were locked and loaded.

But, in nothing short of a true Hollywood twist, we never got the chance. That's when the news broke about the infamous Fuhrman tapes.

It turned out, Fuhrman had been acting as a consultant with a Hollywood screenwriter for a span of many years, providing thirteen hours of taped audio recordings. In these recordings, Fuhrman not only slung bitter racial insults (e.g., using the word *nigger* forty-one times), but he also talked approvingly of police brutality of black suspects *and* of falsifying police reports to secure convictions.

The tapes (recorded between 1985 and 1994) were part of a long-ranging research project by a screenwriter named Laura

Hart McKinny. In search of authentic background for a screen-play she was writing about sexism within the LAPD, McKinny interviewed a number of male and female police officers. As part of this research, McKinny captured hours of uncensored content from Fuhrman.

The conversations were, by all accounts, shocking.

In these sessions, Fuhrman pontificated on his singular world view, openly denigrated blacks, Jews, Hispanics, homosexu-als, women—any category of people that he felt was lesser than himself.

But beyond language and attitudes, Fuhrman revealed some-thing much more insidious: He *bragged* about violent police misconduct motivated by race. He *flaunted* the ease of planting evidence to secure convictions. He described a systemic culture within the LAPD of intimidation and abuse.

According to Fuhrman, these behaviors were all just part of the game. And to be good at the game, you had to possess cer-tain attributes. "You've got to be a borderline sociopath," Fuhrman told McKinny. "You got to be violent."

And it went on. Fuhrman was part of a fraternal group in the department called M.A.W.—"Men Against Women." As I'm sure you can surmise given the clever sobriquet, MAW members shunned or refused to work with female officers. Women were called names like "Critter" and "Hench Monkey." This hostility (as reported after the trial) left female officers feeling unsafe performing their duties, fearful that they would not be provided backup in the field.

Fuhrman also downplayed accomplishments that women earned within the department. He claimed that women in leader-ship positions "are either so ugly or they're a lesbian or they're so dyke-ish that they are not women anymore." Fuhrman was even caught disparaging Judge Lance Ito's wife, LAPD Captain Peggy York, claiming that she "fucked and sucked her way to the top."

But Fuhrman *still* wasn't finished. He had interesting remarks on the Simpson trial and his role in it. In his last recorded con-versation with Laura Hart McKinny on July 18, 1994 (a little more than a month after the murders and a few weeks after the preliminary hearing), she asked Fuhrman whether the exposure of his stance on racism might get him removed from the case. He brushed the notion aside: "I'm the key witness in the biggest case of the century. If I go down, they lose the case," he gloated. "The glove is everything. Without the glove—bye, bye."

As he boasted to McKinny during the taped interviews, Fuhrman was both supportive of, and experienced in, planting evidence to frame people. He knew that there was incriminating blood residue on the glove *at least two months* before the police lab ever examined it.

He also shared with McKinny his motivations to stay in the case. "The funny thing about it is, just like the attorney said, 'For the rest of your life this is you, "Bloody Glove Fuhrman." If you don't make it pay off, you're going through all this for nothing.' So, go for Shapiro, he's an asshole."

In view of Fuhrman's acute awareness of the glove and its importance to the prosecution's case, one should note his response when I asked him in March 1995:

> Q. *Did you believe that you would be an essential witness if you were the first to find an important piece of evidence?*
> A. *Well, I couldn't make that determination at that time, sir. I didn't even know what the implication of the glove was.*

This was, of course, the same Detective Fuhrman who described his first perception of a glove at the murder scene on Bundy by referring to "them," during the preliminary hearing.[1] The chemical tests for the substances on the glove, and attempts to identify possible sources of those substances, were not undertaken until more than two months later, in October 1994. Fuhrman's denial was incredulous. Even at the preliminary hearing, Fuhrman already knew that this glove would be the subject of the principal effort to connect *someone* to the murder scene. *How did he know that?* How could he be so sure—in July 1994—that some other evidence, such as a bloody knife with traces of the blood of both victims on it, wouldn't be found before the trial commenced, and thus weaken the prosecution's almost total reliance on "the glove" from Rockingham?

But once the Fuhrman tapes—as they came to be known—came to light, the trial was shaken to its very core. Prosecutors watched helplessly as the testimony of their key witness vaporized into the ether, and the defense felt an overwhelming vindication. The tapes proved what we already knew about Mark Fuhrman: We were not dealing with a blunt instrument. He was a vindictive viper—*one whose head had just been lopped off by a guillotine of his own making.*

* * *

The discovery of the Fuhrman tapes was a gift to the defense. But it was also one of the finest examples of the kinds of juicy fruits that can be bared through meticulous, thorough investigation. Our investigator, Pat McKenna, is a man who leaves no stones unturned. And at this moment, his efforts turned up a very ripe peach.

When Pat wasn't in the courtroom, he occupied a small office in Johnnie Cochran's suite. His was the unpleasant task of sifting through the myriad of junk phone calls flooding the office, looking for those few plausible snippets of information which *might* lead to useful evidence. The receptionist was soon trained to ward off the craziest of the stories, and to send anything with possibilities along to Pat. The delicate job of evaluating these slices of incoming information was Pat's, and although I have worked with many top-notch investigators over the years, no one comes close to his superb skill as getting witnesses—even those who are hostile initially—to open up to him. In fact, many wound up considering him to be a friend.

One call passed to him in the afternoon of July 7, 1995, came from a man in the movie business in the San Francisco area who claimed to know something about some audiotapes containing racially repugnant statements by Mark Fuhrman. Pat contacted the gentleman, who said that he had been working with a producer who tried to sell him on a story about how badly female police officers were treated by their male colleagues in the West Los Angeles area. The male voice declined to identify himself, doubtless not wanting to be involved.

The production had not moved forward, but the caller remembered the lady's first name as "Laura," and had a note in his file that he believed to be her home phone number in the Winston-Salem area of North Carolina. He gave it to Pat.

When Pat dialed the number, a man answered. He was the husband of Laura Hart McKinny, and confirmed she had indeed been working on a project with a Los Angeles cop. She was teaching at a local university and would be home soon. Pat left his number, and silently crossed his fingers. He assumed that Ms. McKinny was attuned to the ongoing case, and Fuhrman's role in it. He did not expect her to be friendly to the defense if she returned the phone call at all. Many times, witnesses will simply stonewall the defense because it carries no badges.

Not surprisingly, when McKinny called Pat, she was not pleased to hear from him. Pat sensed a tightness in her response when he introduced himself as an investigator for the defense. It seemed like it might be a short, uninformative conversation. He told her that he believed she had some audiotapes involving Mark Fuhrman and said that he would like an opportunity to review them. When he sensed that she was about to hang up on him, he turned on Maximum McKenna:

"Mrs. McKinny, I've been in this business for more than twenty years, and I have worked on little but this case since its beginning, and although it is unusual, I am sure beyond any doubt that Simpson had nothing to do with the murders of his former wife and Ron Goldman. Please just give us half a chance."

Mrs. McKinny hemmed a little bit, but finally answered Pat: "Call my lawyer, Matt Schwartz in Los Angeles."

Schwartz turned out to be a highly professional gentleman and a good lawyer. When Pat called him and asked for an appointment for me to see him, he arranged it immediately, and I went to his office. He was a handsome man with a warm smile who specialized in entertainment law. He had listened to the tapes.

"They contain a lot of language you will love," he said. "I watched your cross of this guy. I think you've got him on the run. These could bury him."

I frowned. "'*Could*,' you said. Are you telling me the tapes might be unavailable?"

"At the moment they are," he replied. "I told her to keep them in North Carolina, out of reach of a California subpoena, until I had a chance to talk with whoever showed up asking for them, which is now you."

"Is there some reason they are to be withheld? That could mean a trip to the North Carolina courts?"

"Quite so," replied Schwartz. "That may be our answer."

Schwartz explained that he was hired to help Ms. McKinny find an interested buyer, and copyright the materials she has produced, and protect her in other ways. "If I just hand you the tapes, I am probably waiving most of what she could own," he said. "Some would say that's not good lawyering."

"I would be one of those critics," I replied. "What do you propose as a solution?"

"Fairly simple," Schwartz said. "You sue us in North Carolina, stating your need for the tapes. I will object and protest, claiming that this is a private work of art and cannot be confiscated by being placed in the public domain through use in a court proceeding. I will lose, but I will have done all that I can to protect the work."

His offer made sense. I picked up the phone in his office and called my good friend and colleague Bob Craig, an attorney in Burlington, North Carolina.

"Bob, I have a hot potato in my lap, and I need a lawsuit faster than you can blink." I explained the situation as briefly as I could. We discussed keeping his court complaint as simple as possible, to avoid legal bottlenecks or harangue along the way, although Matt had assured me there would be none of that. Bob filed the next day and asked for an immediate hearing.

Back at the office, after court, I explained to members of the defense team the discovery. Since I had lived and practiced in North Carolina, I offered to get the tapes and bring them back, to be filed with Judge Ito. "On second thought," I said, "Perhaps the North Carolina court could use a dose of Johnnie's famous oratorical skills. When a hearing is set, I can go prepare the stage for a grand entrance." The suggestion was a hit with Johnnie. As he nodded his approval, Bob Shapiro piped in.

"Easiest thing is, Gerry Uelman and I can go and get them. That way you guys can keep going with the case." Nobody paid much attention to Bob anymore at that point. He did garner attention when he started trying to engineer a plea of guilty without the authority or knowledge of his client and co-counsel, which almost got him fired. But he had largely been benched, and his offer to help out in North Carolina was ignored.

Bob Craig got us a quick hearing before the Honorable William Wood in the Superior Court. When I arrived in Winston-Salem the day before to scout the scene, I learned that Craig's secretary had received a call from Judge Wood's clerk suggesting that the judge would be pleased if Craig made the presentation to him. I told Craig—who was not pushing at all—that this was not to be. This was Johnnie's show. He accepted that without a murmur, but I had an ugly sense of foreboding from the court's message. Might we pay a price if the local boy didn't get to shine, or was Judge Wood possibly a bit racist himself? His father had been a judge when North Carolina was anything but a haven for African Americans. I lived in North Carolina from 1954 to 1956 when *Brown v. Board of Education* was roiling the nation. I worried some about disregarding the judge's stated preference.

The hearing before Judge Wood began smoothly enough. The judge took all counsel back in chambers and listened to a few of the tapes. The ones offered him were particularly vitriolic. Judge Wood wasted little time.

"Mr. Simpson's defense is obviously entitled to these materials," he said with what sounded like finality. "We will be back in court and have a *very brief* hearing on the matter, then I will rule." I caught the deep emphasis on the word *brief.* I'm not sure that

Johnnie understood that the demand for brevity was not a request or suggestion, but tantamount to a directive.

We returned to the courtroom, and things started downhill quickly. From the approach Johnnie took to the tape issue, he felt that a polemic on racism needed to be in the record. He rumbled in stentorian tones about the injustices involved and did a little preaching about the need for justice here. But he was arguing a point he had already won to a judge who had plainly warned that he didn't want to hear it.

As Johnnie spoke, Judge Wood's ears began to get red. He rose and stood behind his chair, glowering. Then he turned briefly to stare at the books in the case behind his bench. Then he waved Johnnie to silence. Matt Schwartz argued simply that the tapes were the basis for an artistic work about male police discrimination, and that allowing them to be taken for court publication would siphon off all their value.

Judge Wood had heard enough. He ruled in favor of McKinny, agreeing that artistic work—even that in process—deserved protection. The judge then went into his chambers, and the many lawyers and press representatives in the courtroom began buzzing that Johnnie had "snatched defeat from the jaws of victory!" To the extent that this may have been true, one must understand that the habit and culture of California lawyers routinely involves windy oratory that is ten or more times its ordinary length. I have watched for the many years I have tried cases in that state for the trial judges to clamp down on lawyer loquaciousness, but I fear that is not in the cards. Johnnie was simply doing what his colleagues do: talk on and on, as though motions could be won by the number of words in counsel's argument rather than their cogency.

To rectify this situation, I gathered up Bob Craig and an outstanding North Carolina trial lawyer named Joe Cheshire, and we descended on the appellate court in Raleigh with a stack of pleadings.

Two weeks later, we got a favorable ruling from the Court of Appeals, and the tapes were delivered to Judge Ito's court.

The crisis was averted, but only for the moment.

* * *

When the tapes arrived, they were transcribed, then played in open court for the lawyers, litigants, press and spectators, but because they had not been admitted into evidence, *not the jury.*

The tapes were (and are today) as startling as advertised. The sneer evident in Fuhrman's voice when he spoke enthusiastically of putting "niggers in a pile and burning them" was palpable. According to an article by Knight Ridder reporter Mark Davis,

His words, vicious and biting, spewed like acid from a ruptured pipe and stunned the standing-room-only crowd.

"How do you intellectualize when you punch the hell out of a nigger?" he asked in one portion of an interview he had with screenwriter Laura Hart McKinny, who spent nearly the entire day testifying. "He either deserves it, or he doesn't."

In another instance, Fuhrman bragged that he and a fellow officer had beaten four suspects so badly that the officers were covered with blood—so soaked, he recalled, that they even had to wipe blood off their badges.

Internal affairs investigators cleared police in that episode, Fuhrman said on the tape. Then he laughed. "I mean, we could have murdered people and got away with it," he said.

And in a third interview, Fuhrman admitted falsifying reports to get a conviction: "That's putting a criminal in jail," he said. "That's being a policeman."

The news of Fuhrman's comments rocked the LAPD, striking a deep blow within the organization. Media reports contended the tapes may have been the worst thing to happen for the department since the Rodney King beating in 1992. Davis reported:

They prompted one police officer who'd worked with Fuhrman to disavow his former colleague, who retired earlier this year and now lives in Sandpoint (Idaho).

"These (tapes) do not represent me at all," Detective Philip Vannatter said when court recessed for lunch.

District Attorney Gil Garcetti called a quick news conference to defend the department. Garcetti, who is in charge of Simpson's prosecution, said he was angry and embarrassed over the Fuhrman tapes. "I'm angry that a police officer ... has uttered such hateful words, and has apparently harbored some vile thoughts and feelings," he said.

"I'm embarrassed for the city, and for the Los Angeles Police Department. I'm embarrassed because this is— these words, misconduct or apparent conduct by a police officer, is not, and I underline this, is not representative of the vast, vast majority of police officers in Los Angeles."

Garcetti said he was also angry because the tapes had altered the focus of the trial from Simpson to Fuhrman.

"We are not in court to protect or defend Mark Fuhrman, we are here in court every day to seek justice."

To hear Gil Garcetti complain about the spotlight shifting toward the LAPD showed again just how much the city wasn't "getting it." Rather than acknowledge that they kept *and promoted* a flagrantly racist cop who, by his own admission, wasn't fit for the job and unable to testify with any credibility, they attempted to deflect attention away from the reality of Fuhrman's venality, and get the public to overlook it.

The fingers they were pointing were at everyone but themselves.

***

Just when it seemed that the trial atmosphere had set new records for bizarre trials, the tapes offered the courtroom yet another bombshell.

Judge Lance Ito was married to Peggy York, an LAPD captain in the West Los Angeles District. She was the senior female in the department, and generally much admired. As the tapes spewed out their hatred for African Americans, Jews, and women, suddenly a phrase erupted that had everyone gawking, wondering whether to believe their own ears: Fuhrman had said that Ms. York was believed to have made her advance through the ranks "on her back."

I have seen many wild developments explode in courtrooms over the years, but surely this incident was the most gripping—even breathtaking—of all. Looking at the judge's face, he was shaken to the marrow bone by this denigration of his wife. He took a brief recess, then returned and read a statement:

> I love my wife dearly and I am wounded by criticism of her, as any spouse would be, and I think it is reasonable to assume that that could have some impact. As I mentioned, women in male-dominated professions learn to deal with this and those who are successful I think we all observe are tougher than most. But having said that, the appearance of a reasonable concern that this court could impartially rule on these material issues is there and I feel I have an obligation then to recuse myself from two issues: One, the scope of the impeachment that is available of Mr. Fuhrman through these tapes because one might suspect that this court would have a motivation to punish Mr. Fuhrman and thereby make wider the scope of impeachment. Someone might reasonably be concerned about that. One might also be concerned that this court, in trying to express its impartiality, would bend over backward the other way and restrict it. In either event there would be concern about this court's ability to act impartially in this matter. I therefore recuse myself from the issue of the tapes themselves and specifically whether or not Captain York is a material and relevant witness for rehabilitation and/or impeachment of Detective Fuhrman, as the case may be. This matter is

therefore—this particular issue is therefore transferred forthwith to department 100 for the reassignment. I'm going to order counsel there forthwith for the purposes of selecting a court to hear the matter, to schedule the matter, and to set up a briefing schedule. I think I've had my staff running on the lexis word search and we come up with an incredible number of transcripts that are going to have to be reviewed by the receiving court. I suspect I won't get a Christmas card from the judge who gets this case. My guess is this is seven to ten days' worth of work. What I propose to do is order counsel back for three o'clock so that we can finish with Miss Kestler, which I would like to do that and we will proceed with Mr. Ragle, if I hear no objection, so the trial at least can progress while those other issues are being resolved.

He was obviously plagued with uncertainties concerning his impartiality in ruling on the tapes, and whether Captain York might be needed as a witness to refute what Fuhrman had said about her reputed accomplishments. Any decent lawyer's heart would go out to a judge who—through no fault of his own—had found himself in such an untenable situation.

Johnnie saw the danger immediately. Marcia Clark would make a strong move for a mistrial, knowing as she did then that the case was already lost to her. She wasted no time in doing so, claiming that Judge Ito had been deprived of the ability to be impartial, and thus should not rule on which of the tapes should be heard by the jury. She wanted him to step down there and then.

The chief justice of the Superior Court learned of Fuhrman's accusation about Captain York and sent in Supervising Superior Court Judge James Bascue to evaluate Judge Ito's ability to continue to serve. He then transferred the issue to Judge John Reid. I was assigned to attend a closed hearing before Judge Reid, in which the issue of impartiality would be thrashed out. It seemed to me that he quickly became suspicious of the prosecution's application for disqualification, and then a quick segue to a motion for mistrial, something most prosecutors would attempt to assiduously avoid by breathing fiery oration.

Fortunately for the defense, Judge Reid was no greenhorn. He listened patiently to both sides, and ruled that although surely wounded, Judge Ito was strong enough to exercise judicial wisdom. The case would continue.

The public has not the faintest idea of how close the Simpson case came to going over the cliff that day; very few of the reporters on scene had a proper appreciation of the length and breadth of our plight, or how we escaped by the skin of our teeth. Had a mistrial occurred, O. J. would have remained in jail. The trial costs had already become enormous, and there was not enough money to pay them out again. Further, retrials are slow, dull affairs. There are few surprises. There is an extensive transcript record limiting the testimony of every witness who gave evidence in the first trial and providing counsel a plethora of opportunities to haggle, nit-pick, and argue with what was said on the earlier trip to the witness stand. The media tend to lose interest quickly in old news, and it is just a miserable experience to endure, especially if you're running the case.

CHAPTER 14
Fuhrman Pleads the Fifth

While we on the defense team felt we'd uncovered the "holy grail" in the Fuhrman tapes, we would find yet another hurdle before us.

After a few days of deliberating which portions of the tapes the jury could hear, on September 1, 1995, Judge Ito made a surprise decision that sent shudders through everyone who had heard the damning contents of the recordings.

Of the thirteen hours of taped conversations, Judge Ito allowed jurors to hear only *two* short references from Fuhrman using the word "nigger." This meant that Fuhrman's boasts of brutalizing and framing suspects as part of his regular police duties, surely the most damning aspects of the tapes, would be kept from the jury.

Judge Ito underlined his decision by stating that the two excerpts he would allow the jury to hear were references to Fuhrman using the word "nigger," which directly contradicted Fuhrman's sworn testimony that he hadn't used the racial slur in the past ten years. One was a transcript of the original tape where Fuhrman told Laura Hart McKinny, "We have no niggers where I grew up." In the second audio reference, McKinny asked him why black Muslims lived in a certain area in the city. Fuhrman answered, "That's where niggers live."

While ugly, these statements were hardly the most incrimina-
tory portions of the sixty-one tape and transcript references the
defense team had asked the court to allow the jury to hear. But
Judge Ito was resolute, stating that Fuhrman's description of misconduct in other cases were not relevant to the Simpson investigation. "It is a theory without factual support," the judge wrote.

Not surprisingly, angry and distressed reactions to this decision were both swift and widespread. The usually cool and composed Johnnie Cochran held a press conference outside his Los
Angeles office where he called Judge Ito's ruling "perhaps one of
the cruelest, unfairest decisions ever rendered in a criminal court."

In contrast to his usual affable and unflappable style, Johnnie's
features displayed a kind of controlled indignation I'd never seen
before and never saw again. His accusations of bias and partiality
were couched in terms that anyone could understand, and there
was a point at which I thought he might well be hauled up before
the bar association for treating the judge with contempt. However,
upon reflection, this seemed less likely, because a procedure of
this sort would have drawn into question—at least on the issue of
mitigation—whether or not the ruling was on its face so foul as to
provoke a reaction of this sort from almost any thinking lawyer.

Peter Neufeld, the New York partner of Barry Scheck, had
even more biting remarks about the decision. "It is a victory for
racism. It is a green light for a rogue and racist cop to engage
in brutality, evidence tampering and the fabrication of probable
cause with impunity."

Media reports of the public's reactions were also emotional.
The *LA Times* reported some in the black community felt hurt
and confused by the ruling. "'We certainly expected more than
this," said Geraldine Washington, acting president of the National
Association for the Advancement of Colored People's Los Angeles
chapter. "People are calling us from all over this country. The
phones are busy. From the tone of the calls, it is a feeling of disbelief and outrage."

Still others, like District Attorney Gil Garcetti, applauded the
ruling. In a written statement, Garcetti said, "While we decry

racism, these tapes are for another forum, not this murder trial," adding that the focus should be on Simpson and the evidence, not the LAPD.

The firestorm dissipated rapidly, and Judge Ito stood by his ruling.

* * *

While we were somewhat stonewalled regarding what we hoped the Fuhrman tapes would prove to the jury—that Fuhrman's testimony as to any part of this case could not be trusted—we still had other witnesses who could attest to Fuhrman's bigotry.

One was Laura Hart McKinny herself. The jury didn't get to hear much from the tapes because of Judge Ito's ruling, but McKinny did testify that they contained more than forty uses of the word *nigger* and that Fuhrman used the word very "casually."

"It was nothing extraordinary. It was part of conversation," she said.

Natalie Singer, who had refused to allow Fuhrman into the apartment she shared with a friend, testified that Fuhrman had told her that "the only good nigger is a dead nigger."

Kathleen Bell, the real estate agent who worked near the Marine recruiting station where she met Fuhrman, told the jury that Fuhrman wanted to kill all blacks. He also was enraged and disgusted by interracial couples. Bell's voice caught with emotion when she quoted Fuhrman as saying, "If I had my way, I'd gather … all the niggers would be gathered together and burned."

The women's testimony seemed to concern the jury, as they listened carefully and took notes. The prosecution, who tried to limit the number of witnesses allowed to testify about Fuhrman's racism, were sullen and had little in the way of cross-examination for Singer and Bell—a wise move, if ever they had one.

* * *

On September 7, 1995, two days following the presentation to the jury of Detective Mark Fuhrman's racist history, he took the stand again, this time outside of the jury's presence where he invoked his Fifth Amendment rights.

The *LA Times* reported,

> A somber, stony-faced Detective Mark Fuhrman asserted his 5th Amendment rights against self-incrimination three times Wednesday, refusing to answer questions posed by defense lawyers who charge that he framed O. J. Simpson.
>
> "Was the testimony that you gave at the preliminary hearing in this case completely truthful?" defense attorney Gerald F. Uelmen asked in a quick, pointed confrontation with Fuhrman, who has told jurors he found a bloody glove at Simpson's estate. "Have you ever falsified a police report?"
>
> And most strikingly, "Did you plant or manufacture any evidence in this case?"
>
> After each question, Fuhrman leaned over, whispered to his attorney and then sat stiffly straight to answer: "I wish to assert my 5th Amendment privilege."
>
> As Fuhrman's testimony ended, Simpson hunched over the defense table, buried his face in his hands and appeared to cry.
>
> Jurors, who waited in an upstairs lounge during Fuhrman's brief but electrifying appearance, did not get to hear the exchange. But Uelmen said he would ask Superior Court Judge Lance A. Ito to instruct the panel today that Fuhrman had taken the 5th Amendment.
>
> Defense sources said it is unlikely that Fuhrman will appear in front of the jury.
>
> Fuhrman's decision to keep silent means that he will not rebut other witnesses' statements that he repeatedly used racial slurs and boasted of inventing charges against suspects. Nor will he attempt to explain any of the

comments he made in a series of taped interviews—comments that contradict his sworn testimony that he never used the word "nigger" in the last decade.

On the advice of his lawyer, Darryl Mounger, Fuhrman said that he would take the 5th Amendment on any question regarding the Simpson case.

* * *

A year after he refused to testify further in the case, Mark Fuhrman reached a settlement with the California attorney general allowing him to avoid a possible four-year jail term for perjury. Instead, Fuhrman's no contest plea to perjury landed him three years of probation and a $200 fine.

"It is important to understand that, as a result of these charges, this plea and this sentence, Mark Fuhrman is now a convicted felon and will forever be branded a liar," said California Attorney General Dan Lungren.

Lungren added that Fuhrman would never be a police officer again in the state of California.

"He is also now the ultimate impeachable witness—a convicted perjurer."

CHAPTER 15
The Fencing Match Continues

P rior to Fuhrman taking the stand, the government had put on several witnesses whose testimony, the prosecution believed, would establish its theory of the case. These included Detective Tom Lange, the senior detective who, along with his partner Philip Vannatter, who took over the investigation from Detectives Ron Phillips and Mark Fuhrman, and then Vannatter himself. But before these important principals testified, the government had put on the stand the first police officer on the scene—Patrolman Robert Riske, and then after him, his superior that day, Sergeant David Rossi.

In long sessions of direct testimony, followed by equally long cross-examinations, the two officers described the crime scene. Marcia Clark tried hard to show that the police had been careful to protect whatever evidence they gathered and we tried even harder to show just the opposite.

Johnnie Cochran, in his cross-examination of Officer Riske, established that the patrolman had not taken a photo of a melted cup of ice cream, but Clark came to his rescue on rebuttal by getting him to say that gathering evidence was not his job. On direct, she had asked him how many bloody gloves he had seen, and he had answered "One."

As for Sergeant Rossi, Riske's superior, I took him—vigorously—through a long and detailed cross, trying to trip him up on the details of his story. When he said that he had approached the bodies of the two victims by walking through some plants alongside a walkway, and that he'd chosen that approach because there were no footprints in the dirt, I reminded him that another officer had already walked that way, and thereby suggested that he, Rossi, hadn't looked for footprints carefully enough; that the investigation was carelessly and sloppily handled, as the defense had been alleging from the beginning.

Our attack on the LAPD police and their handling of the case drew a strenuous reaction from the other side. Many members of the Los Angeles City Council showed up at a meeting wearing blue ribbons to signal their support of the police department. One morning, so did defense team member Robert Shapiro, until we prevailed on him to remove it.

Johnnie Cochran and I both accused the officers of failing to record evidence that might have helped establish the time of death—another important element in the case—because it bears directly on whether Simpson had an alibi for the time of the murders. By the time Detective Tom Lange took the stand three weeks into the trial we were still hearing testimony from the first officers to arrive on the scene.

On direct examination, Marcia Clark got Detective Lange to testify that there had only been one killer, which contradicted our assertion that there had been two. And she also got him to try and shoot down our other assertions that the killings had been drug related. Prior to Lange's testimony, Johnnie Cochran had offered up a defense theory—that the reason for the murders had been a debt owed by Nicole's guest, a friend named Faye Resnick, to certain purveyors of cocaine, which remained unpaid, and the *New York Times* went right after it, reporting under the headline "Simpson's Lawyer Hints Slayings Were Mistake by Drug Dealers":

The chief defense lawyer and the chief police investigator in the O. J. Simpson case continued their seemingly endless fencing match today, delving into topics like the rate at which ice cream melts and the murder methods used by Colombian drug lords. The lawyer, Johnnie L. Cochran Jr., elaborated on his assertion that Nicole Brown Simpson and Ronald L. Goldman were not the victims of a jealous former husband but of irate drug dealers who had set out last June to kill one of Mrs. Simpson's friends—one of their customers—instead. Continuing his effort to offer some plausible alternative to the prosecution's case, Mr. Cochran suggested that the very brutality of the killings indicated that the perpetrators were drug dealers out to collect a debt, and that the real target was Faye Resnick, who was living with Mrs. Simpson, and taking drugs, around the same time.

The prosecution viewed LAPD detective Philip Vannatter, who took the stand a week after Mark Fuhrman, as a very important witness for their side. And, in a sense—but a very different sense—so did we. Detective Vannatter, Tom Lange's partner, was the last of the ten LAPD members the prosecution put on the stand to introduce its evidence against O. J. and, simultaneously, to shoot down the defense theories of a drug-related killing and of a police conspiracy against Simpson. How could there have been a conspiracy, it implied, when so many different cops worked the case, some of whom did not even know one another?

Bob Shapiro was given the opportunity to cross-examine Vannatter, and I was asked to help him prepare. For a lawyer who'd never handled a major witness in a murder case before, Bob Shapiro did a workmanlike job. He got Vannatter to admit that a blanket taken from Nicole's house and used to cover her dead body, might have been left at Bundy by Simpson on an earlier visit, which could explain why a hair resembling Simpson's had been found on the body of Ron Goldman. Shapiro also scored by establishing that while Simpson had a cut on his left hand, there was no cut on the left-hand glove. But Chris Darden, the attorney for the prosecution, countered with this helpful answer from Vannatter:

"I believe during the struggle the left-hand glove was lost and dropped on the ground, and that's when the cut occurred, when the hands were not protected. So...There's no significance to [the fact there was no cut on the glove]."

All in all, Vannatter did not hurt us very badly. He did help establish the government's timeline, relying wholly on Pablo Fenjves's claim to have heard barking at 10:15 p.m. that night, which, if the jury accepted it, would be bad for the defense. But I believe he came across to the jurors as a crusty veteran cop who was wedded to the old LAPD way of doing things, and uncomfortable with, if not also skeptical of, modern investigative methods. My feeling was that the jury didn't warm to him.

The government then called Kato Kaelin, Simpson's shaggy-haired, would-be actor, non-paying houseguest, to the stand to testify. He said that on the night of the murders, he did not see O. J. from 9:35 p.m., the time they got back from having a hamburger, to 10:55 when the limo driver was outside the gate and saw a figure in the home's entryway. According to the prosecution, this meant Simpson had time to commit the murders and then get home to clean up before his trip to Chicago.

With his boyish good looks and quirky, outgoing personality, Kaelin had become a TV crowd favorite when he testified at the preliminary hearing. In fact, one media outlet did a survey that claimed 74 percent of the country knew who Kato Kaelin was, but only 24 percent could identify Vice President Al Gore.

The thirty-five-year-old Kaelin had met Nicole Brown Simpson at a ski resort in Colorado, and they became social friends. Aware that he was an aspiring actor, she offered him the use of her guest room and said he could defray part of the rent by occasionally watching her children. Eventually, however, O. J. offered Kaelin a room in one of the buildings on his estate because he didn't think it "looked right" for Nicole to have an unmarried male living on her property, even though Kaelin and Nicole were not romantically involved.

Juries in lengthy murder trials often appreciate an element of comic relief, and Kaelin certainly provided that. Described by one reporter as "rather childlike," Kaelin was clearly nervous as he waited to be called, and when that call finally came, he all but sprinted to the front of the courtroom, almost knocking over prosecutor Chris Darden.

The loudest laugh line of the entire trial came when Marcia Clark asked if he thought living with O. J. Simpson would benefit his acting career, and he replied, "I don't think we were going for the same parts."

Initially, Clark got the answers she wanted from Kaelin, but later became so frustrated with his obvious attempts not to say anything negative about *anyone* that she asked Judge Ito to declare him a hostile witness.

Clark then pointed out, again, that Kaelin did not know where O. J. had been during the time period in which, the prosecutors say, he killed his former wife and Goldman. She also claimed that on the day of the murders, Simpson was upset about the tight dress Nicole wore and about her efforts to limit his time with his daughter at her dance recital. This, Clark sought to convey, is what led later that evening to murderous rage. Shapiro, on cross-examination of Kaelin, tried to portray Simpson's behavior that day as unimportant.

Kaelin, it appeared, did not want to say anything that would cause anyone to be upset or angry with him. As one reporter wrote, "the aspiring actor ... was less definitive, struggling simultaneously to placate opposing lawyers, reconcile his own varying recollections of events and define the subtle gradations of what he called Mr. Simpson's 'upsetness.'"

As Johnnie Cochran later wrote, "Many adjectives have been employed to describe America's most celebrated houseguest; perhaps 'feckless' would be the kindest. ... His only real purpose seemed to be to make sure nobody was mad at him, no matter what that might cost other people, including O. J., from whom he had been freeloading."

The next significant witness was Allan Park, the limo service driver who picked up O. J. on the night of the murders and drove him to LAX for his flight to Chicago. His testimony is crucial because it turned out to be the *only* statement the jury in this case asked to review during their deliberations. Let's examine why.

Because Allan Park was substituting that night for his boss, Dale St. John, Simpson's regular driver, Park got to the Rockingham estate early, arriving at 10:22 p.m. He drove slowly up and down the street three times to make sure he had the correct address. At 10:39, having verified the address, he waited outside the Ashford Street gate until Simpson came out of his house at 10:55.

During her inquiry, Marcia Clark got what she wanted from Park, at least in part: He testified that he never saw O. J.'s white Bronco parked anywhere in the vicinity. However, on cross-examination (by Johnnie Cochran) he *also* said he didn't see any cuts on his passenger's hand, which bolstered the defense's contention that O. J. did not cut his hand in a struggle with Ron Goldman.

Allan Park also, and most importantly, told Clark that at 10:55 p.m., after he buzzed the house several times with no response, he saw someone "come into the entranceway" of the house. He described someone who was "six foot, 200 pounds," and when asked if that person was Caucasian or African American, he said, "Black."

Clark then asked, "Did you form an opinion as to whether this person was a male or a female?" And the witness replied, "No."

According to Park, at that point he again buzzed the house and a voice he recognized as Simpson's answered the phone. "He told me that he overslept, that he just got out of the shower, and he'd be down in a minute," Park told Clark, the jury, and the television cameras.

What's important here is that Park testified that he saw a dark figure in the *entryway* of the house. He didn't testify that anyone crossed in front of his headlights, which were shining across the driveway. The prosecution had hoped that Park would testify that he saw the figure coming across the lawn, but the fact remained that he saw this figure only in the *walkway*.

Marcia Clark, in her closing argument on September 26, 1995, told the jury that Park had seen a dark figure "walking at a good pace up the driveway"—a clear misrepresentation of what Park actually had said. Although O. J. never got the opportunity to testify on his behalf at the trial, he later would tell television talk show host Larry King that it *was* him in the entryway, having just brought a bag out from inside the house to load into the limo.

When the jury deliberated, the only thing they asked to review was Park's testimony. It was clear there was some confusion about what he actually said on the witness stand, and what Marcia Clark had mischaracterized in her summary.

As it turned out, Park's testimony did not mesh with Clark's paraphrasing. Armanda Cooley wrote in *Madam Foreman: A Rush to Judgment*, the book she did with two other jurors: "[Cochran] asked him where the man was walking, and he traced the path as Mr. Park answered, and when he ended he circled it. ... My problem was Mr. Park never did say he saw O. J. walking in a specific area on that driveway. He said walkway."

It was the government's contention that at around 10:15 p.m. on June 12—the time based mainly on the testimony of Pablo Fenjves—Simpson had killed Nicole Brown Simpson and Ron Goldman, then drove two miles home in his Bronco.

O. J. told the police that at the time of the killings, he was at home watching a Clint Eastwood movie on television and fell asleep. Listings confirmed that the film in question was broadcast that night. O. J. also said the Bronco never moved from its parking spot on Rockingham Avenue, and produced a witness, Rosa Lopez, the neighbors' live-in housekeeper, to corroborate his account. But Lopez turned out to be a very poor witness. Her memory was hazy, her command of English wanting, and she contradicted herself by telling Judge Ito she had a reservation to fly home to El Salvador when she hadn't yet made one.

Even though Lopez's statement would have supported O. J.'s version of where he was when the murders were committed, she presented too many problems and we decided not to use her as a witness on the stand. It also did not help that we, the defense, which had told the judge and the prosecution we had no notes or tapes of Lopez's interview, belatedly discovered there *was* a tape. It made us look as if we'd been hiding something from the other side. Not our finest moment.

CHAPTER 16
DNA: The "Mountain" Becomes a Molehill

We did not challenge the underlying reliability of DNA testing methods; we attacked the way that the evidence was gathered and processed. We had a 21st century technology and 19th century evidence collection methods.

—Barry Scheck, June 18, 2014, *Los Angeles Times*

It was now time for the government to put on its blood evidence. It appeared at least initially as if the prosecution had a strong case. This was certainly how the media portrayed it. The prosecution, including District Attorney Gil Garcetti, claimed repeatedly that it had "a mountain" of DNA evidence.

The blood evidence fell into three categories:

1. Evidence that was correctly collected, tested, and identified, but these results did little to provide proof of guilt or innocence, or,

2. Evidence that was correctly collected, tested and identified, and *seemingly* incriminated Simpson, or,

3. Evidence that was incorrectly gathered, handled, and was subjected to PCR testing because of the minute quantities involved. It could not have been correctly identified under those circumstances.

To help unravel this, let's start first with a short primer on DNA. According to the National Institutes of Health (NIH), DNA is defined as: "the hereditary material in humans and almost all other organisms. Nearly every cell in a person's body has the same DNA. Most DNA is located in the cell nucleus (where it is called nuclear DNA), but a small amount of DNA can also be found in the mitochondria (where it is called mitochondrial DNA or mtDNA).

The information in DNA is stored as a code made up of four chemical bases: adenine (A), guanine (G), cytosine (C), and thymine (T). Human DNA consists of about three billion bases, and more than 99 percent of those bases are the same in all people. The order, or sequence, of these bases determines the information available for building and maintaining an organism, similar to the way in which letters of the alphabet appear in a certain order to form words and sentences.

Once a lab gets blood samples, it tests them by using one of two standard methods: RFLP (restriction fragment length polymorphism) or PCR (polymerase chain reaction). RFLP is the older, well-studied, time-consuming test that yields DNA results that provide a very high degree of certainty. The RFLP test requires a minimum of 25 to 50 nanograms of DNA. PCR, the newer and highly sensitive technique, can be performed with only 0.5 nanogram (50 picograms) of specimen available, because of the ability through PCR to clone—and thus multiply—the actual sample.

The distinction between the two methods would become important. We knew the prosecution was going to put on scientifically trained witnesses who would testify under oath that their tests proved O. J. Simpson's and the victims' blood was everywhere they needed it to be: at both Nicole's house and O. J.'s own home, and in his white Bronco.

However, we felt that when it was our turn to present evidence, especially in relation to testimony about blood, we could show the jury that the prosecution's case was thin to the point of transparency. We intended to prove that DNA evidence is only as sound as the people collecting it and the methods in which it is stored and analyzed. Slipshod gathering and cataloging methods peppered with underlying, sinister motivations lurking within certain members of the LAPD at that time would conjure at the very least reasonable doubt in the deductive minds of reasonable people. We were ready to show the press-created "mountain of blood evidence" for what it really was: a Potemkin village.

* * *

Let's break down the blood evidence that the prosecution offered in detail as it pertains to the Bundy crime scene and Simpson's Rockingham estate.

First, the crime scene:

Blood Drops on the Walkway at Bundy

There were five blood drops consistent with O. J. Simpson's DNA that were gathered on June 13, 1994, on the walkway at the Bundy property. The drops totaled 84.1 nanograms—the equivalent of four pinheads of DNA evidence. Of those five drops, four were so small they had to be tested using the PCR (cloning) method, which requires just 0.5 nanograms of DNA. The defense argued from the start that this testing method was fraught with problems, particularly regarding the laboratory's methods. The Scientific Investigation Division (SID) at the LAPD had only begun PCR testing earlier in 1994. Defense witness Michele Kestler, head of the LAPD crime lab, admitted under oath that technicians had no clear set of policies and procedures other than a four-year-old draft manual that hadn't been updated.

PCR testing is highly susceptible to contamination. Even trace amounts of errant DNA, such as aerosols, can taint the results. A facility like the LAPD Crime Lab that didn't follow the strictest of guidelines in handling and processing samples had a high chance of contamination, thereby marring the results.

The biggest flaw of the many inflicted upon the evidence by the LAPD lab gathered from the scene at Bundy Drive is that Simpson's reference sample (the blood sample that he gave police) was processed *along with* evidence samples. This is crucial because this unorthodox practice administered by untrained technicians where aerosols can linger in the air greatly increases the chance of cross-contamination of the evidence samples. The reference sample was also mislabeled and that mistake was dubbed by the lab as a "clerical error."

LAPD criminalist Collin Yamauchi testified that when processing evidence samples from the Bundy scene, he first tested Simpson's reference sample. Shockingly, he went on to testify that when he opened the tube of Simpson's blood, it spurted up through the ChemWipe® covering the tube and landed on Yamauchi's gloves. He said he changed his gloves, but he couldn't be certain if he disposed of the gloves *inside* of the evidence processing room, where the evidence testing occurred, or in another receptacle outside of the testing area.

Yamauchi also testified he did not change papers between handling the reference and evidence items. Gary Sims, of the California Deptartment of Justice, testified that this practice created "unacceptable risk" for contamination.

Sims also went on to testify that all the blood drop samples were "degraded" or "substantially degraded" due to LAPD's collection and storage methods. Samples were stored in plastic bags (a known foul in evidence gathering) and kept in a hot vehicle for hours without refrigeration.

The Rear Gate at Bundy

Three blood swatches were analyzed from the rear gate at Bundy that were consistent with Simpson via the PCR testing method. While investigators testified the "smudges" on the gate were viewed the morning after the murders, they were not collected until July 3, 1994—*21 days after the murders.* However, the evidence showed no signs of degradation, according to Sims, despite being exposed to three weeks of sunlight, moisture and bacteria.

Defense DNA testing expert John Gerdes, PhD, told jurors, "It doesn't seem to make sense to me. You should see about the same amount of degradation and, in fact, on (sample) 117, which is an older sample, it should have more degradation."

As Barry Scheck would ask the jury in his closing argument, "These samples (from July 3) are not degraded. *How can that be?*"

Prosecutors could offer no explanation.

There was also evidence that the samples contained EDTA, a preservative found in purple top tubes used in blood draws. Was blood taken from Simpson's reference tube and placed on the gate? We posed this question to the jury. After all, at the grand jury proceedings and the preliminary hearing, prison nurse Thano Peratis testified that he drew 8 cc of Simpson's blood at Parker Center after he'd given his statement to police. Yet Simpson's reference sample in police custody had only 6.5 cc. Prosecutors said the 8 cc was just an estimate, but we contended 1.5 cc of Simpson's blood were missing. Where did that blood go?

The Left-hand Glove at Bundy

This glove had 0 nanograms of Simpson's DNA. Nor did it have any cuts or holes in it.

Blood Drops Found on the Rockingham Driveway, Foyer, and Master Bathroom Floor

Of the four drops found at Simpson's estate, three were tested using the PCR method, which again is highly susceptible to contamination. We also argued these drops were inconclusive as Simpson had told police he had a minor cut after golfing that day. Therefore, his DNA in these places would be consistent with where they should be.

And there's another twist in this scenario: During the trial, the jury learned that Detective Vannatter took Simpson's reference blood sample that he'd given to police *back to the Rockingham home* to give to criminalist Dennis Fung while that team was still processing the crime scene. Why would a veteran detective return to a scene with evidence incriminating a suspect? Sloppy police work at best, and suspicious for more cynical minds.

Blood in the Ford Bronco

Of the blood evidence found, the Bronco appeared, on its surface, to be the most important to neutralize. When Mark Fuhrman and the detectives arrived at the Rockingham house at 5:15 a.m., to 5:30 a.m., and found the gates on both Rockingham Avenue and Ashford Street closed and locked, Fuhrman noticed the Bronco parked on Rockingham and, alone, examined it. He called Detective Vannatter over to the Bronco and pointed out a dark smear on the outside door of the vehicle, about a quarter inch long.

After the vehicle was impounded, several areas of the Bronco were swabbed for DNA, including the outside door handle, instrument panel, steering wheel, center console, and carpet. Almost all DNA traces of these areas were consistent with Simpson, which are easy to explain as he often drove the vehicle and he told police in his statement that he had cut his hand at home that day and that he often has small scrapes and nicks from golfing and other activities. There was a trace amount of both Simpson's and Nicole's blood on the steering wheel.

But of the swatches, the most significant was the finding of the console, which the prosecution's DNA expert witness, Gary Sims, testified on May 15, 1995, that those blood samples found in the Bronco matched those of O. J., Nicole, *and* Ron Goldman, which the jury had not heard before. This looked bad for O. J. because there was no way to explain how it got there other than criminally. But again, we had several factors playing in the background that pointed away from Simpson as the suspect.

We had already established through Mark Fuhrman's testimony that there was a period of close to fifteen full minutes where Fuhrman roamed the Rockingham property unaccompanied. We believed he had the bloodied glove from the Bundy crime scene, and that before dropping it, he used it to contaminate the Bronco. We also had an expert witness, Dr. Henry Lee, prepared to testify that the blood stain on the console in the Bronco appeared consistent with a "smearing" motion, a detail we felt indicated that the blood was placed there.

Then there were the collection methods. Criminalist Andrea Mazzola, new to her role and still in field training, used the *same* cotton swab to dab the various spots of blood on the interior of the vehicle, which would contaminate the samples. There was also video footage of Mazzola, while gathering evidence from the Bundy Drive scene, not changing her gloves between handling items. Another nod to careless police work.

Finally, the defense had tow truck driver, John Meraz, who said the Bronco was shunted around a tow yard, left unlocked, and that it was never completely secure. He knew this because Meraz testified he took dry cleaning receipts from the vehicle as souvenirs. With unauthorized people entering the vehicle, it called the prosecution's case into question.

The Right-Hand Glove at Rockingham

The now infamous "bloody glove" in the Simpson case, found by Mark Fuhrman behind Kato Kaelin's room, had DNA markers of Simpson, Brown, and Goldman.

Of the ten areas of the glove that were matched, two areas at the wrist notch of the glove were consistent with Simpson's through PCR testing. This wrist notch is the same area that criminalist Collin Yaumachi wrote his initials on the glove *after* getting blood from Simpson's reference sample on his lab gloves (and potentially on his table and workstation.)

Defense witness Dr. Gerdes testified that the minute amount of Simpson's DNA and where it appeared on the glove would be consistent with cross-contamination.

In addition to thoroughly investigating the LAPD's DNA laboratory methods, we did some field work on our own as it pertains to the glove found by Fuhrman at the Rockingham home. We went *proactive*, to borrow one of the FBI's favorite words.

A critical matter concerning the right glove was its condition when "found" at the Rockingham property by Fuhrman, then by other detectives. When it was retrieved and bagged by the crime lab of the LAPD, the "substance" coating its surface—later clearly identified as human blood—*was still moist.*

There would seem to be but three possible explanations for the presence of the glove at Rockingham in the early morning hours of June 13, 1994:

1. O. J. Simpson put it there. If O. J. had dropped the glove, it could have been no later than 10:50 p.m. on June 12, since he boarded his limousine for the airport fifteen minutes later. That would have left it exposed to the atmosphere until at least 5:30 a.m. on June 13, when it was "discovered."

2. Whoever killed Nicole and Ron Goldman took it from the scene and put it in this unlikely spot, hoping to draw suspicion away from himself and toward Simpson.

3. Mark Fuhrman, upon discovering that his moment of glory was to be denied him by the "old pros" from Parker Center, decided to embed himself in the case. Grabbing a plastic baggie from the trunk of the police car, he scooped the right-handed glove from the Bundy scene, and tucked it in his pocket or perhaps his sock. Remember: *Fuhrman* suggested the trip to Rockingham and led the way; *Fuhrman* jumped the perimeter wall; and *Fuhrman* went alone to the dark pathway. He was gone for fifteen minutes, and then "discovered" the still moist glove.

To test our theory about the wet glove, I decided to conduct an experiment, which we videotaped. On the night of June 12, 1995, when the atmospheric conditions were almost identical to those which prevailed one year before, Pat McKenna and I—with the help of Dr. Robert Huizenga, who drew McKenna's blood—took two Aris Lite gloves very similar to the ones left by the killer (or killers) and smeared them with McKenna's blood.

One glove was placed in a plastic Ziploc® bag such as the ones that Fuhrman admitted to carrying in the trunk of his cruiser, and the other glove was left unprotected. Both were placed as close to the exact spot where Fuhrman said he found the glove on the morning of June 13 a year earlier at about 5:00 to 5:30 a.m. The two gloves were inspected and photographed hourly, beginning at 11:00 p.m.

By 5:00 a.m. in our experiment, the unprotected left-handed glove was completely dry, and the right-handed glove contained in the plastic covering was still wet. The conclusion is inescapable that the glove that was acquired at the scene of the crime had been placed in an airtight container, removed from that container, and deposited at the Simpson home at about the time Fuhrman disappeared and handed Kato Kaelin off to Vannatter.

Pat McKenna submitted a detailed report of our reconstruction of the glove location and condition, but the results of this experiment were never heard by the jury. Judge Ito decided not to let them observe the findings or hear them read aloud. However, the jury did hear that the glove was wet when discovered, and some testimony that, under normal circumstances, the blood would have been dry within two hours.

The Sock

Another piece of evidence was a sock found in O. J's bedroom. Through reliable RFLP testing, the sock was confirmed to have had a droplet of Nicole's blood on it as well as Simpson's. But there were several problems for the prosecution regarding the sock, involving issues with improper collection, storage, and potential tampering of the evidence.

To begin, there were questions around how and when the sock was collected at the scene, based on evidence provided by the LAPD themselves. Police photographs and video of the Rockingham residence show time-stamped discrepancies as to when the sock first appeared on the floor. A police photographer, Willie Ford, testified that he saw no sock when he videotaped Simpson's bedroom at 4:13 p.m. on June 13, 1994. But a police evidence collector said he picked up the sock at about 4:30 or 4:40 p.m.

Next were the reported observations of trained criminal investigators of the sock itself. Initial inspection of the sock upon collection at the Rockingham scene showed no visible signs of blood. Thereafter, it was examined at least twice more by at least five trained criminalists in the crime lab over the next two weeks. Each inspection showed *no observed blood* on the sock. It wasn't until August that the LAPD crime lab reported a blood droplet was found on the garment. A thoughtful next question would be, "If that was never noted before now after several careful inspections, could that blood have been placed there through careless handling and/or malicious intent?"

Then, the placement of the blood drop on the sock created a curious problem. The droplet went *completely through* the sock at both ankles, a clear indication that no foot was in the sock when the blood drop got on it. Our expert witnesses, Criminalist Herbert MacDonell and Dr. Henry Lee, both concluded a stain of that type could not have occurred had the sock been worn when the blood got on it.

When Gary Sims testified that the blood on the sock found in O. J.'s bedroom matched Nicole's genetic markers, defense attorney Barry Scheck asked, "Do you know from your own personal knowledge how and when that blood got on the sock?'

"No," Sims replied.

Finally, one must consider the timing of when news broke about the DNA testing showing that the blood drop contained Nicole's DNA. On September 26, 1994, news reports were surfacing that a leak within the LAPD reported the sock found at the Rockingham residence had a drop of blood matching Nicole's DNA. However, that was the same day the sock was sent to Cellmark to do the genetic testing. Cellmark didn't submit its findings until November 17. This raises the question: *How could police investigators know in September that the blood drop on the sock would belong to Nicole?*

* * *

Indeed, we felt there was enough murkiness surrounding the infamous sock, glove, and other evidence to raise more than just reasonable doubts in the minds of the jurors. But we had another issue looming on the very near horizon: *The jury clock was still ticking.* When the state began its case regarding forensics the first week of April 1995, five jurors had been dismissed for various reasons. By the time prosecutors wrapped up their case on the physical evidence, it was the first week of July, and four more jurors had been dismissed. We were down to just two alternates and in peril of running out of the number of jurors and alternates the state would accept to proceed with the case. Such a calamity would almost certainly mean a mistrial.

This left us having to leave out important witnesses such as Dr. Kary Mullis, the Nobel Laureate and inventor of PCR. As mentioned, Dr. Mullis was prepared to testify about the fallibility of this method based on the gathering techniques at the scenes. Even for a witness of such importance—there just wasn't time. The world never heard what Dr. Mullis had to say, which would have gone a long way to show that the bulk of the prosecution's "mountain" of DNA had to be discarded.

CHAPTER 17
Peeling Back the DNA Layers

W hen it was time for the prosecution to present its blood evidence, it relied primarily on five different witnesses: The LAPD criminologists Dennis Fung, Andrea Mazzola, and Collin Yamauchi; Robin Cotton of Cellmark Diagnostics, the Maryland lab that tested the various blood samples; and US Department of Justice analyst Gary Sims.

Of this team of forensic scientists from both the police and the private sector, the first significant government witness was Dr. Robin Cotton, the director of the well-respected Cellmark Diagnostics. The prosecution used Dr. Cotton to tutor the jury in the fundamentals of DNA testing. Each juror was given a transparent sheet of X-ray film called an autoradiograph, and for two days Dr. Cotton explained how to read its patterns. In contrast to previous days, the jury appeared wide awake and focused, often viewing the overhead display and taking frequent notes. According to the *Chicago Tribune*, "Cotton's patient and understandable presentation had observers likening her to everybody's favorite high school biology teacher."

Still, the subject matter was complex, and despite this difficulty, the media easily accepted the government's evidence rather than admit it didn't fully (or in some cases, even partially) understand it. Many dutifully reported the conclusion of Dr. Cotton that, "In fact, the bands . . . match the bands in Mr. Simpson," and that Nicole Brown's DNA matched the DNA found in the sock. For the first time, jurors heard direct, rather than circumstantial, evidence claiming that O. J., (or to be accurate, *his blood,*) had been at the murder scene. And while this didn't prove he was the killer, it appeared to put him there, which the prosecution had always contended, and we had always denied. Johnnie Cochran, when asked by the media about the impact of Dr. Cotton's testimony, was his usual optimistic self, stating that he didn't think her testimony was "damaging at all. We listened to the evidence and moved ahead. We'll see during cross-examination."

Now it was time for the prosecution to bring out its LAPD criminologists Dennis Fung, Andrea Mazzola, and Collin Yamauchi.

"Fung was the witness O. J. Simpson's acquittal depended on, the key to discrediting the blood evidence," Larry Schiller and James Willwerth later wrote in *American Tragedy*. "Behind Fung, already examined were Vannatter, Lange, and Fuhrman. Ahead were Andrea Mazzola and Collin Yamauchi. But Fung was the key."

Enter Barry Scheck.

As I said earlier, Bob Shapiro did some good things when he put the defense team together, and one of his best was to hire the whiz kids from New York, Barry Scheck and his partner Peter Neufeld. Both professors of law as well as being private practitioners and the co-founders of the Innocence Project in which they used their extensive knowledge of DNA to overturn the convictions of many inmates who should never have been imprisoned in the first place.

Scheck cross-examined Dennis Fung, the LAPD's lead criminologist on the case, and Neufeld took Fung's junior associate, Andrea Mazzola.

In his time before the grand jury, Fung had been impressively calm and professional, so when Scheck announced that he planned to attack the criminologist, fellow defense team member

Gerry Uelmen was shocked: "You'll *attack* him?" to which Barry replied, "He's covering up for a lot of people. I have it on video-tape, and I have it in the records."

Counting his direct examination by prosecutor Hank Goldberg, Dennis Fung spent nine days on the stand, five of them being his cross-examination by Scheck. Contrary to his smooth performance earlier, under Scheck's rapid-fire questioning, Fung's answers sounded hesitant and at times contradictory.

For example, after establishing that last summer Fung had told the grand jury that he, not Mazzola, had collected most of the blood evidence, Barry showed a videotape of Mazzola collecting the glove found at 875 South Bundy, plus other critical pieces of evidence. Fung had to concede that his earlier testimony was not correct. Fung had also told the grand jury that on June 13 at Simpson's house, he'd personally taken a vial of O. J. Simpson's blood from lead detective Phil Vannatter. But Scheck used a different video—a news camera shot of Fung and Mazzola leaving the Rockingham house that day with Fung empty-handed and Mazzola carrying a black garbage bag.

On the stand, Fung remembered that the garbage bag contained the vial of blood. This was important because it was yet another example of substandard police work. We later learned that one of the dismissed jurors said the question of what had happened to that blood sample made her suspicious. In fairness to the two criminologists, Fung and Mazzola, they were simply following the instructions given them by their LAPD superiors, instructions that were just plain wrong and contrary to proper evidence-gathering procedures, especially DNA evidence.

Linda Deutsch, the veteran courtroom journalist, noted the irony of the fact that thanks to Scheck's cross-examination of Dennis Fung, the blood evidence that the government thought would convict Simpson had become a major defense tool.

When Fung stepped off the stand, he did something I'd never seen before in all my years in courtrooms—he walked over to the defense table and shook the hands of everyone within reach—including the defendant, O. J. Simpson!

After Scheck was finally finished, it was the turn of his partner, Peter Neufeld, the other young attorney from New York. It was Peter's job to cross-examine Dennis Fung's second in command, Criminologist 1, Andrea Mazzola. (Fung was a Criminologist 111, the highest ranking.)

Counting her direct examination by the government and Neufeld's long and, by necessity, often repetitious cross, Mazzola was on the stand for four days, during which time tempers frayed and flared until Judge Ito chastised everyone but the jurors. He even kicked two reporters out of court because they talked when he had called for silence.

Neufeld was trying diligently to get the witness to admit that she had exposed the blood samples to cross-contamination in the Los Angeles Police Department laboratory; and he also suggested she had, in her testimony, covered up for both her own negligence and that of her colleagues.

But Mazzola held firm that she had done neither. There was one small human bit: After Peter Neufeld mispronounced the criminologist's name, calling her "Mazzoler," he apologized, blaming the mispronunciation on his Brooklyn roots.

The prosecution, which must have thought Fung and Mazzola would be on and off the stand relatively quickly, had discounted the thoroughness of the two young New York lawyers. Barry and Peter gave notice to the government that the defense planned to mount a very serious challenge by exposing the LAPD's sloppy ways of collecting and analyzing the kind of scientific evidence with which they were attempting to convict O. J. Simpson.

One of the defense team lawyers suggested that—on his deathbed—the last thing Dennis Fung would hear would be the voice of Barry Scheck shouting, "How about *that*, Mr. Fung?" And, clearly Judge Ito agreed, for late in Barry's cross, he called us to a sidebar conference, and said, "He's like a deer caught in the headlights. When are you going to let him go, Mr. Scheck?"

The job of cross-examining Dr. Cotton was also given to Peter Neufeld. At first, he appeared to be making little headway, as Cotton calmly deflected his machine gun-like barrage of questions. A smart and experienced expert witness, she directed her answers to the jurors, seldom looking at her interrogator. But I thought Neufeld did score on the reasonable doubt meter. He asked, "As a scientist, Dr. Cotton, have you ever heard the expression, 'Garbage in, garbage out'?" The prosecution objected to the question, and Judge Ito sustained it, and then helpfully added that even non-scientists know the expression. Neufeld had made his point to the jurors: If they believed the lab had received questionable evidence—the garbage *in*—then they could ignore Cellmark's findings, the garbage *out*. Through his questions, Neufeld had managed to suggest to the jury that despite what Dr. Cotton, the government witness, said, the defense believed differently. The police lab technicians had improperly handled—carelessly or *on purpose*—the cotton swatches they used to pick up bloodstains at the crime scene, and that, as a result, the DNA on the swatches had disintegrated to a point where they were useless as crime scene evidence. The defense alleged that tampering had occurred downtown in the police evidence processing room, where the swatches were stored with bloodstains collected from Simpson's driveway and foyer, and along with a vial of his blood. We also managed to suggest that the police had used its sample of Nicole's blood to stain the socks.

Neufeld reminded jurors that I had argued earlier that blood found inside Simpson's Bronco could have been planted by Mark Fuhrman. I had alleged that the glove was found on Simpson's property because the emotionally unstable and racist Fuhrman, who had found the glove at Bundy, had brought it to Simpson's estate. There, he smeared it inside the Bronco, and then claimed to have "found" it on Simpson's property.

Neufeld asked Cotton to assume that Simpson had cut himself recently and walked out to the Bronco and bled in his car. Judge Ito sustained an objection to the question, but Neufeld suggested an explanation for Simpson's blood was found inside.

Neufeld asked Cotton to make another assumption, that "some other person had come into contact with Nicole Brown Simpson's blood and made a smear on the steering wheel." Judge

Ito cut him off, and Neufeld then asked, hypothetically, if some-one had "touched Mr. Simpson's blood and touched Nicole Brown Simpson's blood and touched that steering wheel." Judge Ito again cut him off, sternly instructing jurors to "disregard the implica-tion of that question," and recessed the court for the day.

Although the judge was clearly displeased with his queries, Neufeld had made his point to the jurors—whose job it would be to weigh the defense's conspiracy theory against the evidence presented by the prosecution.

Next on the stand for the government was Gary Sims, a sen-ior criminologist from the state of California's crime lab. Sims, like Dr. Cotton, was a well-respected and very experienced expert witness. Barry Scheck acknowledged this by asking Sims if either he or Dr. Cotton were part of a conspiracy to tamper with the evidence in the case. When Sims gave the obvious "no" answer, he actually smiled. Scheck's intention was to show the jury that there was a vast difference in the way the labs run by Robin Cotton and Gary Sims collected, stored, and analyzed blood evidence and the way the LAPD did it.

Scheck's hours-long cross-examination of Sims was so detailed that few people in the courtroom could follow all of it, but that didn't worry Scheck because he had a secondary purpose: He wanted Sims's description of how carefully his lab dealt with evidence to be in sharp contrast to that of the government's next witness, Collin Yamauchi, the young and not very experienced LAPD criminologist who had handled the blood samples before they were tested.

On direct examination by the prosecution's Rocky Harmon, Yamauchi almost gave the defense a major break. Harmon was attempting to protect the criminologist—who'd already admitted he'd mislabeled a vial of O. J.'s blood because of a "clerical error"—from questions he'd undoubtedly get from the defense, and asked, "Based on what you've heard in the media before you did the test in this case, did you have an expectation what the outcome of these tests would be?"

"Yes," replied Yamauchi, "I heard on the news that he's got an airtight alibi, he's in Chicago and, you know, it's his ex-wife and this and that, and he's probably not related to this thing."

When it was Scheck's turn to cross-examine Yamauchi, he immediately tried to use this admission as a way to introduce the statement O. J. had given to the police on his return to Los Angeles, but Scheck was unsuccessful. We very much wanted to play that tape for the jury because it contained exculpatory explanations—in essence, it would give an early and favorable look at what Simpson had said to the detectives without any help from legal counsel. Judge Ito wouldn't hear of it. Nonetheless, we were pleased that the jury got to hear the word *alibi* again.

Barry Scheck and Collin Yamauchi eventually got on one another's nerves, and Scheck became openly sarcastic. At one point, after a long and complex answer by the witness, the defense lawyer asked, "Are you finished?"

In a defiant tone, Yamauchi responded, "I am."

"Then," snapped Scheck, "would you please answer my question?"

Barry crossed swords with Marcia Clark after he had asked Yamauchi directly, "When you were talking with Mr. Fung on the morning of June 14th, did you know that detectives at robbery-homicide had taken a statement from Mr. Simpson earlier that day?"

Clark reacted angrily and said she would report Scheck to the State Bar for asking a question that "any lawyer with half a brain, with an I.Q. above five," would know was not proper. Most judges would have berated counsel for using such insulting language against an opponent before the jury, but not Judge Ito.

The jurors seemed intrigued by Yamauchi's discussion of blood staining his gloves, a point that we defense attorneys deemed critical, and his admission that some of O. J.'s blood had gotten onto Yamauchi's work table and on his gloves, which he had to throw away and replace with a clean pair. That testimony had to have left a less-than-impressive picture of the LAPD evidence lab procedures in the minds of the jurors.

CHAPTER 18

Footprints, Fibers, and the Glove That Wouldn't Fit

It took prosecutors seven weeks—from the end of May to the Fourth of July weekend, 1995—call its final eleven witnesses in what they had to sense was a losing battle.

Of that group, there were only two of whom I considered potentially "heavy" witnesses. One was Bill Bodziak, the FBI's top footprint and foot impressions analyst, who had written an authoritative book on the subject; and Doug Deedrick, head of the bureau's lab section that handled hair and fiber analysis and comparison. I had been assigned to cross-examine both witnesses.

There was also another new explosion coming our way about the gloves. We would all discover—during a live court exhibition—that *they didn't even fit Simpson,* another bizarre twist in a case that continued to be fraught with them.

The Footprints

For the state's witnesses, the first of the possible "big guns" to take the stand was Special Agent Bill Bodziak, who brought with him several enlarged photographs and drawings. He helped shed light on the science of footprint and foot impression analysis. He explained that foot impressions are three-dimensional in nature and can be left on any surface which is malleable: Snow, mud, clay, or wax. These result when a foot "sinks into" the surface upon which it is stepped. When available, foot impressions afford some insight into the size and weight of the suspect.

Footprints, on the other hand, are two-dimensional and are generally found on a hard surface. Any substances on the foot or shoe causing the impression may well be left behind. The focus of Bodziak's testimony related to footprints leading back and forth between the alley behind Nicole's house where the murderers' vehicle was probably parked, and the scene of the murders where both bodies were found.

Those prints leading from the vehicle toward the scene were discernible, but had little or no blood mixed in. Those prints going from the scene back toward the vehicle led up some steps and through an alley, initially had generous smears of blood within them, which faded as the person walking got further from the murder site. Bodziak pointed to his enlarged sketches and explained the differences between these prints. After extensive research, he had concluded that the shoes which left the foot impressions were manufactured by Bruno Magli, an Italian company. A search of Simpson's home had revealed no Bruno Magli shoes, but only a pair of indoor slippers (with dissimilar soles) made by that same company. The prosecution was very keen on establishing by any means it could that Simpson had owned Bruno Magli shoes in the past, to support the argument that he could have worn them while committing the murders. No such evidence ever emerged during the criminal trial.

The size of the shoe was determined to be size twelve, a common male shoe size. The size O. J. Simpson, Mark Fuhrman, and millions of other men wear.

When I first studied Bodziak's illustrated footprint trail before he took the witness stand, I noticed what appeared to be a significant anomaly. During his direct examination, the prosecution carefully avoided any mention by the witness of this odd feature among his findings. The footprint evidence showed that one suspect on the initial crime scene, left the scene after the murders and then returned to the areas of the bodies before fleeing again to the getaway vehicle. This was important because it added more time to the clock. If the jury felt our testimony of timeline witnesses was accurate, the window in which Simpson could have perpetrated these killings just got impossibly small.

I feigned only a slight interest about footprint technology generally and Bodziak's experience with it as an expert. When he was turned over to me for cross-examination, I explored briefly the limitations suffered by the whole science of footprint technology, and a significant number of relevant issues that his testimony had failed to address. In most cases, it was because there simply was not enough trace evidence available to him to support further opinions. During his direct examination he had omitted any mention of an anomaly in the footprints he had described.

"Mr. Bodziak," I said, "there is something unusual about the footprints you have been describing for us, is there not?"

"What do you mean, unusual?" he responded.

"Looking at the footprints shown on your diagram, running from the scene of the murder to the back alley, would you say that there is more than one track?"

Bodziak's face clouded, as if he had hoped this moment would never come. "Yes, there do appear to be two different sets of footprints both going and coming from the back alley to the scene."

"And you have told us that from the prints left by the blood on the soles of the shoes, your research indicates that these are Bruno Maglis, correct?"

"That was my testimony," replied Bodziak, somewhat impatiently.

"Now then, since you have pointed to four distinct tracks—that is, two shod feet walking in each direction for a total of four trips—is it possible that two killers wearing identical shoes made those two sets of tracks?" The near impossibility suggested by the question was intended to antagonize him.

"You're talking about two different pairs of shoes of the same size manufactured with identical sole patterns worn by two men. That is not possible, indeed, *it's silly.*"

"And therefore it is plain to you, Mr. Bodziak, that a single person, wearing shoes whose soles had a singular pattern walked from the area where the killers' vehicle was parked, out the alley toward the front of the property, then back again. That same pair of shoes returned to the scene where the bodies lay, then returned through the alley to the vehicle. Is that what your diagram shows?"

"That would appear to be the case," said Bodziak.

"As if the killer had left something important in the vicinity of the bodies, and went back to the scene to retrieve it?"

"It's possible," he replied unenthusiastically.

"You are well aware that both victims were killed with sharp instruments, a knife or knives, are you not?"

"I believe that has been established by evidence already in the case," he replied.

"You are also aware that as of this date no murder weapon has ever been found, isn't that so?" Bodziak agreed.

"Would you agree that it's likely that a killer was departing the scene when he realized he had left the knife behind, and walked back to retrieve it?"

"That seems to be a possibility." He nodded.

"And you have also learned that at about the time the homicides took place, there was a good deal of commotion in the vicinity, principally from the barking of dogs?"

"I've been told that there were some disturbances at the time of the crime, I'm not sure of their extent."

I was inclined to ask him: "And the area was sufficiently illuminated so that any person whose face was well-known in the neighborhood would have run an awful risk going back to the murder scene to retrieve the weapon, isn't that so?" But it was an argumentative question, which would have been excluded as such, and could be better used in final argument.

Nonetheless, the attack on Bodziak, touted earlier as a critical witness for the prosecution who had important testimony implicating Simpson, backfired on them.

Given the facts described earlier, the very few minutes available to Simpson to leave the crime scene, dispose of all weapons, footwear, blood, and other clues, and then clean himself up before appearing at his front door to board the limousine were now further rendered all but impossible by the evidence of the killer's return to the scene, even if it took only a minute or two. That was time that couldn't be spared. We had succeeded in getting Bodziak to unwittingly help the defense case.

The Hair and Fibers

The government's second potential powerhouse witness was Douglas Deedrick, a well-known hair and fiber expert from the FBI laboratories in Quantico, Virginia. Based on the pretrial materials furnished, I understood that he would make comparisons between the human hair samples found, among other items, in a blue knit cap which was discovered at the scene of the murders, and which later became internationally famous when Johnnie Cochran wore it through part of his final argument.

Unlike many of the other types of forensic scientific evidence where a "match" can ultimately be declared between a suspect item and an exemplar whose source is well established, the science of hair and fiber technology has not yet achieved that status. DNA cannot be determined from a strand of hair without the follicle attached. The best that an expert can do after a comparison examination is to express an opinion that there is a degree of similarity between the suspect's and a strand of hair in evidence, or that they are consistent.

Deedrick had been an agent for more than twenty years, and was well respected in his field; indeed, he could be considered

FBI laboratory royalty. I expected him—like Bill Bodziak—to be a tough witness to corner.

In Deedrick's testimony, the prosecution planned to focus on twelve hairs collected from the knit cap found at the crime scene; one hair on Goldman's shirt; one hair found on the Rockingham glove; rose-beige fibers on the cap and glove; and black/blue cotton fibers on Goldman's shirt, the Rockingham glove, and the sock found in Simpson's home.

Deedrick, as Bodziak had done, used an array of enlarged photographs and drawings to illustrate and support the testimony he intended to give. These were to be expected in any major case like Simpson's, however, I was more than a little taken aback by a report given to me by our computer chief, Howard Harris. Harris often worked for some hours after court had adjourned, organizing and categorizing the defense team's evidence that he had projected that day on a screen so that the whole jury could see the exhibits without having to pass them among them, page by page.

While Harris was going about his ordinary duties, Deedrick engaged him in conversation as he set up his own visual materials on easels for his testimony the following day.

"When Simpson's lawyers see what I've got here," tittered Deedrick as if he had the means to summarily end the litigation, "they will probably be seeking a plea deal."

When Harris repeated this boast to me that same evening, I was somewhat comforted by the fact that I had done an extensive background check on the witness, but I was wary even so.

It may be worth taking a moment to focus on the mechanics of a trial lawyers' preparation when an expert witness—particularly one of long experience—is scheduled to appear. It is my good fortune that over the years I have appeared in court in every state but Montana and have gotten to know and befriend a great many lawyers across this nation. During that time, they had become a network of sorts, and in urgent circumstances would drop whatever they were doing and try to help me out through a series of phone calls, and some court records (which in 1995, were beginning to become available electronically). I was able to track down the occasions in which Deedrick had testified in cases in other courts; in many of these instances, I was able to get my colleagues at the defense bar to assist in identifying those cases where they had opposed this witness, and to get me transcripts of what he had said about his experience as he went from court to court. This strategy comprised a substantial effort, but at the end of the day, I thought it to have been well worthwhile.

When Deedrick took the stand, he appeared confident. He had no idea of the transcripts I had.

I also had accumulated a fair number of learned treatises on the subject of hair and fiber comparison and was prepared to examine pretty thoroughly just how conversant he was with the fine points of a profession that had evolved very gradually over the years. I did have some concern that he had constructed a bomb of some sort and was prepared to dump it in the jury box with little warning.

Specifically, I thought he might cross the line and suggest that whatever he had found that might legitimately be a basis for claiming similarity was in this case a means of positive identification. This worry eased considerably when Judge Ito made it plain that hair and fiber analysis could never be the basis for a "match," but only that two specimens might be "consistent with one another" or "similar."

During the cross-examination, Deedrick and I got into a bit of a verbal scuffle over whether he should use the word *like* as opposed to *similar* in delivering his opinions. After a short give and take, he reluctantly agreed that Noah Webster's famous book had to be respected, and that it described those two words as identical.

Marcia Clark's direct examination of Deedrick was long, detailed, and contributed very little to her effort to tie Simpson to the homicides. Her efforts did, however, produce a moment when I thought Deedrick's alleged "bomb" was about to detonate. He mentioned that the inside of the glove (the right one) found at Rockingham had yielded a dark limb hair. I then remembered that when Simpson had been asked for hair samples directly after the preliminary hearing in July, a dozen or more had been plucked from his scalp by a lab technician, but none had been taken from any other part of his body, including the backs of his hands.

This omission struck me at the time as pretty sloppy police work. After all, the prosecutors had a glove which had clearly been used in the murders and was allegedly found at Simpson's home. He was named as a suspect almost immediately when he returned to Los Angeles on June 13. There had to be a reasonable likelihood that the perpetrator who had worn the gloves had lost one or more limb hairs which were left behind in the muslin lining. It would have been a simple matter for the lab technicians to acquire hairs from the back of his hand, yet no one had asked.

Therefore, during my cross-examination of Deedrick, as expected, he admitted that he had made no analysis of any limb hairs from Simpson because none had been given to him. Nonetheless, I am annoyed with myself still because we missed the chance to examine—and maybe exploit—a comparison to the hair found in the glove with Simpson's, even if the prosecution didn't dare take a close look.

I also picked him up on the "blue/black" fibers. Prosecutors posited that they came from the sweat suit Simpson was wearing as described by Kato Kaelin. However, like all fiber and hair evidence, there was nothing to connect the evidence to Simpson. On cross, Deedrick admitted he never obtained samples of clothing from law enforcement personnel at the crime scene and didn't check to see if the fibers matched the dark blue uniforms of police officers.

Deedrick proved to be an experienced, cautious, and responsive witness. From time to time, he showed a trace of wit, which is usually well received by juries. But he toed the line of propriety when it came to that temptation to slide a "similarity" forward to "identification," and his testimony really did very little damage, especially after I punched holes in its dependability.

"As compared to fingerprint identification or foot impressions identification or the identification of projectiles fired by weapons, this is a much more subjective science, is it not?" I asked Deedrick. He conceded.

"The court has never recognized hair examinations as a positive means of identification and we don't either," Deedrick said.

Before winding up my cross, I could not resist taunting him with a mistake arising from his prior courtroom experiences which—in fairness—was more attributable to laxity and nonchalance than it was to any evil purpose on his part. I got him to admit that he had testified more than a half dozen times prior to coming to Los Angeles for the Simpson case. I had on the defense desk a number of what were obviously trial transcripts. When I began by asking him about a criminal case in Alaska in 1983 where he had testified, Marcia Clark went into a bit of a snit because I had not shown the transcripts to her beforehand. I insisted that unless and until I actually made use of those transcripts, she was not entitled to peek into my cross-examination plans and ammunition. After some give and take, Judge Ito agreed with me.

Deedrick quickly grasped that he had been had and put up no resistance. He admitted that he had been telling juries for more than ten years that he had examined four thousand hair and fiber cases.

When I pointed out that, logically, this would mean that he had examined no cases at all after that trial in Alaska, since the number had not budged, he smiled sheepishly and said, "I guess I just got tired of keeping track."

Doug Deedrick was a man you had to like. As he left the stand, I concluded that he knew all along that none of his evidence would be nuclear, and that he had been having a little fun with Howard Harris. As he left the courtroom while we were in recess, he gave me a subdued grin, and said, "You know, nobody ever did that to me before." I could not resist a retort: "Before you testify again, a recalculation of your historical experience might be in order." With a quick handshake, we said goodbye, and I have not seen him since.

* * *

And then came the moment when it looked as if the prosecution might come tumbling down.

On June 15, 1995, Christopher Darden questioned one of his glove witnesses, Richard Rubin, president of the company that had manufactured the Aris Lite men's glove, such as the ones found at Bundy and Rockingham. When Judge Ito took a recess, I took advantage of the moment to further investigate the "Rockingham" right glove, which had been marked in evidence. I had been eyeing the gloves and thought that they looked small, even for me, and I have a perfectly average size nine hand—regular in every way. It turned out I was right: When I slipped on the right glove, it was quite snug on me. I knew there was no chance they would fit O. J., who has enormous hands. He could wrap either hand around a football the way Sweetwater Clifton of the old Harlem Globetrotters basketball team could envelop a basketball, pretending to dribble vigorously while never letting go of the ball. Those whose adulation for the National Football League goes back to the Simpson era will recall that O. J. rarely fumbled.

I was convinced that if the glove was tight on me, they would look ridiculous on Simpson. But a demonstration of that fact would be far more telling if it were staged by the prosecution, rather than the defense. Rubin was Chris Darden's witness, and I had learned long before that if one wanted to cause Darden to do something silly, a press of his hot button would do the trick.

While the recess was still in progress, I walked up to Darden and said, "Chris, you're a good shit, but you've got the balls of a stud field mouse."

Predictably, he was infuriated. "What the hell do you mean by that?" he demanded.

"What I mean," I replied, "is that you don't have the balls to make O. J. try on that glove. If you don't, I think I will."

As Judge Ito made his way back to the bench, Darden charged and caught up with him.

"Judge," he spluttered. "Mr. Bailey just told me something, and I want the defendant to try on that glove."

Like so many who act impulsively when goaded, Darden got

his wish. Simpson was brought before the jury, and undeniably struggled with the gloves, tugging to get them unsuccessfully to cover his palm and slide over his finger knuckles.

We felt this plainly showed that these gloves could not be his, and the evidence of this assertion was shown repeatedly around the world. That night, the press was chanting that the defense may have turned the case around in its favor, spawning Johnnie Cochran's famous proclamation to the jury in his closing argument: "If it doesn't fit, you must acquit."

CHAPTER 19

The Defense Begins

MR. COCHRAN: Good morning, Miss Simpson.

ARNELLE SIMPSON: Good morning.

MR. COCHRAN: Miss Simpson, are you acquainted with the gentleman at the end of counsel table there, Mr. O. J. Simpson?

MS. SIMPSON: Yes, I am.

MR. COCHRAN: How are you acquainted with him?

MS. SIMPSON: I'm his daughter.

MR. COCHRAN: And do you have other brothers and sisters?

MS. SIMPSON: Yes, I do.

MR. COCHRAN: And tell us about your brothers and sisters, their names and approximate ages.

MS. SIMPSON: Jason, Sydney and Justin . . . Jason is 25, Sydney is 10 and Justin is 6.

MR. COCHRAN: And you are still young enough that I can ask this. How old are you?

MS. SIMPSON: 26.

MR. COCHRAN: And you are the oldest of the Simpson siblings?

MS. SIMPSON: Yes, I am.

MR. COCHRAN: What was your date of birth?

MS. SIMPSON: 12/4/68.

MR. COCHRAN: Something unusual about that date?

MS. SIMPSON: I was born the same day my dad won the Heisman trophy.

***

With that, the defense of Orenthal James Simpson was underway. We could have opened the defense case by putting on our time-line witnesses followed by the various people who saw a friendly, affable, i.e. *normal*, O. J. on June 13, 1994—*before* he got the news of the double homicides. But Johnnie decided to go with a soft opening so that the jury could hear from people who—even if they were family members—had always viewed Orenthal James Simpson as a good man. So, before he got into the substance of his direct examination, Johnnie wanted to show the depth of the family's support for O. J. In my opinion, as usual, Johnnie Cochran was right.

MR. COCHRAN: What is your mother's name?

MS. SIMPSON: Marguerite Thomas.

MR. COCHRAN: Is she present in Court today?

MS. SIMPSON: Yes, she is.

MR. COCHRAN: Is she the lady with the flower on with the yellow?

MS. SIMPSON: Yes, she is.

The jurors really didn't need Johnnie Cochran to point out to them that O. J.'s female support team of daughter, sister, and mother, also included his ex-wife Marguerite (something I'd rarely seen in my many murder trials) because all four were wearing yellow, which one observer called the "Simpson team colors." On leaving court the day she had testified, Arnelle told the media, "Yellow is a sign of hope—a happy color. We wanted it to be a happy day."

Through Arnelle, Johnnie brought out that, based on her observation, in the months before the murders, O. J. was not hostile toward Nicole and certainly not stalking her. In fact, Arnelle said that when she had pneumonia, he brought soup to her at Bundy Drive.

Some commentators said that Johnnie spent too much time on such family matters as pets, their names, and when they lived and died. But in doing so, he managed to paint the picture of a close, loving family, *and* he elicited the helpful testimony that when one dog died and it was decided to bury him in the front yard, O. J. was too upset to dig the hole and Nicole had to do it.

Johnnie also got in the testimony that O. J. was chronically late, which dovetailed with his behavior just prior to leaving for Chicago on June 12:

> MR. COCHRAN: Let's talk a little bit about your dad's traveling habits, as you knew them, and we are talking now about the period after January of 1994. Let's say between the period of January and June of 1994. Have you ever been around when your dad was getting ready to leave for a trip?
>
> MS. SIMPSON: Yes.
>
> MR. COCHRAN: Can you describe for us any particular things about his getting ready, his packing habits and those sorts of things?
>
> MS. SIMPSON: He would usually do everything last minute . . . there has always been an ongoing joke within the family that we would always say, Dad, you would have to get ready and he would always say, I would be ready before you would be. And I would always prepare an hour before and he will get dressed in the last fifteen minutes before we would have to leave. He has done this for years.

Johnnie addressed the night of June 13, when O. J. arrived home, distraught. Several family members and friends gathered to comfort one another. While most stayed in the family room of the home, O. J. had retired to his upstairs bedroom. Arnelle and a few people went to check on him.

MR. COCHRAN: And when you were up there at that point did you have any further conversation with your dad?

MS. SIMPSON: Yes.

MR. COCHRAN: And again, you can't tell us about that conversation, but how did your father appear or seem to you this time when you saw him laying in his bed where he had the washcloth across his forehead?

MS. SIMPSON: Very tired, umm, kind of lifeless. He was just—so hard to explain because there was so much going on and it was so emotional, and I was just trying to comfort him because he just seemed like he didn't know what to do.

MR. COCHRAN: All right. You had never seen him that way before?

MS. SIMPSON: No, never.

Then Johnnie questioned Arnell about Ron Shipp, the friend who talked about O. J.'s dreams of killing Nicole.

MR. COCHRAN: The time that you saw [Ron] Shipp until the last time you saw him that evening, did he always have a drink in his hand?

The prosecution objected to this question and after rephrasing it, Arnelle testified that she really couldn't say.

As it turned out, we needn't have worried about how the jury viewed Shipp. In 1996, three of the African American female jurors (Armanda Cooley, Carrie Bess, and Marsha Rubin-Jackson) in their book, *Madam Foreman: A Rush to Judgement*, gave Shipp little regard. This is what Rubin-Jackson had to say about Ron Shipp:

"Very early on in the trial the witnesses were primarily Los Angeles police officers and detectives with the exception of Ron Shipp who stood out to all of us. I felt Ron basically saw an opportunity where he could make some money, *and I felt he was lying about that dream* [Italics added]…Ron Shipp is someone most of us didn't believe for a number of reasons. He appeared to be an alcoholic and I think he was a groupie. I seriously do. I'm not going to believe the part about the dream, but to me, his testimony was all about notoriety. That's what I thought. I really thought he was trying to cash in. And because of that I couldn't put any weight on the dream part."

"I know Ron Shipp used to go by O. J.'s and he used to run people by there that he knew. But I discredit Ron Shipp for two reasons," Carrie [Bess] pointed out. "Number one, after he got irritated he jumps and says, 'O. J. just wants to use people. That's all why he kicked me out.' It looks like he's so angry that he'll say anything to get back at him"... [But, wrote Marsha Rubin-Jackson], "Even though Ron Shipp had a drinking problem, it doesn't mean he wasn't telling the truth. Because in every bit of slander there's a trace of truth. But the point is whether you're going to pick the part that you need to pick out and stick to it."

Arnelle Simpson was followed on the stand by her aunt Carmelita Durio, O. J.'s younger sister, and then Eunice Simpson, their mother, both of whom gave testimony that supported the defense contention that Ron Shipp had been drinking on the night he claimed to have heard O. J. speak of the killing-Nicole dream. Eunice testified that Shipp looked "spaced."

Eunice Simpson got up out of her wheelchair, assisted by Carl Douglas. A strong witness from an emotional standpoint, the dignified seventy-three-year-old African American woman who had raised her four children by herself, working nights for twenty-eight years in the psychiatric ward of San Francisco General Hospital, responded to Johnnie's gentle questioning by telling the jury how all the members of her family—but especially O. J.—suffered from rheumatoid arthritis.

When Cochran was finished, Chris Darden—wisely—had no questions for Eunice Simpson.

The next two defense witnesses were women who testified to the intensity of the O. J. Simpson-Paula Barbieri romance which we wanted the jury to know about because it contradicted the government's claim that O. J. was obsessed with Nicole to the point of homicide. After that, we put on six timeline witnesses—Danny Mandel, Ellen Aaronson, Francesca Harmon, Denise Pilnak, Judy

Telander, and Robert Heidstra—first daters, neighbors, and dog walkers. They each established *our* version of the timeline, which, in my opinion, was always our strongest defense.

The Timeline

Mandel and Aaronson, the first-and-only-time daters, resisted intense cross-examination and stuck to their story that when they walked past Nicole's condo at 10:25 p.m., they saw or heard no signs of mayhem. This was vitally important because it was ten minutes later than when the government—which needed to show a larger window of time for Simpson to have been the killer—said the bodies were already dead and lying near the gate.

The other four defense witnesses took some flak on cross-examination in relation to previous statements as to the exact time, but no one "caved."

Harman confirmed there was no noise on Bundy Drive at 10:20 p.m.; Pilnak confirmed the time of her telephone call; Telander said when she left Pilnak's residence just before 10:30 p.m., there was no noise, and Heidstra, the witness who heard Ron Goldman shout his last words, was firm in his determination that he heard shouts at 10:40.

But the prosecution may have hurt itself, in the eyes of the jury, when Darden seemed to be condescending toward Robert Heidstra, one of the neighborhood's least affluent citizens, who made his living detailing the fancy cars of his rich neighbors. Darden said that Heidstra "washed cars" for a living, hardly the same thing. He also had asked Heidstra if he was in this country legally.

Darden didn't get Heidstra to budge off his testimony and at one point, in his questioning, things got almost metaphysical when Darden asked him, "Have you heard that saying, you know, when a tree falls in the forest there is no one there to hear it, it doesn't make noise?" Heidstra hadn't heard that and looked as puzzled as most of the jurors did.

After the witness finished his testimony, one reporter summed up his appearance by writing, "But the most dramatic testimony of the day came from one of Nicole Brown Simpson's neighbors. Robert Heidstra testified that around 10:40 p.m., while he was standing near her condominium, he heard two men arguing. One yelled 'Hey! Hey! Hey!' Heidstra said. The other male voice shouted back, but Heidstra said he could not make out what the other voice was saying because Nicole Brown Simpson's Akita dog was barking hysterically. 'Then I heard a gate slam, bang!' he said. The prosecution had placed the time of the murders at about 10:15 p.m., giving Simpson time to commit the murders and return home to catch a limousine ride to the airport. The defense wanted to push the murders as close to 11 p.m. as possible because at that time it had Park and Kaelin at witnesses."

Denise Pilnak, the woman who recalled calling her mother that night before hearing the dog, was the *only* timeline witness who could provide indisputable documentary evidence supporting her recollections. She "set the clock" for the start of the murders because her telephone bill *proved* that the murders *had not yet begun* before 10:28 p.m. as that was when, according to her bill, the call ended. Pilnak's account of her activities—following the call and before hearing the dog—pushes that barking back to 10:35 or 10:36 p.m. *at the earliest.*

CHAPTER 20
An Affable Murderer?

Once the timeline was established, it was time to demonstrate another key pillar: demeanor.

I called Captain Wayne Stanfield—the American Airlines pilot who flew the plane to Chicago on the night of the murders—to testify as to O. J.'s behavior on that fateful night. Stanfield had left the cockpit and brought his logbook for Simpson to sign, and they'd chatted, in the first class cabin, for about twenty minutes. The pilot's description of O. J.'s behavior hardly fit a reasonable man's idea of how one who had recently butchered two human beings would act.

A curious aside to the appearance of Captain Stanfield is that it might never have occurred but for chance. As late as August 1995, no one in the media—or the lawyers for either side—knew, or attached any significance to, the name Wayne Stanfield.

But one day Jane Wells, a special correspondent for CNBC News who'd been covering the Simpson case on a daily basis for her network, decided to join her husband to take their dog to the vet, a friend of her husband's. Like Wells's husband, both the vet and Stanfield were former military pilots. Her husband and the vet were chatting and, overhearing their conversation, Jane Wells got quite a shock:

As I walked into the vet's office, I overheard my husband and the vet mention "Wayne," and how "Wayne" had flown Simpson to Chicago the night of the murders.

"Wayne" was Wayne Stanfield, a neighbor of the veterinarian and a Navy buddy of my husband's. Stanfield was the American Airlines captain who did indeed fly Simpson to Chicago the night of June 12th. I learned from my husband and the vet that once Stanfield found out there was a celebrity on board that night, he went back to first class during the flight to say hello. Stanfield shook Simpson's hand and asked him to sign his pilot logbook for June 12, 1994. Simpson did, signing, "Peace to You." Most importantly, Stanfield could not recall seeing any cut on O. J.'s finger, a crucial point for the defense, as Simpson claimed he cut the finger in his Chicago hotel room after learning of the killings. Prosecutors contended that he cut it while committing the crimes.

But that moment in August 1994, no one in the media knew this story. My husband had been sitting on it for weeks.

Inside the veterinarian's office, steam started pouring from my ears. I tried to keep my cool. I said, calmly, "Do you know what I do for a living? Do you know what helps pay the bills? Stories. Specifically, O. J. Simpson stories." My husband gave me a level look and replied, 'If you keep talking to me like that I won't call Wayne for you.' He made me promise to be cordial to his friend, and I was. Wayne provided me with a copy of his logbook showing O. J.'s signature, described for me his experience, and I broke the story. Other stories would follow over the next three years, but this one was the closest I got to six degrees of O. J. Well, the closest I know of. There may be other connections, but my husband won't tell me.

My direct examination of Captain Stanfield established that on the night that the government claimed Simpson had brutally stabbed two people to death just hours earlier—one of them his former wife whom the government claimed he still loved to the point of obsession—O. J. Simpson appeared calm and pleasant. And, as far as the pilot could determine, he had no cuts on either of his hands. Stanfield testified that O. J. did not act like a man who had done what the prosecution claimed he'd done.

Similar testimony was given by the next two witnesses, Michael Norris and Michael Gladden, two airport workers who asked for the Juice's signature when he got to the airport—and received it, even though he was running quite late for his flight.

The defense then called Howard Bingham, O. J.'s acquaintance who was on the same flight. Bingham, a photographer who'd specialized in taking pictures of Muhammad Ali, was himself rather famous. However, unlike O. J., he had a coach ticket, and at one point he got up and went up to first class and spoke to Simpson for about a minute and a half, and then also saw and talked with him while they both waited for their luggage in Chicago.

Bingham testified, briefly, that in their short visit, Simpson appeared to be the genial O. J. he'd known for years. Under Marcia Clark's friendly cross-examination, he admitted that they were, at best, acquaintances, not good friends. But from the defense standpoint, we were pleased with Bingham's testimony because he too described a relaxed O. J. who looked and sounded "normal." And while they were not best buddies, he had seen and interacted with the defendant before and knew what his "normal" demeanor was and was not.

Our next witness was Hertz Corporation employee Jim Merrill, whom a distraught Simpson had called (at home) at 8 a.m. on June 13 for a ride back to the airport. Merrill described an extremely upset O. J., as did Dave Kildruff, another Hertz employee with whom Simpson, having given up on Merrill who was stuck in traffic, had ridden to O'Hare. Both men described Simpson as almost sobbing.

Then it was time for Mark Partridge, one of the defense's most important witnesses.

On June 13, 1994, the morning after the murders, unable to book a first class seat on either American or United, O. J. had taken a coach seat on the American flight. He sat in the first row of the coach section in the aisle seat on the right-hand side; in front of him on the bulkhead was an air-to-ground telephone, which Simpson immediately asked to use.

Seated next to O. J. was Mark Partridge, a Harvard-trained patent lawyer from Chicago who couldn't help but overhear as a frantic Simpson was hurriedly making a series of phone calls. It was clear to Partridge that something had happened the night before to Simpson's wife and that Simpson was frantically calling many different people trying to find out what had happened. Soon realizing that these calls involved something quite serious, Partridge made handwritten notes, and then later wrote a letter— copies of which he sent to both the prosecution and the defense— outlining in substantial detail all his observations.

On cross, Marcia Clark elicited from Partridge that O. J.'s first call had been to his lawyer, Skip Taft, implying that this was unusual behavior for a man not yet accused of any crime. On redirect, Johnnie established that Taft, in addition to being one of Simpson's lawyers, was also a longtime friend.

* * *

Mark Partridge was followed on the stand by the next defense witness, Dr. Robert Huizenga, and what follows is most of his direct testimony.

MR. SHAPIRO: You are a physician and surgeon licensed to practice in the state of California?

DR. HUIZENGA: Yes, I am. I practice internal medicine.

MR. SHAPIRO: And when did you see Mr. O. J. Simpson first as a patient?

DR. HUIZENGA: I saw him first at noon on June 15, 1994.

MR. SHAPIRO: And was that at someone's suggestion other than Mr. Simpson's?

DR. HUIZENGA: It was at your suggestion.

MR. SHAPIRO: Would you tell the ladies and gentlemen of the jury what type of examination you conducted of O. J. Simpson on the 15th, Wednesday?

DR. HUIZENGA: Well, when he came I did a very thorough history. Subsequently, a physical examination... In my initial history with Mr. Simpson he kind of presented with that whole array of the typical post-NFL injury syndromes. He had, of course, a number of head concussions when he was playing with the Buffalo team. Specifically, he had initially a surgery on his left wrist all the way back to 1965 which significantly limited the motion in his left wrist and caused him continuing pain. He had multiple fractures, which is pretty common in football, and had visibly enlarged knuckles which also can be associated with either fractures or osteoarthritis or other rheumatologic arthritic conditions. He had significant knee complaints. And he had subsequently on his left knee had four surgeries.

MR. SHAPIRO: Let me just see if we can put this in perspective. The first thing you told the jury was that he had a typical post-NFL syndrome. Break that down and explain what you are trying to convey to the jury.

DR. HUIZENGA: Well, when I first saw him in the office, which as I said was noon, we squeezed him in during the lunch hour, he basically was visibly limping as he came down the hall. You know, that is the first thing that strikes me. And he really was not walking properly.

MR. SHAPIRO: What is your opinion as to the condition of his knee based on your examination and the medical histories that you reviewed?

DR. HUIZENGA: He had severe wear and tear arthritis of the left knee and was a strong candidate in the relatively near future for a total knee replacement.

MR. SHAPIRO: In your opinion how would that affect his mobility on the day you saw him?

DR. HUIZENGA: On the day I saw him he had significantly limited mobility because of the knee and actually another ankle problem that we haven't discussed, and I think would be significantly limited in terms of fast walking, certainly in terms of slow jogging, it would be very difficult, if not impossible, that day.

MR. SHAPIRO: Now, let's go above the waist. Did you do any examination between—let's talk about the wrist.

DR. HUIZENGA: The left wrist. He sustained an injury, the exact nature of which I'm not exactly clear, in 1965, but needed surgery in this area. When I did an exam, usually the wrist should come up something like ninety degrees and it should kind of flap down also at about ninety degrees, so you estimate these things in the office. And his left wrist really was only able to come up about thirty or forty degrees. This is not an exact science, but you know, you kind of estimate 45 degrees, and he did not seem to break that plane. And when you forcibly tried to move it up, you know, there was no give and [no] pain.

MR. SHAPIRO: Was there any other injuries that you observed in the arm areas?

DR. HUIZENGA: He had damage to his elbows such that when he would try to fully extend —again, the elbow should extend 180 degrees, to be perfectly straight, and he had what we call a flexion contracture.

MR. SHAPIRO: Any other observations of the upper torso?

DR. HUIZENGA: Umm, he had multiple scars, keloids over parts of his upper body and the back, and of course the fingers and the elbows and forearms and hands. He was somewhat bowlegged, you know, in addition to the limp we described, and I think those were the—in addition to the finger things that we talked about, the large— enlargements, those were the major findings.

MR. SHAPIRO: Did you notice any inflammation in the hand area?

DR. HUIZENGA: Yes, I did. He had multiple areas that were enlarged, these bony enlargements on his joints.

MR. SHAPIRO: Which hand were you referring to?

DR. HUIZENGA: This is the right hand.

MR. SHAPIRO: When you saw him on the 15th did you have any opinion as to how these conditions would affect his mobility?

DR. HUIZENGA: Well, he was visibly limping to my eye, and my initial impression was that it was mainly the osteoarthritis or the wear and tear disease. But I think that really he is limited, specifically lower extremities, by his arthritis, and he certainly was limited to a way on the 15th of June where he would have a very difficult time moving quickly in his lower extremities.

MR. SHAPIRO: This is not a condition, in your opinion, that came on within two days, is it?

DR. HUIZENGA: No, I don't believe that is—I think that these are long-lived symptoms.

MR. SHAPIRO: Is that the way Mr. Simpson appeared on the 15th in your office?

DR. HUIZENGA: Yes. Initially I was looking over every part of his head, including his scalp, for any evidence of hematomas, which is a—after you get some direct trauma, a little bleeding under the skin, think bump, you know, you know it as a goose egg. We were looking very carefully for scratch marks. I was looking for any area of a chipped tooth and ran my fingers around all of his teeth in his mouth. We were looking for any evidence that anything—had kind of pulled on his ears and looked very carefully behind his ears and examined his skin. In addition, I did a very careful physical exam of his nose. I do that routinely, looking for any evidence of the use of cocaine and his nasal passages were entirely normal. Looked very carefully on his neck for any evidence of pulling or tugging or any bruise.

Basically, a bruise is some evidence of direct contusion without laceration, and saw none. There was no purpura which is a black and blue type of mark if you break a blood vessel under the skin. There was no evidence of change in skin color other than some of these old darkly pigmented evidences of old abrasions and the multiple cuts you get as a football player.

MR. SHAPIRO: Specifically did you find any evidence of bruising, scratches, cuts or abrasions?

DR. HUIZENGA: No, I did not.

MR. SHAPIRO: Did you examine the right hand for any cuts or abrasions?

DR. HUIZENGA: Yes, I did. There is a jagged laceration that extends from the distal interphalangeal joint of the fourth left finger and it comes in almost a snake-like fashion and just it—it slices coming down in this way (Indicating), and then it almost seems to change in the plane and then it is a deeper cut.

MR. SHAPIRO: Thank you. Did you observe this injury on Mr. Simpson on the 15th, as well as the 17th?

DR. HUIZENGA: Yes, I did.

MR. SHAPIRO: Would you describe that to the jury?

DR. HUIZENGA: Okay. Okay. On his third finger he had a lesion that had the appearance of a fishhook and basically from the top it came down and kind of fished in a direction toward his fourth index finger.

MR. SHAPIRO: Do you have any opinion as to … as to how the injury above the knuckle was caused?

DR. HUIZENGA: I believe it was by some sort of a sharp object.

MR. SHAPIRO: Not a knife?

DR. HUIZENGA: A knife is a possibility, but to me the edges looked a little bit ragged, but that was a possibility, but it seemed to me to be more consistent with glass, but certainly a sharp object can do that.

MR. SHAPIRO: In this wound, do you have an opinion as to what is more reasonable as the cause for that injury?

DR. HUIZENGA: This wound, as I said, was one of the—appeared to be slightly cleaner than the others, but I think for the constellation of all the wounds it seemed more likely that glass was the cause...

MR. SHAPIRO: Now, are there certain types of activities somebody with the conditions that Mr. Simpson suffers from be incapable of doing?

DR. HUIZENGA: Yes, there are. Relatively sedentary things since his cardiovascular shape wasn't really that good that really don't need, you know, quick movement on that knee and of course over the period of that time his ankle, which was bothering him at that time.

The next day, the *New York Times* reported, "Dr. Robert Huizenga testified that Mr. Simpson, ravaged by disease and battered by being 'banged against the turf' as a football player for too many years, was unable to walk properly and barely able to jog, let alone run as a fleeing murderer with a plane to catch might have had to do. Dr. Huizenga described Mr. Simpson, 48, as a man whose damaged right ankle made him limp, whose left knee needed to be replaced and who could neither move forward nor laterally with ease."

But as weak as Dr. Huizenga had made Simpson sound in his direct examination, assistant prosecutor Brian Kelberg got the doctor to say on cross that O. J. was, in fact, strong enough to kill two people.

* * *

The prosecution's case lasted twenty-three weeks. The defense's lasted ten. During our first week, the defense had moved things along nicely—which we hoped the jury noticed and appreciated—putting on twenty-two witnesses.

In our second week, we put on nine witnesses, one of the most important being LAPD photographer Willie Ford, who'd taken pictures in O. J.'s home and bedroom on June 13, the day after the killings. Criminologists Fung and Mazzola had said they'd collected the bloody sock at 4:13 p.m. that afternoon, but Ford's video, taken at 4:00 p.m., showed no sock. The prosecutors said they hadn't turned Ford's video over to the defense because it was "administrative," not evidentiary.

Two more witnesses testified for the defense about the sock, Dr. Fredric Rieders and Herbert MacDonell, both of whom gave testimony that cast doubt on the prosecution's claims that the blood on Nicole's back gate and the blood on the socks implicated O. J. Reviewing the lab reports, Dr. Rieders testified the two evidence stains both contained a high amount of EDTA, a chemical used in test tubes to preserve blood, but that is not created naturally in the human body. This supported the defense theory that the blood was planted. On cross-examination, Marcia Clark tried to diffuse Dr. Rieders's testimony in this case by showing that he had made a mistake in an old case.

But, as the *New York Times* reported: [B]efore the jury, Ms. Clark struggled with the doctor, ultimately dredging up a purportedly botched diagnosis he made five years earlier in an effort to discredit him. Dr. Rieders brushed her aside with the impatience and assurance of an old professor, becoming the most important defense witness to hold his own on cross-examination.

Next, Herbert MacDonell, a member of the International Association of Blood Stain Pattern Analysts and supervisor of forty-three "blood-stain institutes," obviously impressed the media. A *New York Times* reporter wrote:

Lawyers for O. J. Simpson today began a three-pronged effort to prove a conspiracy by the police to frame their client, arguing that rogue officers planted blood on a sock, planted a bloody glove behind Mr. Simpson's house and planted rigged laboratory test results with the press.

The defense advanced the first prong when their blood-splatter expert stated that blood on the sock found at the foot of Mr. Simpson's bed had got there by touch rather than by splatter and that some of that blood had seeped through, something that could not have happened had Simpson been wearing it at the time.

A prosecution scientist had previously testified that the blood found on the ankle of the sock—blood matching Nicole Brown Simpson's—had been splattered on it. But the defense expert, MacDonell of Corning, N.Y., scoffed at that.

He testified that could only be the case if Simpson had a hole through his ankle exactly matching the position of the two blood spots.

CHAPTER 21
The Defense Wrap-up

In *"American Tragedy,"* Larry Schiller and James Willwerth wrote about the phase of the trial when the prosecution had just finished its case and the defense was set to begin:

> Plainly, the prosecutors knew they were about to lose the biggest case of their careers. They were pissed, [Carl] Douglas said to himself; we're kicking their asses. As a federal public defender, he's never once met a prosecutor who'd lost gracefully. Now, the atmosphere in court had changed. There was none of the semi-sincere camaraderie everyone had been at pains to display back in February. The opposing attorneys hardly spoke to one another now. Even the trash talk had slowed down. No more of this search-for-truth bullshit. Clark and Darden were down to the basics. Attack, attack, and then attack again.
>
> Simpson knew the game his team was playing. But as team owner he reminded them, "Don't anyone get cocky." He had said it all the way back when Barry Scheck destroyed Dennis Fung in April. "I played football for twelve years and I never spiked the ball after a touchdown," he told them. "I just handed it to the ref, or I dropped it. Don't you guys get cocky." It was an almost constant refrain.

The prosecution, of course, saw things differently. Marcia Clark later wrote, "At this point, we were beginning to get excited. The defense was making our case for us, tossing us meatball after meatball. The jury *had* to be thinking that an innocent man would have a better case to present."

We, the defense, still had a number of key witnesses to present, but when several more jurors were taken off the panel by the judge, the possibility of a mistrial began to haunt us. As mentioned earlier, in California, a non-capital trial can continue with as few as six jurors, *but only if both the defense and the prosecution agree to do so.* Marcia Clark—who, despite her seeming confidence, had to know things weren't looking good for her side—made it crystal clear that she would not agree to proceed with fewer than twelve jurors. So, we had to shift into overdrive, and put on what turned out to be our final twenty-one witnesses in seven weeks.

Two of the most significant were world-class scientists: Dr. Michael Baden, the former chief medical examiner of New York City and the New York State Police, and Dr. Henry Lee, arguably the top forensic expert on the planet.

In its case, the government had put on Los Angeles County coroner Dr. Lakshmanan Sathyavagiswaran—even though he had not performed the autopsies of Nicole and Ronald Goldman— who'd testified that each of the killings could have been accomplished in less than a minute. Dr. Baden shot that theory full of holes "in testimony that was brisk, graphic and gruesome, leaving the victims' families and Mr. Simpson alike with eyes watering, Dr. Baden suggested that the struggle was much more protracted. Both victims were conscious, resisting and capable of screaming, taxing the skills and nimbleness of a sole strong perpetrator, the doctor said," according to the *New York Times.*

Dr. Henry Lee testified that it looked to him as if the blood evidence appeared to show tampering. For example, under Barry Scheck's direct examination, Lee testified that of seven swatches that were collected and sent to laboratories for analysis that showed Simpson's DNA, four of the swatches had "transfer stains." This meant that when the swatches were packed in paper the morning after they were collected, the swatches still held moisture. Lee said, in his experience, blood swatches take no more than three hours to dry, and at least thirteen hours had passed before being packed in paper.

Our theory was that police could have replaced the swatches with reference samples of Simpson's blood, thereby guaranteeing a DNA match. Lee said he could not explain why the swatches were still wet.

"The only opinion I can give under these circumstances is something [is] wrong," he said. When the government tried to have that opinion stricken from the record, Judge Ito, in one of his rare pro-defense rulings, denied the motion.

Meanwhile, as the case trundled on, and as Judge Ito was privately evaluating the Fuhrman Tapes and their admissibility, the jury was showing signs of wear. The judge, seeing their edges beginning to fray, issued them a pep talk. The *New York Times* reported,

> Judge Ito told jurors that they had been sequestered longer than any other jury in California history, having surpassed the 225 days served by a jury that in 1971 found Charles Manson and three female members of his 'family' guilty of murder in the Tate-LaBianca slayings in Los Angeles in August 1969. Thursday was this jury's 226th day of sequestration.
>
> And there will be more days, Judge Ito promised…
>
> "In talking to you individually and in observing you, I know that you are a very tough and tenacious group of people," the judge said. "I know you've made a commitment to see this matter through."

The talk seemed to buoy the sequestered panel a bit even as they had further time to cool their heels as he took time to deliberate over the tapes.

After portions of the tapes were played, whereby jurors heard only two very mild snippets of Fuhrman using the N-word, which were less than electrifying, our only hope at another shot to get the "bad stuff in" was his anticipated reappearance on the witness stand with the resumption of his previously interrupted cross-examination. However, when we learned that Fuhrman intended to take the Fifth Amendment to every question, Gerry Uelmen was given the honor of presiding over this ritual.

We closed the defense case (reluctantly) by putting on two of the most colorful characters to testify in the entire trial. Brothers Larry and Craig Anthony (Tony the Animal) Fiato, were mobsters who came to court straight from the Federal Witness Protection Program to say that while waiting to testify against former fellow Mafia members, they'd had beers with Detective Philip Vannatter. Larry testified that the veteran LAPD detective said that at the time he and Fuhrman and Detective Lange went to O. J.'s house, Vannatter already considered O. J. a suspect, which directly contradicted his earlier testimony and illustrated our assertion that investigators were in a rush to judgment.

Craig Fiato's testimony was less damning in that he explained he embellished his statement against Vannatter to aggravate the FBI agent watching over the Fiatos. "I was only pimping him," he scoffed.

After the Fiatos testimony, and determined not to end on a thud, we also put on one more rebuttal witness, Herbert MacDonell, to testify about glove shrinkage. The prosecution had claimed the reason that the gloves did not fit Simpson was that blood contracted the leather. MacDonell attested that drying blood could not shrink leather.

* * *

There are two nightmare developments that can drive a criminal defense lawyer crazy. The first is when the defense confronts the decision to have the defendant testify and there are good reasons to do so and good reasons not to do so. The second occurs when there has been a long and arduous trial, which could go either way, and the potential for a mistrial looms. In the Simpson case, Johnnie Cochran and I got hit with both of these dilemmas.

O. J. Simpson promised to be an excellent witness. He spoke well, had a genial manner about him, and a pleasant demeanor. His story was logical, straightforward, and would withstand tight scrutiny. He was unlikely to lose his temper over minor insults.

Now here's where the second legal asteroid comes into play: the threat of a mistrial. A mistrial occurs when either a mistake made during trial is so egregious that it cannot be corrected by language from the trial judge or, in California, when the jury dwindles below twelve members. In a mistrial, the only remedy is to start the case over again. In this case, ten alternates had already been dismissed in eight months of trial. This left us with two alternates, and we felt that if the trial ground on, we could easily lose three more jurors, leaving us with eleven and either side could call for a mistrial.

The probability of losing more jurors left the defense in a quandary: Should we end the trial as quickly as possible to avoid a mistrial? Or should we risk adding more witnesses to the stand to bolster our case? Did we feel confident enough that we could rest our case now, believing the jury would find Simpson innocent?

Of the remaining witness we had yet to call beyond O. J. himself, was Nicole's neighbor Tom Lang, our critical timeline witness, who said he saw two men in a white pick-up truck in front of Nicole's condo seemingly arguing with a woman in dark clothing. And we had DNA pioneer Dr. Kary Mullis to refute the PCR findings along with veteran forensic psychiatrist Dr. Bernard Yudowitz, who was prepared to testify that Simpson fit none of the psychological markers of a person who had murdered two people.

Of these witnesses, I felt Tom Lang was the most compelling because I believe he was the only person who may have seen the killer or killers that evening. I believed (and believe to this day) that his testimony would have gone a long way in proving

Simpson's innocence, or at the very least cast a longer shadow of doubt for the naysayers. But Johnnie was hesitant to put him on the stand for reasons that he and I hotly debated in a closed-door meeting in June. It was, in the course of this long and demanding trial, the only time in which we disagreed in what could be considered a meaningful way.

Johnnie believed Tom Lang posed two problems for the defense:

1. The police report regarding Lang's statement claimed that he said the woman he saw was wearing a "long, white dress"—and Nicole was wearing a black one the evening of her death. However, this was an *error* on the part of the police record and not what Lang had told the reporting officer. Johnnie felt the faulty police record would be difficult to dispel and open a hole for the prosecution.

2. The white Ford 350 Lang said he saw that evening looks not unlike (from the front grill area) a Ford Bronco. Lang, himself had owned three Ford 350 trucks and surely knew the difference, but again, Johnnie thought it was another potential crack that the prosecutors could exploit to their advantage.

After a brief, and somewhat passionate back and forth, Johnnie won out. He was lead counsel in the case, after all, and the trial progressed without rancor, or at least that was how I felt—that is, until weeks later when Mark Fuhrman took the stand to exercise his 5th amendment rights. As I sat in court prepared to deliver the coup de grâce, Gerry Uelmen jumped from his seat and took the podium to question Fuhrman.

I was surprised by this move, which Johnnie had arranged without including me on the discussions, but I remained ultimately unruffled by the veiled insult. I was glad to be in attendance because after Gerry had finished his questioning and took his seat, I was there to direct him to return to the podium to posit the most critical question:

UELMEN: I only have one other question, your honor.

COURT: What was that, Mr. Uelmen?

ULEMEN: Detective Fuhrman, did you plant or manufacture any evidence in this case?

FUHRMAN: I assert my 5th amendment privilege.

While I had wished that Johnnie had spoken with me about the last-minute change, I'm happy to say it had no lingering effect on our friendship. This was a topsy-turvy trial and wrinkles and dust-ups often came from every direction.

After careful consideration on whether to put Simpson on the stand to testify on his own behalf, we felt that the prosecution would drag out their cross-examination until three jurors expired in the jury box if necessary, so badly did they want a mistrial. Having Simpson testify would prolong the trial and risk a mistrial, which would have been catastrophic. We had always intended to have O. J. testify and had spent hours with him to prepare, but the clock was running down. However, I believe if O. J. had taken the stand to tell his account of that evening and withstood what would have surely been a vigorous cross-examination, he would have further convinced the jury of his innocence. But, more importantly, I believe he would have converted much of the court of public opinion who felt he was guilty. It would have given him the voice to cut through the abundant media commentary that branded him guilty.

When Judge Ito asked Simpson to state for the record his decision not to testify for his own defense, O. J. stood before the court (but outside of the jury's view) and stated, "Good morning, your honor. As much as I would like to address some of the misrepresentations about myself, and my Nicole, and our life together, I am mindful of the mood and stamina of this jury. I have confidence, a lot more it seems than Miss Clark has, of their integrity and that they will find as the record stands now, that I did not, could not, and would not have committed this crime."

And with that, 361 days after jury selection began, the defense rested—if that is the right word.

CHAPTER 22

Closing Arguments and Deliberation

The next important stage in the Simpson trial was the closing argument for each side. Usually, the prosecution goes first, then the defense, and then, in most instances, the government gets another chance to address the jury because it, not the defense, has the burden of proof. The prosecution must prove—*beyond a reasonable doubt*—that the accused did it; the defense does not have to prove the opposite. And in this case, to convict, the jury would have to go further and find that no reasonable hypothesis of innocence could fit the facts that had been proven to the jury's satisfaction.

On Tuesday, September 26, 1995, Marcia Clark led off for the government, to be followed that same day by Christopher Darden. Johnnie Cochran and Barry Scheck would make the defense's closing arguments.

When Clark stood up and began her argument, the ordeal of the nine-month long trial showed on her face and in the dark circles under her eyes. (She later revealed that she had an abscessed tooth that required emergency dental work, fitted into her already near-impossible schedule.) But she rallied to her cause and soon hit her stride, trying despite the difficulty of having to explain away the prosecution's problems caused by Mark Fuhrman; the sloppy police work; and the unexplained thumps on Kato Kaelin's wall. Knowing there was no way she could rehabilitate her one-time star witness in Fuhrman, Clark launched an opposite tact by asking and then immediately answering her own questions:

MARCIA CLARK:
Did [Mark Fuhrman] lie when he testified here in this courtroom saying that he did not use racial epithets in the last 10 years? Yes. Is he a racist? Yes.

Is he the worst LAPD has to offer? Yes.

Do we wish that this person was never hired by LAPD? Yes.

Should LAPD have ever hired him? No.

Should such a person be a police officer? No.

In fact, do we wish there were no such person on the planet? Yes.

But the fact that Mark Fuhrman is a racist and lied about it on the witness stand does not mean that we haven't proven the defendant guilty beyond a reasonable doubt. And it would be a tragedy if, with such overwhelming evidence, ladies and gentlemen, as we have presented to you, you found the defendant not guilty in spite of all that because of the racist attitudes of one police officer.

To put it mildly, I found that argument a bit of a stretch, and I thought that the jury did too. My judgment was affirmed later that year when the book from three female jurors was released. In *Madam Foreman: A Rush To Judgement,* they wrote, "The only thing I didn't like about Marcia was her expressions. She had a strong case. She believed in her case. Maybe she was just showing me that she was frustrated. ... [My only criticism of her] was based on how she projected her examination with the witnesses. It made it seem like we were on a different level. I know everybody doesn't have a college degree, but there's such a thing as common sense."

The next problem that Clark had to deal with in her final argument was the unquestionable presence—as the defense had shown so clearly—of sloppy police work. Again, the lead prosecutor "fessed up":

> The defense has thrown out many, many other questions. They've thrown out questions about whether LAPD has some bad police officers. Does the scientific division have some sloppy criminalists? Does the coroner's office have some sloppy coroners? And the answer to all these questions is: Sure, yes, they do. That's not news to you. I'm sure it wasn't a big surprise to you.
>
> But those are not—they're important issues. You know, we should look into the quality control. Things should be done better. Things could always be done better in every case, at every time. There's no question about that.
>
> We're not here to vote on that today.
>
> The question is what the evidence that was presented to you that relates to who killed Ron and Nicole—what does that tell you? Does that convince you beyond a reasonable doubt?

Next, Clark turned to the question of those three mysterious thumps on Kato Kaelin's wall:

> The defense would have you believe, ladies and gentlemen, that the defendant's appearance on the driveway just two minutes after the thumping on Kato's wall is a coincidence.[1]
>
> And the defense would have you believe that the thumping and the appearance of that glove—the defendant's glove—were unrelated events.
>
> And the thumps themselves: Just think about that. Regardless of where or how they happened, just the fact that they happened shortly after the murders at the defendant's house and just before the defendant walked up his driveway[2] in dark clothing, like the dark blue or black sweat outfit that Kato described: He just put those facts together.

And you realize what has happened. The defendant came back from Bundy in a hurry. Ron Goldman upset his plans and things took a little longer than anticipated. He ran back behind the house—that dark, narrow, south pathway. You all saw it. You were there in daytime. But imagine how dark it is at night. That dark, narrow south pathway—thinking he could get rid of the glove, the knife in that dirt area in the back. You recall, back behind the guest houses there's a dirt area. It's just all dirt, not very well tended.

But he was in a hurry. He was moving quickly down a dark, narrow pathway overhung with trees, strewn with leaves and in his haste, he ran right into that air-conditioner that was hanging over that south pathway. And running into that air-conditioner caused him to fall against the wall making the wall of Kato's room shake.

Marcia Clark wrapped up her closing argument by comparing the state's case against O. J. to a jigsaw puzzle in which the picture isn't clear until the final pieces are fitted into place. She used a visual aid that, when completed, showed a puzzle on which O. J's face did not appear until the very last piece was added.

And now let me summarize for you what we have proven.

One piece of the puzzle: We've proven the opportunity to kill. We've given the time window in which he was able to kill because his whereabouts were unaccounted for during the time when we know the murders were occurring.

We have the hand injuries that were suffered on the night of his wife's murder—to the left hand, as we know the killer was injured on his left hand.

We have the post-homicidal conduct that I told you about: Lying to Allan Park, making Allan Park wait outside. Not letting Kato pick up that little dark bag. His reaction to Detective Phillips when he made notification. When Detective Phillips said to him, "Nicole has been killed," instead of asking about a car accident, the defendant asks no questions.

We have the manner of killings, killings that indicate that it was a rage killing, that it was a fury killing, that it was not a professional hit. The manner of killing that indicates one person committed these murders. One person with the same style of killing.

We have the knit cap at Bundy. We have the evidence on Ron Goldman's shirt of the blue-black cotton fibers, the defendant's hair.

We have the Bruno Magli shoe prints, size 12—all of them size 12, his size shoe—all of them consistent going down the Bundy walk.

We have the Bundy blood trail: His blood to the left of the bloody shoe prints. We have the blood in the Bronco—his and Ron Goldman's.

We have the Rockingham blood trail, up the driveway, in his bathroom, in the foyer.

We have the Rockingham glove with all of the evidence on it: Ron Goldman, fibers from his shirt; Ron Goldman's hair; Nicole's hair; the defendant's blood; Ron Goldman's blood; Nicole's blood. And the Bronco fiber. And the blue-black cotton fibers. We have the socks and we have the blue-black cotton fibers on the socks. And we have Nicole Brown's blood on the socks.

And when the screen showed the last piece of the jigsaw puzzle going into place, Clark said, dramatically, "There he is."

Although the analogy was hardly unique, she presented it fairly well. But glancing at the jury, I didn't think they were all that impressed. And they weren't. As the three female jurors later wrote in their book: "Near the end of Marcia Clark's closing argument, one of the jurors broke down and cried. It was such an emotional speech. I thought, *Jesus Christ. Please. Somebody help me. Get these people to understand that I am not totally illiterate here. That we don't need this...*emotional appeal in order for us to reach a decision."

But the jurors were in for even more emotion when prosecutor Chris Darden got up the same day to make the government's second closing argument. At its outset, he, too, felt it necessary to trash Mark Fuhrman, the cop who'd once been the bedrock of the state's case.

> Everybody knows you can't send a message to Fuhrman, you can't send a message to the LAPD, you can't eradicate racism within the LAPD or within the LA community or within the nation as a whole by delivering a verdict of not guilty in a case like this where it is clear, and you know it is clear, you feel it, you know it, you know it in your heart, you know it. . . .
>
> This case is about this Defendant, O. J. Simpson, and the "M" word, murder; Not about Mark Fuhrman and the "N" word.

Darden also hammered on the prosecution's "motive" mantra. But first, he correctly reminded the jury that "motive is not an element of the crime charged and need not be shown." Despite this directive, Darden then spent a considerable amount of time telling the jury that Simpson was capable of "extreme rage, jealousy and violence," describing him as a "burning fuse." And while motive is not an element of the offense of murder, getting a conviction *without* showing a motive has always been difficult.

* * *

And then it was our turn.

> JUDGE LANCE ITO: We're now ready to proceed with the defense argument. Mr. Cochran, you may proceed.
> JOHNNIE COCHRAN:
> We met approximately one year and one day ago, September 26th, 1994. I guess we've been together longer than some relationships, as it were. But we've had a unique relationship in this matter, in that you've been the judges

of the facts. We have been advocates on both sides. The judge has been the judge of the law. We all understand our various roles in this endeavor that I'm going to call a journey toward justice. That's what we're going to be talking about this afternoon as I seek to address you. ...

Now, in the course of this process, what we are discussing [are] the reasonable inferences of the evidence, I ask you to remember that we're all advocates, we're all officers of this court. I will recall the evidence and speak about the evidence. Should I misstate that evidence, please don't hold that against Mr. Simpson. I will never intentionally do that. In fact, I think you'll find that during my presentation, unlike my learned colleagues on the other side, I'm going to read you testimony, what the witnesses actually said, so there'll be no misunderstanding about what was said about certain key things....

Now, in this case, you are aware that we represent Mr. Orenthal James Simpson. The prosecution never calls him Mr. Orenthal James Simpson, they call him defendant. I want to tell you right at the outset that Orenthal James Simpson, like all defendants, is presumed to be innocent. He's entitled to the same dignity and respect as all the rest of us. As he sits over there now, he's cloaked in a presumption of innocence. You will determine the facts of whether or not he's set free to walk out those doors or whether he spends the rest of his life in prison. But he's Orenthal James Simpson, he's not just the defendant. And we on the defense are proud, consider it a privilege to have been part of representing him in this exercise and this journey toward justice. Make no mistake about it. ...

You've heard from the jury instructions ... We don't have to do anything. We don't have to prove anything. This is the prosecution's burden, and we can't let them turn the Constitution on its head. We can't let them get away from their burden. It's my job, one of my jobs, is to remind you of that and to remind them of that, that that's their burden.

They must prove Mr. Simpson guilty beyond a reasonable doubt and to a moral certainty, and we will talk about what a reasonable doubt means.

And so now as we have this opportunity to analyze the facts of the case, I agree with one thing that Mr. Darden said, to this task I ask you to bring your common sense. Collectively, the fourteen of you have more than five hundred years of experience. I know you're all young, but you multiply that fourteen, you won't hold that against me, I don't think. Five hundred years of experience. You didn't leave your common sense out in that hallway when you came in here, and we're going to ask you to apply it to the facts of this case.

If you look at everything in a cynical fashion, you heard this morning, "A-Ha. There was a knapsack over," or a knap bag or some little bag they were talking about, "over in the driveway." Well, if you're a golfer, isn't it reasonable to assume there's golf balls in there? And you put that in your golf bag. What's the big deal? Because they've got to try to theorize and try to explain anything, explain everything, which they can't explain. They weren't there. They rushed to judgment, and it leads to this kind of wild speculation. You have to do that when you don't have a case, and that's all you've seen them do, time after time after time. ...

So, we know that Kato had some concerns, he was looking around. We know that at some point, Mr. Simpson comes down the stairs carrying the Louis Vuitton bag or whatever, and then Mr. Simpson leaves about eleven, 11:02, for the airport. That's pretty clear, based upon the evidence. And, you'll recall that Ms. Clark again gives Mr. Simpson five minutes to rush in. According to her theory, he rushes in, changes clothes, disposes of all these clothes, showers, packs, does everything, and comes downstairs and [she] says, composes himself. Now, can you imagine that? I mean, who do they think they're talking to? In five minutes, he does all these things, and then they tell you that, you know, "Under this post-homicidal way you act, you get yourself all composed and you just do this." This is preposterous. They're not experts. They can't testify. Those are just their wildest, rankest theories. You use your common sense when they tell you things like that.

[On the night of the murders] O. J. Simpson was O. J. Simpson, the way he always appeared, by the people who knew him and talked to him . . . But the reason they can't explain his demeanor and the way he acted like he'd always act, they then talk about, "Well, you can't tell who's a murderer." And those are all real convenient words, aren't they? But they fly in the face of reasonable activity by a reasonable man on that particular night.

So, there's Allan Park. O. J. Simpson comes down within five minutes of the time that they believe he goes upstairs. No time to dispose of bloody clothes. What about blood on the carpet? What about dirt on this white carpet? How does he shower? How does he get dressed? I mean, does it make any sense at all? Does it?

Park himself says the golf bag was already packed and ready to go when he pulled into the driveway, and Ms. Clark went to great trouble to tell you how credible she thought Mr. Park was and how he tried to lay everything out. And, I think, by and large, we agree with that. But I think if you're going to quote Mr. Park, you ought to quote him accurately and not attempt to mislead, or whatever. ...

So we know that Mr. O. J. Simpson was preparing to leave for this trip that had been long planned. And when we summarize, then, the two timelines, it seems to me that their timeline is not even reasonable. It doesn't make any sense. It's a much less credible version than the testimony you've heard from our witnesses. Their version does in no way disprove the defense timeline. We don't have to even put that forth, but we did. There, then, must be a reasonable doubt.

Consider everything that Mr. Simpson would have had to have done in a very short time by their timeline. He would have had to drive over to Bundy, as they've described, in this little, limited time frame when there's not enough time, killed two athletic people in a struggle that takes five to fifteen minutes. Walked slowly from the scene. Returned to the scene, supposedly looking for a missing hat and glove, and poking around. Go back to this alley a second time. Drive more than five minutes to Rockingham, where nobody hears him or sees him. Either stop along the way to hide these bloody clothes and knives, et cetera, or take them in the house with him, where they'll [the prosecution] still [be] hoisted by their own petard because there's no blood, there's no trace, there's no nothing. So that's why the prosecution has had to try and push back their timeline. Even to today, they're still pushing it back, because it doesn't make any sense, it doesn't fit. That's why they abandoned Ellen Aaronson, why they abandoned Dan Mandel, why they didn't want to call Denise Pilnak, why they didn't want to call Robert Heidstra. That's why we're now hearing this preposterous add-on of time that the thumps may have occurred at 10:15. That's Ms. Clark's wish list, but that's not the evidence in this case.

Where Chris Darden told the jury that the police were not on trial in this case, Johnnie reminded them that they most certainly were. As an organization that had been heavily criticized in recent years, the LAPD had a very good reason to manufacture evidence in this case and move into the winner's column.

Gee, how would all these police officers set up O. J. Simpson? Why would they do that? I will answer that question for you. They believed he was guilty. They wanted to win. They didn't want to lose another big case. That is why. They believed that he was guilty. These actions rose from what their belief was, but they can't make that—the prosecutors can't make that judgment. Nobody but you can make that judgment. So when they take the law into their own hands, they become worse than the people who break the law, because they are the protectors of the law. Who then polices the police? You police the police. You police them by your verdict.

The point I was trying to make, they didn't understand that it is not just using the 'N' word. Forget that. We knew he was lying about that. Forget that. It is about the lengths to which he would go to get somebody black and also white if they are associated with black. That is pretty frightening. It is not just African Americans, it is white people who would associate or deign to go out with a black man or marry one. You are free in America to love whoever you want, so it infects all of us, doesn't it, this one rotten apple, and yet they cover for him. Yet they cover for him.

Johnnie concluded his summation by thanking Chris Darden for telling the court that the defense had, "in a textbook fashion," impeached Mark Fuhrman.

* * *

The second lawyer to make a closing argument for the defense was Barry Scheck, who had done a good job of showing that the LAPD criminologists had created, to use his phrase, "a cesspool of contamination."

MR. SCHECK:

Ladies and gentlemen of the jury, good morning... Let me join with everybody in thanking you for your service. I can—the frustration, the loneliness, the sacrifice you have made in this sequestration is something that we understand or we are trying to understand. As the Judge has pointed out a number of times, my colleague, Mr. Neufeld and I, we are from New York City. More specifically, we are from Brooklyn, and we've been out here quite unexpectedly for a lot of months. And I remember when that detective from Chicago testified about having those keys that you stick in and out of the doors and little lights go on, umm, every day going in and out of those doors again and again, and again like Groundhog Day, everything repeating itself, the monotony, the loneliness, the frustration. We sit around and we talk sometimes in amazement at how you deal with this and how appreciative we are and—well, it is just really an honor and a privilege to present this case to you. And as lawyers that dealt with some of the forensic evidence in this case, which was detailed and complicated, and I'm sure I speak for myself, Mr. Blasier, Mr. Neufeld, Mr. Clarke, for the Prosecution, Mr. Goldberg, that we had a job. Our job was to make it simple, to make it cogent without sacrificing any meaningful detail. That is our job. And I can't tell you how appreciative we are because you paid attention, you were patient, you followed the evidence. I know that. I watched it. Now, you know it is our job to make it simple, to make it cogent without sacrificing detail that was important, and sometimes we let you down. I know that. Some days when we were talking about some of this, it was hard, and we came back to it again. And I think both sides tried to clarify the issues as much as we could, but you never let us down, because those were long days, but you were more than fair with us. I know you followed and paid attention to this evidence. So it is a privilege and honor to have presented that evidence to you and I must also say that standing before you right now is a terrifying responsibility. It is a terrifying responsibility because we think the evidence shows that we represent an innocent man wrongly accused.

MS. CLARK: Objection, objection.

By this point in this marathon of a trial, there was plenty of antagonism between the lawyers on opposite sides, but Barry Scheck and Marcia Clark were clearly the most contentious pair. The previous week, in a heated exchange in the judge's chambers, when Barry had made an objection, Marcia had snapped, "Shut up, Scheck." He clearly remembered that comment, so he wasn't at all surprised when she started to object during his final argument, which is often considered to be rude. Later, when it was again her turn to argue in the rebuttal phase of the prosecution's closing statement, he returned the favor, objecting some sixty times, which had to be a record number of objections during a time when lawyers, traditionally, make no objections.

In his closing arguments, using a series of slides, Scheck laid out our main scientific arguments, one by one, slowly (at least, slowly for him).

Any laboratory has to have three things: You have to have rules and training, you have to have what is known as quality assurance, and you have to have chain of custody and security of the evidence. Well, what have we heard about rules and training at the Los Angeles Police Department laboratory? Well, this laboratory is run without a set of rules. That everyone knows. They don't even have a manual. Think about that. That is extraordinary. And then they have this draft manual and it is ignored by the criminalists, Fung and Mazzola. They don't know what is in the draft manual, what procedures there are. And then the laboratory director, Michele Kestler, well, she was the acting laboratory director. Actually, one of the real problems here is at the time of this case, the head of the laboratory was a police officer, not a scientist, but Michele Kestler, she had that draft manual on her desk for four years going through it. And she says, well, some of this is no good and they didn't get around to it, so that is how you become a black hole.

The testimony is clear in this case they did not give their criminalists training in state-of-the-art techniques, in particular of great relevance here, there was no DNA training for the evidence collectors. Now, that has got to be a significant point. Miss Clark told you in the opening statement that collecting, preserving bloodstain evidence for purposes of DNA testing was as simple as going into your kitchen and cleaning up spillage. Now, we all know, we all know that is not true based on what we've heard in this case. ...

May we have the next slide, please. Quality assurance. That is a term that is used in bureaucracies and hospitals and laboratories, any places where you are trying to deliver service with integrity. What is going on here? There is a failure to document how you collect the evidence, a fundamental duty as Dr. Lee showed you, remember, with that chart, fundamental duty of the criminalists to document the evidence. In other words, where it was picked up, how it was picked up, when it was picked up.

Scheck then attacked the LAPD's slipshod training of its criminalists, particularly when compared with the technicians at Cellmark.

There was no serious supervision of these people (at the LAPD). That is just clear. You saw it. This lab was not inspected. This lab is not accredited. This lab is not subjected, certainly the DNA, to external blind proficiency testing which you know, which you know, is what you need. Dr. Gerdes told you about that. Everybody talked about that. This national research council report, DNA technology in forensic science.

Could we have the next slide? Now, this is critical. Chain of custody and security. There is absolutely nothing more fundamental to preserving integrity of forensic evidence than a chain of custody, than having security. You have to know what you are picking up. You have to be able to document it, otherwise bad things can happen and nobody can trace it. In this case, they did not count the swatches when they collected them. They did not count the swatches when they got back to the laboratory and put them in the tubes for drying. They did not count the swatches when they took them out of the tubes and put them in the bindles. We don't know how many swatches they started with. They didn't book the evidence in this case for three days. They kept it in the least secure facility, the evidence processing room, for three days, without being able to track the items. The lead homicide detective in this case, and we have talked about it a little and we will talk about it some more, is walking around with an unsealed blood vial for three hours. It is unheard of.

Think about the Bronco. They finished doing the collection in the Bronco and then it is abandoned literally for two months. There is a box you are supposed to check off, give special care if you are going to check it for biological evidence, not checked off. It is sent to Viertel's tow yard. It is abandoned for two months. There are no records of who went in and out of that car. There was a theft. Everybody was around in there.

When Scheck was through, Johnnie Cochran gave the defense's last plea for an acquittal. In the week before final arguments were to be held, Johnnie had asked each member of the defense team to list the fifteen most important questions for the jurors to answer. He collected the submissions, and then formulated them for use in his final argument:

JOHNNIE COCHRAN:
There may be 1,000 such questions in a case like this which could be put to [Marcia Clark], but we intend no such exercise. I do think, after careful deliberation, that it might be fair to suggest fifteen questions, just fifteen

questions which literally hang in the air in this courtroom at this moment. And as the time approaches for you to decide this case, for us to hand the baton to you. I offer these questions now as a most important challenge to the Prosecution, the Prosecution which claims that it has met its burden in this case. If that burden has in fact been met, you will be given logical, sensible, credible, satisfying answers to each of these fifteen questions. If the questions are overwhelming and unanswerable, they will be ignored or you will be told that the Prosecution has no obligation to answer questions. If you are given anything less than a complete sensible and satisfactory response, satisfying you beyond a reasonable doubt to these fifteen questions, you will quickly realize that the case really is transparent and you will think about the scenario that I just went through for you and that the term smoke and mirrors that you heard about doesn't apply to the Defense. We proved real hard things for you, things that you can see, things you could take back in that jury room. And accordingly, you would have to find Mr. Simpson not guilty.

When I'm concluded, for Miss Clark's convenience, should she decide to deal with these very troublesome questions, I'm going to leave her a written list of these questions here when I conclude. Let me go over these fifteen questions with you just briefly.

1. Why, there on the monitor, did the blood show up on the sock almost two months after a careful search for evidence? And why, as demonstrated by Dr. Lee and Professor MacDonell, was the blood applied when there was no foot in it? Do you think that is a fair question in this case? Let's see if she can answer that question.

Question no. 2. Why was Mark Fuhrman, a detective who had been pushed off the case, a person who went by himself to the Bronco, over the fence to interrogate Kato to discover the glove and the thump, thump, thump area?

No. 3. Why was the glove still moist when Fuhrman found it if Mr. Simpson had dropped it seven hours earlier? As Agent Bodziak told you, as Herb MacDonell has told you, blood dries very rapidly.

If Mark Fuhrman, who speaks so openly about his intense genocidal racism to a relative stranger such as Kathleen Bell, how many of his co-workers, the other detectives in this case, were also aware that he lied when he denied using the "N" word yet failed to come forward?

Why did the Prosecution not call a single police officer to rebut police photographer Rokahr's testimony that Detective Fuhrman was pointing at the glove [at Bundy], before, before Fuhrman went to Rockingham? That is around 4:30 in the morning.

If the glove had been dropped on the walkway at Rockingham ten minutes after the murder, why is there no blood or fiber on that south walkway or on the leaves the glove was resting on? Why is there no blood in the 150 feet of narrow walkway or on the stucco wall abutting it?

No. 7. For what purpose was Vannatter carrying Mr. Simpson's blood in his pocket for three hours and a distance of 25 miles instead of booking it down the hall at Parker Center?

No. 8. Why did Deputy District Attorney Hank Goldberg, in a desperate effort to cover up for the missing 1.5 milliliters of Mr. Simpson's blood, secretly go out to the home of police nurse Thano Peratis without notice to the Defense and get him to contradict his previous sworn testimony at both the grand jury and the preliminary hearing? Peratis was never sworn. We were never given notice.

Why, if, according to Miss Clark, he walked into his own house wearing the murder clothes and shoes, there is not any soil or so much as a smear or drop of blood associated with the victims on the floor, the white carpeting, the doorknobs, the light switches and his bedding?

If Mr. Simpson had just killed Mr. Goldman in a bloody battle involving more than two dozen knife wounds where Mr. Goldman remains standing and struggling for several minutes, how come there is less than seven/tenths of one drop of blood consistent with Mr. Goldman found in the Bronco?

No. 11. Why, following a bitter struggle allegedly with Mr. Goldman, were there no bruises or marks on O. J. Simpson's body?

No. 12. Why do bloodstains with the most DNA not show up until weeks after the murder, those on the socks, those on the back gate?

No. 13. Why did Mark Fuhrman lie to us? Why did Phil Vannatter lie to us?

No. 14. Why did the sock show up almost two months after a careful search for evidence, and why was the blood on it applied when there was no foot in it?

And, finally, 15. Given Professor MacDonell's testimony that the gloves would not have shrunk no matter how much blood was smeared on them, and given that they never shrank from June 21st, 1994, until now, despite having been repeatedly frozen and thawed, how come the gloves just don't fit?

I'm going to leave those questions for Miss Clark and we'll see what she chooses to do with and about them. That will be her choice. But I think you have a right to demand answers if you are going to do your job in this case. It seems to me you will need to have answers to those questions. Now, there are many, many, many more, but as with everything in this case, there comes a time when you can only do so much. We took fifteen as representatives, but I can tell you we had more than fifty questions, but fifteen will be enough, don't you think? I think so. ...It is now up to you. We are going to pass this baton to you soon. You will do the right thing. You have made a commitment for justice. You will do the right thing.

By your decision you control his very life in your hands. Treat it carefully. Treat it fairly. Be fair. Don't be part of this continuing cover-up. Do the right thing remembering that if it doesn't fit, you must acquit, that if these messengers have lied to you, you can't trust their message, that this has been a search for truth. That no matter how bad it looks, if truth is out there on a scaffold and wrong is in here on the throne, when that scaffold sways the future and beyond the dim unknown standeth the same God for all people keeping watch above his own. He watches all of us and he will watch you in your decision. Thank you for your attention. God bless you.

* * *

THE COURT:

All right. Ladies and gentlemen, contrary to our previous schedule, I'm going to recess for the evening at this time. We will resume tomorrow morning at nine o'clock. And the lawyers have promised me that we will finish this case. One of the conditions—that we go over until tomorrow morning—is that we will finish tomorrow afternoon with the rebuttal arguments by the Prosecution. I will instruct you and the case will be yours tomorrow afternoon. And I hope—hopefully we will at least get it far enough to have you go in, select a Foreperson to preside over your deliberations, and then Mrs. Robertson has a list of the exhibits and everything that will be presented to you so you can get organized for the coming days. All right. Having said that, please remember all my admonitions to you. Don't discuss the case, don't form any opinions about the case, don't conduct any deliberations until the matter has been submitted, do not allow anybody to communicate with you with regard to the case. See you tomorrow morning, nine o'clock. All right. We will be in recess.

* * *

On Friday, September 29, Marcia Clark rose to speak the last words the state of California would get to say in its attempt to convict O. J. Simpson of the murders of Nicole Brown Simpson and Ronald Goldman. She was as ready as she'd ever be, but so was Barry Scheck. As Larry Schiller and James Willwerth later wrote in *American Tragedy*: "Scheck objected so often that before long Ito furiously warned him to stop. During an argument over Marcia's use of personal references while the jury was absent, Scheck objected out of turn.

"'Sit down,' Ito shouted, livid, pointing his finger at the attorney.

Scheck was almost daring the judge to cite him for contempt. Peter Neufeld was delighted. All along, he'd hoped *somebody* would go to jail in this trial. Maybe Barry would make it. A grand civil liberties tradition."

Coolly, Marcia Clark adjusted to withstand the defense lawyer's constant interruptions.

Without stopping to wait for Judge Ito to say "Sustained" or "Denied," she simply kept on speaking, finishing what she had started out to say, confident that Judge Ito would not sustain the objection. Her confidence was not misplaced.

One by one, she covered her main points, claiming that the prosecution's evidence proved, basically, the opposite of what we'd said. And then she closed with a clever refutation, point by point, of Johnnie's fifteen questions of the day before. Then she began her summation:

> None of us wanted to believe that O. J. Simpson would commit murder. We all wanted to believe that our image of him was right. We didn't want to believe that the man we saw in the movies and commercials would do this.
> But he did.
> And the fact that he did doesn't mean he wasn't a great football player. It doesn't mean he never did a good thing

in his life. Nothing takes that away. And it's still here. It'll always be here.

But so will the fact that he committed these murders.

And even though it's a hard thing, still it cannot mean—it cannot mean that you let a guilty person go free. That someone who commits murder is not held accountable for it. He had strength and he had weaknesses. And it's his weakness that brought us here today. and it's his weakness—that's why we're here and Ron and Nicole are not.

Defense would say no motive. No motive. It's one of the oldest motives ever known, ladies and gentlemen. Anger, fear of abandonment, jealousy, loss of control, of Nicole and of himself.

Usually I feel like I'm the only one left to speak for the victims.

But in this case Ron and Nicole, they're speaking to you. They're speaking to you. And they're telling you who murdered them. ...

Remember back in 1989, she cried to Detective Edwards: "He's going to kill me! He's going to kill me!" The children were there. 1990: She made a safe deposit box. Put photographs of her beaten face and her haunted look in a safe deposit box along with a will. She was only 30 years old. How many 30-year-olds you know do that? A will, a safe deposit box. It's like writing: in the event of my death.

She knew. "He's going to kill me."

1993: The 911 tape. The children were there. He was screaming. She was crying. And she was frightened. Think the thing that perhaps was so chilling about her voice is that sound of resignation. There was a resignation to it. Inevitability. She knew she was going to die.

And Ron, he speaks to you. In struggling so valiantly, he forced his murderer to leave the evidence behind that you might not ordinarily have found.

And they both are telling you who did it with their hair, their clothes, their bodies, their blood.

They tell you he did it.

He did it. Mr. Simpson, Orenthal Simpson, he did it.

They told you in the only way they can. Will you hear them? Or will you ignore their plea for justice?

Or, as Nicole said to Detective Edwards, you never do anything about him...

Ms. Clark continued:

> I want to play something for you, ladies and gentlemen, that puts it all together. Let me explain what this is. This is a compilation of the 1989 tape, 911 call, the 1993 911 call, photographs from 1989 beating and the photographs from her safe deposit box and the photographs from Rockingham and Bundy. *[Tape is played.]*
>
> I don't have to say anything else.
>
> Ladies and gentlemen, on behalf of the people of the State of California, because we have proven beyond a reasonable doubt, far beyond a reasonable doubt, that the defendant committed these murders, we ask you to find the defendant guilty of murder in the first degree of Ronald Goldman and Nicole Brown.
>
> Thank you very much.

* * *

The defense team lawyers gave the lead prosecutor generally high marks for her rebuttal argument, but we all agreed on one thing—she had not answered all of Johnnie's fifteen questions adequately. And, as I would learn when I read the book by the three female jurors, the jury didn't think so either. And they didn't think much of the closing argument—from either side.

The whole thing with those closing arguments was I felt it was all a script. Everybody had his or her little script. I hated it because at that point you're supposed to be tying in all the evidence and tying in everything. So we're sitting there and trying to just focus on the issues, and there they are, Marcia Clark, the woe is me and blah, blah, blah trying to get the tear thing. And Johnnie Cochran is going on about Proverbs and this, that, and the other, and the hat routine, and, "If it doesn't fit, you must acquit." You don't need all of that. We tried to wash all of that out and just hear what we needed to hear. We hated it.

When we brought up the subject everybody said, "Wasn't that the most miserable thing you ever had to deal with in your life?"

Hmmm... Apparently, the jury was much further down the road to a verdict than we thought.

* * *

On Saturday, the 28th day of September 1995, after more than eight months of what was then arguably the most excruciating trial in American history, Judge Ito gave the jury its instructions. Just from looking at the jurors' faces, one could see that they were anxious to get on with their deliberations. But it was not to be. Even though the jurors were ready to discuss the case, Judge Ito had plans for the weekend which meant he would be unavailable to superintend any questions or other issues which might arise during their deliberations. So, he informed them that they would not be allowed to deliberate the case until Monday, October 2, when his weekend indulgence was completed.

I thought this to be—for a jury that had been locked up for eight months—very inconsiderate treatment.

On Monday morning, when the jury was actually allowed to begin to discuss their verdicts in the case, I was fulfilling a prior obligation to address a group of executives at a meeting in

Redondo Beach, a few miles south of Los Angeles, on one of my favorite topics: the amalgamation of self-confidence, discipline, and determination which when found within a single personality will produce a person of considerable force.

Because he expected deliberations to be extensive, Johnnie Cochran was in Napa Valley; Scheck and Neufeld had gone back to New York; and Bob Blasier went home to Sacramento. My trusty and invaluable sidekick, investigator Pat McKenna, stayed in Los Angeles.

On the previous Friday, I had done an interview with Paula Zahn of CBS News, telling her that there would be an acquittal after no more than three days of deliberations, and that she and others of her news media cadre were likely to be sorely embarrassed for their smug predictions of a conviction. It would be, I told her, a fine occasion for "I told you so." If recollection serves, she has not spoken to me since. I think I may have been the only lawyer on the defense team who thought the verdicts would be swift, and the results favorable.

As my Redondo Beach lecture was about to begin, I got a phone call from Carl Douglas, the managing partner of the Cochran firm, and a key player in Simpson's defense. He was the lone lawyer designated to go to court that first day of the scheduled deliberations in the unexpected event that something was to happen that day.

The jury, said Carl, wanted to hear a reading of the testimony of Allan Park, the limousine driver who had waited for Simpson for thirty minutes before he finally emerged from his home. Because Park's testimony had been largely corroborative of Simpson's statement to the police and others about his whereabouts at the time of the murders, I did not find the jury's request to be at all distressing. But, I suggested to Carl that he ask Judge Ito to inform the jury that although they would be permitted to hear Park's testimony read to them, it would have to be read in its entirety and not just in little snippets. Carl passed that request along to the judge, who instructed the jury as asked.

Later I received a second, and most heartwarming call from

Carl, who told me that when the court reporter came to the part of Park's testimony where he was asked whether his headlights covered the front of Simpson's home as he waited outside the gate, and whether he had seen anyone pass through them before 10:55 p.m. when Simpson first appeared, his answer was no. At that point, Carl reported, the jury rose and returned to their deliberation room even though the testimony from Park was far from complete, a clear rejection of the judge's instruction.

Shortly thereafter, the jury asked that they be furnished with verdict forms, and about *eight minutes* later two verdicts (one for each victim) were returned to the clerk. Because chief counsel for the defense—Johnnie Cochran—was not available, Judge Ito had the verdicts sealed and announced that they would be published the following morning at 10:00 a.m.

As I was driving back from Redondo Beach, I received a call from Cathy Randa, Simpson's longtime personal secretary (and one of the nicest people on planet Earth) with a request. She asked if I would go to the jail and speak with O. J., because she was concerned that he'd be beside himself with anxiety over the contents of the sealed verdict envelope. She said, and I will always treasure her words: "Lee, you have always had the most positive view of O. J.'s case of anyone on the defense team. I think a talk with you would be really good for him right about now." I assured her that I would proceed to the jail with dispatch, and I did.

When I arrived, the expected horde of reporters from every branch of the media was buzzing around anxiously on the jailhouse steps, and as I ascended, a microphone was shoved just under my nose with a demand that I comment on what many expected would be a likely conviction of my client.

Never having been one to suffer fools, either gladly or lightly, I stomped on this one. "Let me say this just once, and then let's see what's in the envelope. I have been involved, immersed, in this process for just under forty years, and most of you intrepid news folks have seen only its superficial aspects. In the sealed envelope, which will be opened tomorrow, I am totally certain—from the record of what happened today—that there are two acquittals and nothing less."

In my exasperation at what I had long viewed as a mediocre job of reporting a criminal case, I may have added a rude aside such as "And put that in your pipe and smoke it." Admittedly, one of the few joys in the practice of criminal law is the deliciously selfish sight of a prejudiced band of news media hounds being shown up as rank amateurs.

I should point out that this burst of bravado was well founded. The reading of the testimony of Allan Park had obviously been done to satisfy the reservations of a minority on the jury, and when the record showed that during his thirty-minute wait, Allan Park had not seen anyone cross through his headlights, it was apparent that O. J. had not parked his Bronco on the street and walked to his front door during that interval. Once this point was made, the majority—according to Douglas—shot an "I-told-you-so" glance at the sixty-year old white woman who was viewed as the most conservative juror, and said in effect, "Okay, there it is. You were wrong; now let's get back to work."

When, a short time later, the jury asked for verdict forms, it was apparent that the last issue in the jury room had been resolved and the jurors, having just voted unanimously, were ready to sign. The forms were returned eight minutes later. This sequence of events was the source of my complete confidence that the verdicts would be favorable.

Bob Shapiro, on the other hand, despite being inexperienced in the hardscrabble handling of murder cases, let it be known that he was sure there had been a conviction. Indeed, he called Alan Dershowitz, who was committed to handle any appeal that might be necessary, and told him to expect a conviction. When Alan appeared the following morning during a TV interview and said that he was "cautiously pessimistic," it turned out to be a bit embarrassing.

As I entered the jail's visiting room and saw O. J. coming toward me, I expected to find at least some traces of concern on his face. Not so. He was beaming, with a grin that stretched from ear to ear. "Juice," I said, "I came here to bring you glad tidings, but it looks to me like you already know."

A bit sheepishly, he told me that the deputies asked him for his autograph or a photo, explaining that they didn't expect to see him again. He knew the deputies knew how the jury voted, so he was sure he was going to be released.

We spent some time chatting about the case and discussing what he would do once released. He told me that after he had had a chance to breathe a bit, he wanted to see all his defenders at his home to thank them for all that they had done to help him.

The following morning, a goodly number of the world's population were glued to their television sets just before 10:00 a.m. Pacific Daylight Time, the scheduled hour for the publication of the verdicts. I met Johnnie Cochran at his home, and his handshake was strong and his face showed his usual attractive smile. I thought he was optimistic, but perhaps not as confident as I was about the outcome rushing rapidly toward us.

"Are you sure, my brother?" he asked. I tried to relieve his anxiety. "Johnnie," I said, "I've been at this business for a long time. I can smell and feel the verdicts we deserve." He seemed to take some heart from that, but I felt he still had some reservations.

CHAPTER 23

The Verdict

On October 3, 1995, the jurors filed into the court-room—134 days after the trial had begun. Judge Lance Ito asked Orenthal J. Simpson and Johnnie Cochran to rise and face the jury. O. J. stood tall, listening intently.

At 10:07 a.m., the clerk spoke:

"The Superior Court, County of Los Angeles, in the matter of the People of the State of California vs. Orenthal J. Simpson, Case Number BA097211. We, the jury in the above and titled action, find the defendant, Orenthal James Simpson, not guilty of the crime of murder in violation of the penal code, section 187A, a felony upon Nicole Brown Simpson, a human being, as charged in count 1 of the information." A similar result was announced for Ron Goldman.

Johnnie clapped Simpson on the back. Trembling with victory, O. J. whispered only his gratitude, "Thank you... thank you."

Confident though I had been of the outcome, it was nonetheless a solemn moment when, after all these weeks, many of them utterly wasted, the record getting its final, official imprimatur. The wave of emotions and reactions surged through the courtroom, crashing through the outcries, making the simultaneous tsunami almost unbearable. Emotions were high, with the Simpson family wiping away tears of joy, nearly crumpling with relief, while Ron Goldman's sister broke into great heaving sobs.

She was comforted by her father, Fred, who's fury was palpable. The Brown family remained composed but were seemingly in disbelief. Marcia Clark and Christopher Darden were nearly expressionless. I must believe they'd seen this verdict coming.

I think it only fitting to include some thoughts from what may be the most objective and externally observant book on the Simpson case, the book written by the three female jurors. Here is Carrie Bess's impression of Judge Lance Ito reading the verdict to himself just before his clerk read it to the world: "I knew something was funny when he read it, because I could see his color change. I definitely saw the expression on his face change. ... Then the judge asked Mr. Simpson to stand and face us while Mrs. Robertson read the verdict. I thought, *Well, this is it,* and I looked right at him as he turned toward us. The man can't look at everybody at the same time, but somehow I felt he was looking right at me."

Bess wrote, "Oh man, you could see the people looking and you could hear a big old wave of 'AAAHHH,' and then I could hear her—I could hear her just screaming out—Ron Goldman's sister, just screaming. And I could hear 'WHOOOO,' you know, it's like you couldn't hear what they were saying but there was mumbling and it was like a big rolling wave of sound coming at you. And you could hear all this hollering. And all I wanted to do was get out of there. ... At that point I had stopped looking. I couldn't look anymore. I was just trying to hold on. I just wanted him to take his gavel and say, 'Order in the court,' but he didn't."

"O. J. put his hand up like this and waved to us," adds Bess, raising her hand. "And then I looked at Marcia Clark, I looked at the prosecution, and they looked like 'You mother...' you know what I'm saying. All I can hear is this girl just screaming."

Juror Marsha Rubin-Jackson echoed Bess's feelings. "And I said, 'Oh, Jesus,' because I was about to cry too ... I felt so sad for the people that truly believed Justice wasn't served...All I wanted to do at that point was just get up and walk out."

Armanda Cooley continued: "I know the majority of the dismissed jurors also agreed with our decision based on the evidence they heard, but I think it's interesting that they also were aware of the additional information that was kept from us, that Mark Fuhrman had taken the fifth, for example. I learned that Jeanette Harris and Willie Craven would have also voted not guilty."

"The prosecution did not prove its case beyond a reasonable doubt," Harris said. "The evidence was just too questionable."

While the maelstrom that swirled inside the courtroom was sharp and laden with emotion, the immediate reactions outside the courthouse were magnified as the media and public devoured the news and its impact. Feelings about Simpson's acquittal were often divided along racial lines, with people of color believing his innocence while many whites felt he was snatched from the arms of justice by the legal machinations of his defense.

In the following days, the amount of media space given to the verdict in the Simpson case was on a par with the beginning or end of a world war. The *Washington Post* devoted 80 percent of its October 4, 1995, "Extra" edition front page to news and opinion stories about the Simpson case, trial, and outcome. It reported, "The verdict brought to a sudden end the 'Trial of the Century' that had grown over more than a year to a form of national media addiction, mesmerizing millions of television viewers, dominating news coverage and provoking widespread debate about issues of domestic violence, racism, the jury system and police misconduct."

That same day, The *Los Angeles Times,* the hometown paper, so to speak, ran dozens of articles about the verdict in the Simpson case, reporting on such topics as whether or not trials should be televised, along with responses overseas: "The O. J. Simpson trial received mixed reactions abroad. In France, the Simpson saga received scant attention, according to Reuters. One Frenchman even confused the football legend with a cartoon character, presumably from 'The Simpsons,' which has an even bigger following in France. British newspapers remade their front pages to make way for news that the jury had reached a verdict and the story led morning radio and television news bulletins."

It was an historically divisive moment that gave rise to a never-repaired cleft in the American population. After all, people had been promised by the press that the prosecution's case was strong and that a conviction was assured. Linda Deutsch of the Associated Press did a masterful job in reporting the trial accurately and in detail. The quality of print reporting by other journalists was far less admirable.

In Washington, the government voices said what they thought to be politically attractive.

From a handwritten statement to congressional leaders, President Bill Clinton asked Americans to trust in the jury system, reminding them that "the only people who heard all the evidence were the people who were sitting in the jury box." Clinton went on to address what was evident as a racial divide in the opinions of the verdict by many across the country. "In terms of the way Americans see the world differently, that troubles me... I think the only answer to that is for us to spend more time listening to each other and try to put ourselves in each others' shoes and understand why we see the world in different ways and keep trying to overcome that."

According to a Washington CNN report, "White House press secretary Mike McCurry said the president watched the verdict in an anteroom off the Oval Office with some aides, including White House Chief of Staff Leon Panetta. The president was somber as he wrote out his reaction in red ink, according to McCurry. He said the president did not seem surprised by the verdict."

Senate Majority Leader Bob Dole (R) also underlined the importance of faith in the US judicial system. "In America, guilt and innocence are determined by an impartial jury of our peers. In this case, a jury of twelve men and women of different backgrounds were able to come together and reach a unanimous verdict. This tragic episode has been torturous for the families of the victims. My thoughts and prayers—and those of all Americans—will remain with the families of the victims for many years to come."

Still, politicians fell short of endorsing Simpson's innocence. Years after Dole's statement, I would learn that when writer Brian Heiss, who was involved in drafting the remark, suggested that the senator praise the verdict and proclaim Simpson's innocence, his suggestion was, as he told me, "quickly dismissed."

Former housing secretary Jack Kemp, who had played with O. J. with the Buffalo Bills, said the jury's decision should be accepted, regardless of one's personal feelings. "The workings of our system have resulted in a decision which must be trusted," Kemp said. He added that the dominant role race played through-out the trial underscores the ongoing racial strife in the United States. "And while there is still a long way to go, our focus must be on racial reconciliation and healing."

Not all the politicians were so tempered—or constitution-ally correct—in their public comments. Conservative California Republican Congressman Bob Dornan, in his ignorance—and with great arrogance—overruled the jury, saying, "O. J. is guilty 15 times . . . John Cochran is guilty of murder. He (Simpson) won't do any movies; any producer that employs him, I'll be sure, is painted with a big 'S' for 'Shame.'"

* * *

The day after the verdict, an op-ed entitled, "Reasonable Doubt" ran in the *New York Times* by the noted novelist, and very able Chicago trial lawyer, Scott Turow. The essay reminded the American conscience of our judicial duty to uphold the US Constitution. In his treatise, Turow examined the violation of the Fourth Amendment, a cornerstone within the Bill of Rights that keeps the government from excessive intrusion into the lives of its citizens. He criticized not only the manner in which police in the Simpson case gathered evidence, but more importantly, how the LA district attorney's office defended those "arrogant blunders."

According to Turow, it sent a message to the Simpson jury.

When the Fourth Amendment and the other consti-tutional rules restricting police behavior are violated, it necessarily carries with it a strong message to our political minorities that the legal system is a two-faced joker, one that says, "We make the rules and we'll follow the ones we like."

I was an assistant United States attorney for eight years, and I never had a piece of evidence suppressed in a case I handled. This is not because I was such a great lawyer. It was because the federal agents I worked with understood the Fourth Amendment and didn't violate it.

A legal system, like any moral system, is a complex and interdependent social arrangement. No one does good on his own. It requires the constant support, reinforcement and allegiance of all players for each to resist the ever-present temptations to let ends justify means. And that system appears to have broken down in Los Angeles. The jurors were impaneled knowing from the start that this was business as usual.

Nothing the prosecutors could do could convince them that this case was not corrupted by the police department's world-renowned racial hostility.

* * *

In late October, back in Florida, I received a four-paragraph letter from Johnnie Cochran, dated October 26, 1995. It read:

Re: _People v. O. J. Simpson_

Dear Lee:

I wanted to take this opportunity to express to each member of the Defense Team my deep and heartfelt appreciation for your magnificent work in representing our client, Mr. O. J. Simpson.

On Tuesday, October 3, at approximately 10:07 a.m., we all made history. We proved that justice is alive and well in America, and were instrumental in seeing that an innocent man kept his freedom.

O. J. joins me in thanking you for saving his life. This

could not have been accomplished had we not remained a Team, focused on Mr. Simpson's innocence with our eyes consistently on the prize.

It has, indeed, been my privilege to work with each of you. I count each of you as friends, and I pray that our relationship will be a long and fruitful one.

Kindest personal regards,
/s/ Johnnie L. Cochran, Jr.

Johnnie's letter was a fine gesture, but its sentiments were hardly universal. In fact, the opposite would be closer to the truth.

* * *

It took weeks before the ashes from the intense media firestorm surrounding the verdict began to settle. However, the spectacle of those viewing the news announcement, which played incessantly, showed people (predominantly black) cheering wildly on the one hand and others (predominantly white), crying angrily, stoking the embers of racial divide, which glow cherry red even now, after a quarter of a century has passed.

Disappointing as this was to behold, I had no inkling at the time that a man acquitted of two murders by a jury of his peers would be held to such harsh public scrutiny. Those who claimed justice was not served based their opinions almost entirely on broadcasted opinions and rhetoric of media pundits, not having closely watched the trial and the evidence presented.

As for me, I was somewhat surprised at the vitriol heaped my way over my part in helping to dismember a racist cop, without whose perjured testimony, the trial would never have taken place. But, as any good defense attorney learns, you must square your shoulders and be ready to take the blows. It comes with the job.

CHAPTER 24
The Aftermath

I n the following months, more thoughts and commentary would emerge from journalists, legal scholars, and the key trial participants alike. Everyone, it seemed, wanted to weigh in with their thoughts on the "Trial of the Century," joining in what sometimes felt like a snake pit.

While Johnnie Cochran's brief note to the lawyers who had defended O. J. was a fine letter and its tone and kind words were pure Johnnie Cochran, his statement that "we were instrumental in seeing that an innocent man kept his freedom," hardly reflected public opinion. Indeed, in the weeks—and, eventually, years—following the verdict, that statement was closer to the exact opposite of what the majority of the public, especially the white public, believed.

Interestingly, the extent to which race became such a polarizing topic to the public shocked the Simpson trial jury members. Forewoman Armanda Cooley noted that all the jurors—and she stressed that it was *all* of them—were surprised to learn, post-verdict, "that racism was so heavily involved in people's reactions after the trial."

She wrote, "It's important that people know this was not a racist thing. I'm black and Mr. Simpson is black. However, Mr. Simpson lives in a white world. When we signed up to do our civic duty, it was People versus Orenthal J. Simpson, not People versus Racism or People versus the Politicians or People versus Battered Women and Children. I'm just as sensitive to racism as the next person is, but people need to know that was not our cause whatsoever."

Another jury member, Marcia Rubin-Jackson, echoed Cooley's surprise.

"I don't understand how people could say I let someone go because he was black," she wrote. "It really angers me for people to say that because I was a black woman, I let this black man go. If they had proven to me that this black man had killed two people, that black man would be in prison. Simple as that."

Jury member Carrie Bess also expressed surprise that Johnnie Cochran was accused of using race to sway the jury.

"People are saying Johnnie Cochran played the race card right from the start. I didn't pick up on that at all. I know he just kept saying in his opening statement, 'Pay attention to Detective Fuhrman. He's the only one who found all the evidence.' I didn't pick up that Fuhrman was a racist. I just picked up that Fuhrman was lying...

"Johnnie played a race card, but he's a criminal lawyer," Bess contends. "He's supposed to play every card in the deck to get his client off. That's the law. I am surprised that the prosecuting attorneys let it go so far, knowing they had a problem with Fuhrman as opposed to bringing it out to us ... And Fuhrman was the trial. Fuhrman found the hat. Fuhrman found the glove. Fuhrman found the blood. Fuhrman went over the gate. Fuhrman did everything. When you throw it out, what case do you have? You've got reasonable doubt right there before you even get to the criminalists."

While the jury felt race was not a significant factor in Simpson's acquittal, it emerged that even members of his defense wanted to distance themselves from this hot topic that was broiling across America.

Immediately after the trial, Bob Shapiro gave an interview with Barbara Walters during an ABC News special, where he denounced the use of race in the trial. He claimed the race card "was played from the bottom of the deck" and that Johnnie Cochran believed "everything in America is about race." It was an odd statement coming from Bob. It had been his initial strategy to put the LAPD on trial from the moment he discovered, via the *New Yorker*, Mark Fuhrman's lawsuit requesting early retirement for racial bias. I suspect Bob's change of heart was fueled by social fallout that he and his wife suffered within their wealthy circle of white friends and associates who felt uncomfortable with the verdict and the racial discussions it sparked at dinner parties.

Johnnie felt Bob was also deeply offended that he had been downgraded to a lesser role in the trial after it became apparent he lacked experience in such cases. After Shapiro told Walters he would never work with Cochran again, Johnnie told KNBC, the NBC Los Angeles television affiliate, "We did not realize the damage it would do to his ego to not be lead attorney."

Shapiro went on to explain to Walters his rift with me, explaining that he brought me in for my "great wisdom and brainpower," but that I was never intended to be in the courtroom. Shapiro told Walters, "It's a very, very sad point in my life. This is a man who I had a very close relationship with, and I will never have a relationship with him again."

This was not something that has ever caused me to lose any sleep. At the time, I told KNBC-TV, "For the past year, Shapiro's been looking for someone to interview him who wouldn't ask him if he'd ever tried a murder case before. Finally, he found Barbara Walters."

Sadly, Shapiro wasn't the only member of the defense team who felt the backlash of the Simpson acquittal while he rubbed elbows in his affluent, Caucasian, California social circles. A year after the trial, O. J.'s long-time "friend" Robert Kardashian gave a *20/20* interview with Barbara Walters in which he claimed he was "conflicted" by the blood evidence. Though Kardashian had soundly supported O. J. throughout the nearly year-long trial and was privy to every bit of evidence, he told Walters he had his "doubts."

After the interview aired, Kardashian called O. J. and apologized, telling him that he needed the $50,000 from the interview for his "family." Seeing how history has unfolded for his reality TV ex-wife and children and their inexplicable rise to fame and wealth, perhaps Kardashian, who died in 2003, would have been better served to have remained stalwart in his support of his friend rather than weakly cave to the deadly sin of greed for his own benefit.

* * *

In 1996, the books began to roll off the presses, which were inevitable given the global interest in the case. Among the first (1996 and '97) were those by the two major prosecutors, Marcia Clark and Christopher Darden. Viking paid her $4.2 million, and Darden received $1.3 million from (Judith) Regan Books.

Clark, who proved she still didn't get it, wrote in her book, *Without a Doubt*:

> Make no mistake about it, this so-called Dream Team *played the race card*. I'd just like to ask those guys a question: Did it ever occur to you, as you broke your buns getting your spoiled, rich, sadistic jerk of a client acquitted, that you might just be putting public safety at risk? Whole neighborhoods of Los Angeles—and other cities—could have gone down in flames, Johnnie, because of your irresponsible, inflammatory rhetoric. And no amount of revisionist fast talk is going to change the fact that you guys pandered to racism to win. You took a jury itching to avenge Rodney King and inclined it to nullify the law. The result was miscarriage of justice, which, in turn, left many whites gunning for payback.
>
> In November 1996, California voters went to the polls and did something unthinkable. They voted to do away with affirmative action programs in this state. Think about that. Twenty years of social reforms blown away like ashes in the wind. I'm not alone in believing that Proposition 209 would never have stood an ice cube's chance in hell

if white Californians had not been so infuriated by the Simpson verdict. There's all kinds of ways to riot: in the streets or at the ballot box. That's the problem with pay-back. It never stops.

I have one simple answer to Ms. Clark's diatribe: *We were not the ones who put Mark Fuhrman on the witness stand.*

In his book, *In Contempt*, Chris Darden spent less time than Clark describing his reaction to the verdict: "At 10:00 a.m., with 90 percent of the televisions in America tuned in, with commerce pausing to look over its shoulder and the entire world holding its breath, Judge Ito asked Simpson to rise and his clerk, Deirdre Robertson, began reading the verdict. 'We the jury...' Afterwards I was numb...trying to imagine how they could come to a rea-soned decision in just four hours. It was impossible... Instead, they did just what Johnnie Cochran asked them to do. They sent a message."

Several days after the verdict, Johnnie L. Cochran Jr. won another sort of victory by way of his book deal, though he would not have put it that way. As the *Los Angeles Times* reported:

> Johnnie L. Cochran Jr., who repeatedly confounded the legal pundits during his successful defense of O. J. Simpson, stunned the publishing industry Tuesday when he signed the most lucrative book contract yet awarded to a participant in the so-called 'Trial of the Century.'
>
> According to sources involved in the negotiations, the total value of Cochran's deal with the Ballantine Group, a division of Random House, slightly exceeds the $4.2-mil-lion advance obtained just last week by prosecutor Marcia Clark. 'Let's just say we won again,' said a Cochran confi-dant, who asked not to be identified.
>
> Cochran's book, which will be titled *"My Journey to Justice: The Autobiography of Johnnie L. Cochran, Jr.,"* will be published by Ballantine's One World imprint, and is scheduled for release in the spring of 1997. He has yet to

select a collaborator. Another of Simpson's defense lawyers, Robert L. Shapiro, also concluded a seven-figure publishing contract Tuesday. The Century City lawyer will receive $1.5 million from Warner Books for a manuscript titled, 'The Search for Justice: A Defense Attorney's Brief on the O. J. Simpson Case.' According to knowledgeable sources, Shapiro, who will collaborate with free-lance writer Larkin Warren, already has written more than 1,000 pages of his book, which is scheduled for publication in the spring.

The contracts secured by Cochran and Clark are the third- and fourth-richest for a single volume of nonfiction in the history of American publishing. Only Gens. Colin Powell and H. Norman Schwarzkopf have received more— $6 million and $5 million, respectively. Taken together, the advances received by Shapiro and Cochran on Tuesday bring the estimated total already paid by publishers for Simpson-related books to more than $14 million.

"There's a feeding frenzy in progress," said one prominent New York book editor, "and it's not over yet. None of these prices make the slightest sense from a financial standpoint."

"Schwarzkopf's book didn't come close to making back its advance and, now that he's taken himself out of the presidential race, it doesn't look like Powell's will either," said the editor, whose firm was among the unsuccessful bidders for Clark's manuscript. "I'm not sure what Cochran and Clark will tell us about the state of American justice, but these deals speak volumes about the state of American publishing. I'm stunned."

When Johnnie's memoir, *Journey to Justice*, was published in 1996, it concluded with several chapters on the Simpson trial. About the verdict, he wrote:

At home that night [October 2nd, the night before the verdict was to be read] there were phone calls from every member of the team but one. Scheck, Neufeld, Uelmen, Blasier—we all kicked around the sequence of events and, shyly, allowed ourselves the same guarded optimism.

"Here's hoping," said Barry Scheck from his Brooklyn apartment.

I never heard from Bob Shapiro. As I later discovered, he had phoned Alan Dershowitz and instructed him to begin working on the appeal that would follow a conviction. In the meantime, he slipped off to record a television interview with Barbara Walters to be broadcast the following evening. In it, he accused the rest of us of 'playing the race card from the bottom of the deck.' It was a desperate act of contrition for a defense he then believed had failed. ...

At 10:07 a.m., the jury's sealed verdict was handed to Ito to read. As he looked down at it in silence, we searched the jury's faces for clues. Shapiro leaned over and said to our client, [who was] half out of his mind with worry, "It's going to be bad news, O. J. I can tell by the look on Ito's face."

"Be quiet," I snapped.

Seconds later, as the words "Not Guilty" echoed through the courtroom and across the nation, I muttered, "Yes, yes," and allowed my head to slump over onto O. J's shoulder. There is no better support than a man restored to liberty.

When Bob Shapiro's book came out, I was somewhat surprised that he dealt with the verdict in a relatively straightforward manner and did not try to take credit where it wasn't due. This is how he described the crucial moment: "It was all anyone at the defense table could do to remain stable... Instantly, it seemed as though the entire room was in tears... Someone said later that in the moments after we received the verdict, I appeared to literally, physically, step back from the table. And in fact, I did. To me, a trial is a sober, somber event, and a courtroom is second only to a church....And no matter the outcome, no matter the verdict, I've always tried to maintain some measure of dignity and decorum in the first strange moments after a verdict is announced. Cheers and high fives are inappropriate; it's a courtroom, not the NBA playoffs.

Shortly after the verdict had been read, Shapiro, who had promised immediate post-verdict interviews to both Barbara Walters and Larry King, told Johnnie of his plans. Shapiro wrote:

> I told Cochran that I was going to be frank on these programs. "You've got to know what my feelings are about this. It wasn't necessary what you did, what you said. The Holocaust reference, the Nation of Islam guards, raising the issue of race for jury nullification."
>
> He just nodded as he listened to me. "Johnnie, it could have backfired," I said. "We had reasonable doubt walking away, from the very beginning. You didn't have to play that card."
>
> "I appreciate your candor, Bob," he said. "And you're entitled to your opinions. It's just that I don't share them."

CHAPTER 25

The Civil Trial and the Years That Followed

A little more than a year after the not guilty verdicts had been rendered in the criminal cases, a civil case brought by Fred Goldman and the Browns was called for trial in Santa Monica, in West Los Angeles. Had District Attorney Gil Garcetti not directed otherwise, the criminal trial would have taken place there, rather than downtown. Santa Monica is a whole different place from center Los Angeles. Indeed, many consider it to be a whole different place than anywhere else on the planet. It certainly has its own culture, heavily populated by the wealthy entertainment community. The average per capita income in the community in 1995 was just shy of $60,000, and the black population was less than five percent.

Judge Hosaki Fujisaki was presiding in the case, and with a bucketful of harsh rulings, he effectively gutted the case on the first day of trial by rulings on many motions which were just short of horrendous. Indeed, he ruled so much evidence from the criminal case as beyond the plaintiff's reach that defense attorney Bob Baker, an accomplished trial lawyer, voiced his exasperation bitterly. The judge had left so little for him to do as an advocate in the case that he might as well have gone home to wait out the result in the mail, which Judge Fujisaki had all but prearranged.

As a sampler, the judge had ruled out all mention of Fuhrman's racist attitudes, his brutality in the past and willingness to plant evidence to get convictions, and his taking of the Fifth Amendment in the criminal case. He also ruled that any sloppiness of procedure or rule infractions committed by those who gathered the blood and other scientific evidence would be excluded from the jury's consideration. He also ruled that the defense's expert, Dr. Henry Lee, would not be permitted to express any opinion as to the discipline, or lack thereof, practiced by the prosecution's evidence gatherers.

The brutal and highly biased preemptive rulings, which would cause most capable trial lawyers to gag perceptibly, were perhaps small potatoes in the array of problems facing Simpson. His jury alone presented an obstacle which was probably insurmountable. For the media had not gone quietly into "this good night" after they proved to be so inept at predicting the criminal verdict.

The reporters, who had so confidently predicted conviction at the criminal trial, howled at what they passed off as juror bias, ignorance, nullification, and all manner of other bad faith conduct in carrying out their duties. They insisted—with few noble exceptions—that the criminal jury had got it wrong, and that they had it right all along, and that the antics of the Dream Team stole justice. Many of them treated the jurors in the criminal case with pure vilification.

It would be silly to suggest that this blame-shifting effort by the media went unnoticed by the Santa Monica population. In a civil trial the proof only needs to be supported by a probability, not "beyond a reasonable doubt." No juror wanted to be ridiculed as the previous jurors were, or have his family harassed because the evidence didn't seem to firmly connect Simpson to the case.

The civil trial began October 23, 1996, and lasted until February 4, 1997. Unlike the criminal trial, the jury in the civil case was predominantly white.

Just before a two-week Christmas break, Judge Fujisaki allowed plaintiff's counsel, Daniel Petrocelli, to assert in the form of a question to Simpson, who took the stand: "On the evening of June 14, 1994, you went to the offices of *Intercept, Inc.*, a polygraph testing company, and submitted to a test and *failed?*"

In many courts—without the requisite scientific foundation, at very least—would be grounds for a mistrial. But not before Judge Fujisaki. The issue was left for the jury to ponder over the holiday recess.

We thought the judge might have unwittingly cut the defense a break. By all rules of law and logic, plaintiff's counsel had just knowingly opened the door to further exploration of the "lie detector" issue by the defense. We leapt at the opportunity to deliver a mighty blow in favor of Simpson's innocence.

We got tickets for O. J. to fly to Boston, and to be tested in my apartment which was adjacent to our offices there. I called Bob Brisentine—former chief polygraph examiner of the United States Army and universally respected in the profession—to come to Boston and perform a classic polygraph test on Simpson, videotaped for all to scrutinize. The plaintiff would contribute to the reopening of the Simpson trial in January with a bombshell!

But as quickly as the flower of hope had bloomed, it wilted. Bob Brisentine's wife became terribly ill, and there wasn't enough time to substitute another examiner. We would test O. J. some evening after the trial resumed. But Judge Fujisaki had apparently had an epiphany over the break; in all probability, every judge in America had let him know during the holidays that his permitted reference to the "failed" polygraph was dead wrong, and that he should try to correct his error. He did, with dispatch.

As soon as court was called to order in January, the judge ordered that since Simpson—in answer to Petrocelli's question had denied both taking and failing the test— which remained uncontradicted by any physical *evidence* to the contrary—there was no evidence before the jury which was prejudicial, and instructed them to therefore ignore Petrocelli's question and Simpson's answer accordingly.

Then the civil trial focused ultimately on the now infamous shoes. Introduced into the civil trial—but never before seen in the entirety of the criminal trial—were a series of photographs allegedly taken during a Buffalo Bills vs. Miami Dolphins game played in foul weather in 1993. By then retired as an active player, Simpson had been hired by NBC as a sideline reporter, principally updating fans on what was occurring in the locker room after injuries occurred, and other incidental facts not covered by the broadcast booth. Thirty photographs showing Simpson walking along the edge of the playing field wearing baggy grey flannel slacks and suede shoes. These were identified as Bruno Magli shoes.

In both trials Simpson had at all times sworn that he'd never owned Bruno Magli shoes, but only a pair of slippers made by that company. He also claimed that he did not wear the grey slacks depicted. The defense called an expert to testify that the photos had been doctored. Plaintiff called its expert to say that they were not altered from the original. There was no direct tie between these shoes and the Bruno Magli shoeprints found by FBI expert Bill Bodziak at the murder scene, but there seems little doubt that these photos may have contributed to the jury's verdict.

Whatever their rationale, the jurors delivered crushing verdicts in favor of all the plaintiffs, and against Simpson. This verdict has no doubt buttressed the arguments of those who claim that Simpson "beat the rap" in the criminal cases because of the slick performances of his dream team. But this civil verdict, which was allowed to stand because of the lower requirements of proof used in civil cases, makes no logical sense at all.

Usually, the deliberations of a jury are difficult to reconstruct because no record is kept of what they argue amongst themselves, and therefore none is published. But occasionally, when the smoke clears, there remains evidence as to how and why the voting evolved as it did.

First, sometimes questions from the jury to the court seeking clarifications of the instructions, or the reading back of some of the testimony (as happened here) illuminate what would normally remain in the shadows. Additionally, when one or more of the jurors writes about their experience, arguments made in the jury room are often described, and sometimes attributed to the juror who made them. As with the jurors at the criminal trial, three of the civil case jurors published a book together. In it they explain a great deal about the paths that led them to join—rather quickly—in a unanimous verdict.

The first element that a prosecutor *must* prove in pursuing a criminal cases against a defendant is to show that that person had an *opportunity* to commit the crime. The core of the Simpson defense was lack of opportunity. With the timeline evidence presented, there was no way—within the 10:35–10:55 window available that night—that Simpson could have traveled to 875 South Bundy Drive, committed the two murders, then interrupted his escape from the scene by returning to it for some reason (the two-way *Bruno Magli* footprints described by Special Agent Bodziak), drive back to the Rockingham house without getting the car a bloody mess, hide the murder weapon or weapons and bloody clothing, somehow sneak in without Allan Park seeing or Kato Kaelin noticing his arrival, get cleaned up, then answer the front gate phone, then appear at his entrance door ready to travel.

If the jury in the criminal case found as a fact that Simpson had no *opportunity* to commit the crimes, then there was no way that the civil jury could have found otherwise on the same evidence. Simpson was either at 875 South Bundy Drive that night, or he wasn't, and there was no in between. Clearly the criminal jury found as a fact that he wasn't there. In a better system of laws, the civil case would never have been allowed to proceed.

CHAPTER 26
The Polygraph Test

Because it was so badly botched, the polygraph test that was attempted to be performed on O. J.—and its aftermath—needs further explanation.

As mentioned, my initial involvement with the Simpson case had begun with a witching hour phone call from Bob Shapiro, which came too late. Bob correctly thought that having the client pass a polygraph test administered by the former head of the polygraph section of the Los Angeles police department, Lieutenant Ed Gelb, might give the department detectives pause in their zeal to blame Simpson for the murders. But Bob didn't know enough about polygraph testing to fill a yellow sticky note and should have called me *before* he jumped in with both feet. He had met Gelb through me when Ed and I were partners in *Lie Detector*.

Ed Gelb was a confident, forceful man, well respected by his profession. Had he been present when Shapiro showed up with Simpson and Robert Kardashian in tow, things might have gone quite differently. Whereas Shapiro managed to bully the examiner on duty into testing Simpson most unadvisedly, Ed would have sat him in a corner with a gag in his mouth, and had the kind of talk with O. J. that top-notch examiners use as a predicate for all carefully conducted polygraph examinations: a painstaking interview used to determine what the subject knows, what he denies knowing, and sometimes why he is willing to submit to a test.

But, tragically, Ed was in Spain, where he had arranged to do a replication of our show for Spanish TV and was enjoying a strong audience. On duty that fateful night at the Los Angeles office was Dennis Nunnally, with whom I had worked as one of the examiners on our show. Dennis was both experienced and competent; as soon as Shapiro told him that he wanted to test a potential suspect for the murder of his former wife about forty-eight hours before, Dennis informed him that there would have to be a "cooling off" period because a former loved one was involved. He explained that because of the highly charged emotional state of the suspect, reactions to even the most innocuous questions could be greatly exaggerated.

Shapiro would have none of it. He said that Simpson had agreed to surrender to an arrest warrant the following morning, and that he did not want to conduct any testing in the jail. This was the only chance. Dennis agreed to give it a try, despite the fact that he was too rushed to conduct a proper examination, or even to get a detailed briefing on the known facts of the case, and Simpson's version of his whereabouts at the time in question.

A polygraph test produces charts reflecting the body's physiological activity (blood pressure, pulse, breathing, and a galvanic response in the skin) following the asking of questions. These charts, which can be either electronic or printed on paper (as Simpson's were), are called polygrams. To my knowledge, the only person capable of reading and interpreting polygrams who has ever seen the detritus of the Simpson effort is myself, because when Shapiro finally got me on the phone, I told him to discontinue testing immediately. His response was to grab Dennis's charts and take them with him. He showed them to me one day in his office. They were ragged, and in my view all but worthless for interpretive purposes. When subpoenaed to produce them in the civil case, Shapiro answered that he had destroyed them.

What followed was Simpson's excursion the next day to the cemetery where Nicole was buried, and his famous drive back to his home where he surrendered. No effort was made to administer a test to him during the long months before he was free again after the verdict of not guilty.

But the subject of taking a polygraph did not go away. After the post-verdict dust of the civil trial had settled and Simpson was living in South Florida, people asked what he was doing to pursue his stated objective of aiding everyone in every way to discover the identity of—and punish—the true killers of Nicole and Ron Goldman. I discussed this situation with him and formulated a plan. The only hope of successfully reopening a case so badly butchered by the police and prosecutors was an offer of money—a bounty, in plain English—for information leading to the identity of the perpetrator(s). Simpson had little money left after the high cost of defending himself at two trials as well as the huge civil judgment against him of $33 million in favor of the Browns and Goldmans. This all but precluded him from getting his hands on any significant funding to apply to such an effort. But a wealthy third party? Perhaps.

In the post-trial years, I lived in Manalapan, Florida, adjacent to Lantana, where the famous supermarket tabloid *National Enquirer* had its headquarters. Although much derided as primarily a sensationalist publication, I had noted that while the case was in process, the *Enquirer* had ironically done a more respectable job of reporting the facts than many of its highbrow brethren. I also knew that its management was not averse to "checkbook journalism" where it could get an exclusive story by putting cash on the table.

As a final measure of comfort, I knew that their lead law firm was Williams & Connolly in Washington, DC. The founder of that firm, Edward Bennett Williams, was deceased, but he had been a friend and to some extent a valued mentor from the day we had first met in July1960, when I had lunch with him immediately after I had completed taking the Massachusetts bar examination. A year after the civil trial ended, I called Brendan Sullivan, a senior partner in that firm at the time, and put to him a proposal: Simpson would submit to a polygraph examination to determine whether he had had any involvement in the murders. It would be hosted by the *National Enquirer,* who would be permitted to choose the examiner, videotape the test, and own the publication rights to it. If Simpson failed, they would have a blockbuster story to report.

But if he should pass, the *Enquirer* would put up $2 million in a special fund, to be awarded to any person or persons who could supply credible information as to why Nicole and Ron Goldman had been killed, whether such culprits were eventually prosecuted or not. I suspected, and had heard through the FBI rumor mill, that the killers had been executed by the mob for their calamitous mistake in murdering two innocent victims in error. No money arising from this event would go to O. J. or his counsel, and thus would not come within the grasp of those who held judgments against him.

I rather promptly received a green light from the law firm. The *Enquirer* agreed to my terms. To my delight, they selected Bob Brisentine to conduct the exam with no suggestions from me, and without knowing that he had been my first choice for the 1996 Christmas holiday test which had been aborted. The test would be conducted in Brisentine's laboratory. The *Enquirer's* representative and I would observe these proceedings through closed-circuit television. The resulting polygrams, whether they were judged by Brisentine to be "DI (deception indicated), "NDI" (no deception indicated), or "Inconclusive" would be subject to peer review by a panel of Brisentine's senior colleagues.

It looked like the *Enquirer* had bought itself a winner either way. If Simpson flunked, the *Enquirer* would gain heroic status, even from those who thought most of its stories were gossipy trash. If he passed, the story would go on for many months, and sell lots of copies.

But in the Simpson case, "Murphy's law" seems to ever be near at hand. In what I am satisfied was an unfortunate coincidence, some *Enquirer* reporter wrote a short article about O. J.'s daughter. The story was unflattering, to put it mildly, and Simpson was justifiably enraged. "You want me to *trust* these people?" he asked bitterly. "Forget about it," he said. "This whole business! If they treated my daughter that way, what are they planning for me?"

I could not argue. But after sixty-six years of using polygraph tests, I have no doubt that Simpson would have passed cleanly. I also have no doubt that O. J. Simpson's detractors would have called the whole exercise a "fake."

I could not argue. But after sixty-six years of using polygraph
tests, I have no doubt that Simpson would have passed cleanly.
I also have no doubt that Simpson's detractors would have
called the whole exercise a fake.

EPILOGUE

At the end of the day, what does the Simpson case stand
for as one of the monumental trials of American history?
In my view it highlights many of the strengths and weaknesses of our system of jurisprudence, and certainly the plethora
of weaknesses by far outnumber and outweigh—in judicial significance—its few strengths.

First, we must look at the surviving victim families. In a murder
trial, a criminal defense lawyer is often in a tenuous position when
it comes to the survivors of the victim's family and friends. While
there is always compassion for their unimaginable loss, allowing
yourself to get too close to their grief and anger can jeopardize
your client's case and his freedom. This challenge was particularly
difficult in this trial as the families of both Nicole and Ron were
present in the courtroom every day, and in many incidences (particularly regarding Fred Goldman), giving their "guilty" verdict to
millions through the media. Anyone could sympathize with the
inconceivable frenzy swirling around them, forcing them to process their misery in the public eye. And for the defense to rebut
these attacks on Simpson would have proven to be a no-win situation. This trial and the intense milieu surrounding it was no way
for anyone to grieve, and certainly offered no haven for healing.
No one came away with anything good, and the title of Lawrence
Schiller's book, *American Tragedy*, was a fitting summation of the
unfortunate catastrophe.

And what of the prosecutors? For losers who put on a terribly frail case because that is all they had, they made out somewhat better. District Attorney Gil Garcetti offered several excuses for the poor result, but generally prospered. Marcia Clark's book essentially lionizes herself as a heroic warrior; Chris Darden did the same. And they were certainly both paid handsome advances for their books. Both Clark and Darden experimented with other ventures including hosting a television show and making multiple appearances on talk shows to promote their book sales. It is likely that neither lawyer has admitted to this day that the defense didn't *win* the Simpson case; the prosecution blew it, by getting into a sandbox with a viper in the shape of Mark Fuhrman. Obviously, if the case had to be restarted today, convicted perjurer Fuhrman would be totally unavailable as a witness. Without his evidence, would there have been any case at all? Seasoned trial lawyers will have no trouble responding with a thumping "NO," as we have done.

The aftermath of the defense ensemble is much more complex. Lead counsel Johnnie Cochran—a wonderful man and an effective lawyer by any measure—passed away in 2005. He was a good colleague, a joy to work with, and—to me at least—an attentive and agreeable man. Our one dispute throughout the trial was whether to call Tom Lang, Nicole's neighbor, who almost surely got a brief look at the killers. Johnnie feared the time involved might lead a mistrial. I thought Lang's testimony was the best support we had for the notion that others had killed Nicole by mistake, then Goldman as an unexpected arrival, and that Simpson was totally innocent. Johnnie won the day, but I wish he hadn't. As one who has been much scorned for bullying a rabidly racist cop and getting a killer off in the process, I wish Lang was in the record, fully cross-examined, and explaining why an LAPD officer had tried to get him to lie.

On a lighter note, Johnnie's popularity soared when the verdict came in and in its aftermath. Some wealthy lawyers in Florida and Alabama cut a deal with him to start The Cochran Firm, and put up $20 million to open facilities in many cities across the country. They continue to flourish today.

Sadly, during the latter course of the trial, Johnnie mentioned to me that occasionally he was having severe headaches that over-the-counter painkillers could not dispel. I urged him to seek a specialized medical diagnosis, and he made it plain (for reasons he did not disclose) that he did not wish anyone to know about this condition. He would smile wanly and assure me that things would get better as soon the trial was over. Unbeknownst to Johnnie—or anyone else—his headaches were probably the harbinger of a brain tumor that was growing slowly inside his head.

The last time I saw Johnnie Cochran alive was very special. In Palm Beach County, Florida, there is a very well-known and well-respected church called the Tabernacle, whose then pastor was a highly regarded graduate of the Harvard Divinity School. One Sunday it was announced that Johnnie would be giving a guest sermon. The constituency was predominantly made up of African Americans, and the only Caucasians that I recall attending included an acclaimed civil trial lawyer named Bob Montgomery and myself. The sermon was stirring, to say the least, and simply added dimension to a man who in my opinion stood very tall in this too-often forlorn world. It was, in a word, a most memorable experience, and one that I am happy to have had.

During the next decade, the headache that had annoyed Johnnie in 1995 grew slowly but inexorably, and by 2005, it had literally forced the life out of his brain. He passed away on March 29, 2005, at the age of sixty-seven. Along with a multitude of his friends and admirers, I attended the funeral. Of all the excellent lawyers it has been my privilege to know, Johnnie Cochran was one of the most extraordinary.

Carl Douglas, Johnnie's case manager, is out practicing on his own, quite successfully. Carl is a good lawyer, and it was a pleasure to work with him.

Barry Scheck and Peter Neufeld, whom I dubbed "The Gangsters from New York," did an excellent job with the DNA evidence. They effectively showed that it was not the *science* of

DNA that was flawed, but rather those in charge of collecting crime scene evidence were. Their collection techniques were sloppy at best, and as witnesses they seemed untrained and ill-prepared. Scheck and Neufeld pretty much shredded them. Their expertise was genuine, and they gave good value for their fees.

Almost unnoticeable, even though he was the only lawyer to attend most of both the criminal and civil trials, Robert Blasier of Sacramento was a serious contributor to both defense strategy and tactics. Despite nagging health problems, he was a substantial asset. When I wanted to test drive a proposed cross-examination, I would sit alone with Bob and ask him to poke holes in my efforts. He often did, enabling me to make corrections and improvements. I would have been happy to have Bob second chair any trial with me.

As for Robert Shapiro, I do not believe that deep down he was pleased with the verdict. Had there been a conviction, he could have chortled, "I told you so" for turning down his last-ditch effort to engineer a plea to manslaughter.

During the trial, I had obtained, for all counsel at the defense table, small laptop computers offered by Toshiba which sported a built-in printer. Bob had secretly worked out a contract for a book with Grand Central Publishing, and during most of the courtroom hours sat at the table, creating deathless prose. A quick scan would suggest that he had repeatedly saved the day and was principally responsible for the favorable result.

For me, I must mention that it was fashionable for the young reporters covering the trial proceedings to opine—based upon little experience—that "Bailey really needs this one; he hasn't scored big recently." I doubt that these newbies had done much homework on the matter. I had successfully completed a murder trial in March, two months before Simpson came along. And there were many which preceded that one.

I wanted the Simpson case like I wanted chain of angina attacks. I had been burnt too often in California state courts (federal courts are run like a tighter ship, mostly), quoting a fee for a trial of a few weeks, then getting stuck there for months, losing my ass financially. This shortcoming on California's part is badly compounded by the arrival of press interest. The Simpson case was frequently dubbed a "circus" by the media—and in a sense it was—created, sustained, and fueled by poor reporting. I saw the Simpson trial as an ugly experience about to happen. Further, I had never second chaired a major criminal trial before, and didn't like the idea of committee decisions, as inevitably occurs when too many cooks spoil the broth. Had Shapiro remained as lead counsel, I would have snatched the reins from him early on. When Johnnie entered the case, things changed substantially. He was a former prosecutor who knew his way around downtown Los Angeles, and its courtrooms.

At the end of the day, my total income from the Simpson case was $16,800 toward expenses that were many times that amount.

I had gotten myself into a lousy deal, but Johnnie Cochran's leadership made the plight much more palatable.

O. J.'s situation was and is both topsy-turvy and complex. In my view, the press had convicted him handily with its low-grade reporting and high-octane speculation, masquerading as fact. "Fake news" is an apt term. I'm sure he was surprised and dismayed to find that far from being congratulated for a stunning victory, he was assumed to have "beaten the rap" with the help of some "slick lawyers from the East." He took up residence in Florida, where he had many friends, and spent as much time on the golf course as he could. Because I lived there, I sometimes invited several of my acquaintances and colleagues to have lunch with him. The result was always the same. No matter how hostile the mien of the guest might have been initially, without exception, they echoed the words of the late Dr. Yudowitz, the greatest psychiatric expert in homicide as a behavior: "This guy didn't kill anyone and wouldn't kill anyone."

The most delicate task in the writing of this book has been conveying a balanced assessment of the performance of Honorable Lance Ito, the trial judge who presided over the Trial of the Century. Critiquing trial judges is a tricky, and often unfair business. Criticism from the public is often uninformed, semi-illiterate, and in some instances, deranged. Upon the embers of such carping, lower grade reporters are wont to pour raw fuel, as with an attachment fixed to the aft end of a turbojet main engine called an afterburner. I had flown an F-18 Hornet a year or so before: It would climb straight up, vertically. I wish I had had one available during this trial.

Any story that embarrasses the rich and powerful is sure to get space in the local tabloids, and those of other countries. Except for publishing an occasional opinion explaining some ruling, judges have little access to the press or public from the bench. Press conferences are taboo.

Occasionally a trial lawyer who is engaged before the court in a proceeding when the judge has been taking his public lumps will sally forth and come to his defense. I have done it on several cases over the years where the judge is being pilloried, especially when the screeching is based upon their following some direct appellate decision, about which the judge has no choice whatsoever. I have done this in part because I have—as a lawyer who has appeared before more different state, federal, military, and administrative judges in the United States than any lawyer in history–seen a pretty good cross section of those women and men who bestride the bench around the land. I hasten to admit that I have gotten the rosier end of that experience. As a traveling gunslinger with a "reputation," I was often the beneficiary of extended courtesy and cooperation from the bench. My colleagues on both sides sometimes complained that I got noticeably better treatment from the court than they did.

On the other hand, when I drew a "stinker" as trial judge who disliked outsiders, life could be miserable.

Judge Ito surely belongs on the better side of the judicial group. He treated me—and counsel generally—quite fairly in most respects. But the threshold issue is not how well Judge Ito behaved on the bench generally, but how much impartiality he was able to exercise despite the fact that his wife was a "top cop" in West Los Angeles.

It is certainly true that in accordance with the best traditions of the judiciary, Judge Ito did spontaneously offer to recuse himself because of his marital situation. When he posed the question, Shapiro agreed to have Judge Ito preside as if Bob were a wizened veteran of courtroom wars.

One must pause at this point and examine Judge Ito's acceptance of Shapiro's "waiver of bias." In the particular circumstances of this case, was it enough? I think that Shapiro should have explained to O. J. the nuances of having a judge control the trial whose wife was rooting for a conviction and let him consider the matter. Simpson is a smart man and might have sought other opinions from co-counsel. Most important, Judge Ito should have recused himself *sua sponte*, no matter what Shapiro suggested. He was an experienced trial judge who well understood both the probable scope of sensational homicide cases, and who also knew that Shapiro was a babe in the woods.

As the trial got underway, it appeared to me that Judge Ito's rulings on motions and evidentiary issues were pretty even-handed. But I must fault him for lawyer control. Counsel for both sides talked endlessly about comparatively minor points, and they were given what seemed an unfettered license to ramble on and on. Of the still festering open wounds which are the legacy of the Simpson case, is that it wasted so much time and money. (An audit report showed the prosecution's case cost California taxpayers a staggering *$9 million*.)

But then, any of Judge Ito's biased, pro-prosecution leanings, if that's what they were, paled beside the enormity of Fuhrman's cruel and filthy, guttersnipe claim that Capt. York had earned her prestigious rank more with sexual—as opposed to professional—prowess. No judge ought to ever be faced with a sledgehammer blow to the face while presiding in open court. Any yet once the press got hold of Fuhrman's slur and ricocheted it along the international wire at the speed of light, there was no way to unring the bell.

I must confess that we—lawyers on both sides, the judge, and the detectives—dropped the ball badly. All of us—including the judge—should have spotted the offensive language before it became public; it could easily have been sealed and kept far away from the case. As it was, the publication of this slur caught everyone off guard, and the judge was so overcome with feeling he choked up on the bench, stifling a sob.

The publication of the Simpson verdict on the morning of October 3, 1995, was much like the shot heard round the world. It seems unquestionable that the televised sequence of events surrounding the reading of the verdict was seen by more people in more countries than any other prominent event in world history, simply because notice of the event had gone out through nearly every form of human communication known to mankind at the time, probably including some Aborigine drum beats in the far reaches of the Australian Outback. News cameras focused on groups of every description and captured the wildly emotional response which erupted. As I reviewed a few of these later that day, an ugly sense of foreboding sent a chill through my system: it turns out, that chill seemed to have an infinite number of half-lives.

Clearly, a national racial divide had just gotten much worse. African Americans cheered the verdict. Caucasians cried, booed, and wrung their hands. And goaded by an "I told you so," the idea was driven home repeatedly that this had been a racist trial and produced a racist verdict by a predominantly black jury. Some reporters ventured that the jury just wasn't bright enough to comprehend DNA evidence, allowing Simpson to escape. I cannot recall a case where a jury was so unfairly pummeled for simply doing its job and following instructions. And as a result, of course, the story has been sold that Simpson got away with murder.

* * *

I learned over time—sadly—that my client and I were to suffer for years to come, "the damnation of an acquittal." I slowly realized that I was being viewed as a pariah by the white population, for having wielded perverse skills to put a crazy murderer back into the general population. Oddly enough, while Johnnie Cochran has been credited with "winning" the case for twenty-five years now, I have been condemned for doing the same thing.

We who manned the bulwarks of the defense for Simpson did so, with one exception, with unflagging consistency and loyalty. We know in our marrow that he had nothing whatever to do with the homicides. We also know that the case had no racist components, except for the one furnished up by the prosecution: A wannabe detective who hates blacks and Jews, and whose own description of his egregious conduct while slashing the face of justice with the sharp edges of his badge. To convince itself that they had not jumped the gun and arrested Simpson prematurely, the prosecution allowed this charade of a police officer to play "hide the football." In the end, he hid it from them, until it exploded in their faces in the form of his audiotaped braggadocio.

And what of the city itself?

Los Angeles was originally known as "The City of Angels," and perhaps once upon a time it was. But if the angels are still there, they are keeping a low profile. More evident are the gargoyles, gremlins, and goliaths who confound human activity like the tentacles of an octopus. Among the non-angelic entities in the city is the Los Angeles Police Department, which has been in the throes of scandal and turmoil for decades. It has chewed through police commissioners (including some rather good ones) like a buzz saw. The 800-ton gorilla in the city is Interstate 405, where the "low-speed chase" occurred. The main artery in the state, it can jam with no warning, and leave you creeping along at walking speed, inhaling toxic smog in seven corrosive flavors. These are often tinted with aromas emanating from forests, homes—it seems there is always a large fire somewhere, usually several burning at once.

The LAPD, having suffered a beating during the Simpson trial, sunk millions into its Scientific Investigation Division, according to a December 1998 *LA Times* report. "That trial helped shed light on the lab's antiquated equipment and its criminalists' tremendous workloads.

"Poor equipment, inadequate facilities and insufficient personnel are all unacceptable and were in need of remedy," said City

Councilwoman Laura Chick, chairwoman of the Public Safety Committee.

"Since 1995, the LAPD has added 32 employees for the lab, spent about $500,000 on new training programs, and invested about $3 million in facility and equipment upgrades."

But to me, the saddest corner of the sometimes-great state of California is its justice apparatus. A cohort of snails seems to have been chosen many years ago to run and control the judicial system, and they hold forth at their glacial pace. Trials—both civil and criminal—are horribly expensive compared to most other states, in part because of the sluggish way they drag along. They are also protracted because lawyers spend so much time on roadways like US 405, waiting in traffic, charging the client by the hour, often being late for court.

And while each of these shortcomings contributed to the Simpson case, neither they nor their permutations adequately explain the aberration which became The People v. Simpson. Lurking in the recent history of this bedeviled community was a scar on its soul called the Rodney King case. It was, I am satisfied, the triggering event without which the cops would have never tried to pin the murder on Simpson in the first place.

Even though the LAPD officers who were caught on video savagely beating a defenseless Rodney King were eventually charged with assault, the first trial in Simi Valley, a suburb so conservative it was thought by some to be run by a consortium of the heirs of Attila the Hun, did not serve justice. The jurors somehow fantasized that there was room in the disgusting four corners of the video to find some vestige of self-defense for the baton-wielding officers and returned verdicts of not guilty.

The verdicts resulted in such outrage—the second wave, indeed—that the federal government chose to prosecute the same officers in federal court for civil rights violations, and they were—much belatedly—convicted. That, however, did little to assuage the public thirst for revenge, especially among African Americans who understood that a white cop could shoot them down on Hollywood Boulevard and walk away. The city was a keg of dynamite, fuse protruding, waiting for ignition. That flame was unwittingly provided by a racist, twisted, fame-seeking, junior detective who wanted to be aggrandized as the super-sleuth working the Simpson case.

Into this teeming cauldron of hatred and racial divisiveness wandered O. J. Simpson, innocent for the most part of these community troubles. I believe that some higher-up officials in the LAPD saw a chance to make the black community pay for the embarrassment it had brought to the police department, now close to its record high in public disapproval.

With hardly a caution, they jumped Simpson, even though the evidence against him is, and always has been, little more than a cruel joke. Lives have been badly damaged. Millions in public and private funds were flushed away, toward no useful end.

Simpson remains his same affable self, taking each day as it comes, surrounded by many friends of the best kind. But he is perhaps the most prominent defendant in history to win a defense verdict, only to be trashed by millions who have little respect for the system—and thus themselves—with an unyielding presumption of guilt.

To all of those who played fast and loose with the truth while wearing a badge, and to those who allowed, even sometimes encouraged them to do it, an honest look in any mirror should bounce back but one image:

Shame, shame, shame!

Books Cited

Bailey, F. Lee. *For the Defense.* Atheneum, 1975.

———. *To Be a Trial Lawyer.* John Wiley & Sons Inc., 1992.

Cochran, Johnnie. *Journey to Justice.* One World/Ballantine, 1997.

Cooley, Armanda, Carrie Bess, and Marsha Rubin-Jackson. *Madam Foreman: A Rush to Judgment?* NewStar Media, Inc., 1996.

Schiller, Lawrence, and James Willwerth. *American Tragedy: The Uncensored Story of the O. J. Simpson Defense.* Random House, 1996.

Clark, Marcia, and Teresa Carpenter. *Without a Doubt.* Viking Adult, 1997.

Darden, Christopher, and Jess Walter. *In Contempt.* ReganBooks, 1996.

Shapiro, Robert, and Larkin Warren. *The Search for Justice: A Defense Attorney's Brief on the O. J. Simpson Case.* Warner Books, 1996.

A Note about the Trial Transcripts

Visit www.TruthAboutTheOJSimpsonTrial.com for the most factual documentation and analysis of the O.J. Simpson saga to date. From the entire court transcripts to the infamous "Fuhrman Tapes," this explosive website also offers investigation interviews, notes, strategy documents and shocking revelations to support all facets of this book.

Endnotes

Prologue

1 Transcript: Testimony of Danny Mandel.
2 Transcript: Testimony of Ellen Aaronson.
3 Transcript: Testimony of Danny Mandel.
4 Transcript: Testimony of Denise Pilnak.
5 Transcript: Testimony of Judy Telander.
6 Transcript: Testimony of Denise Pilnak.
7 Transcript: Testimony of Denise Pilnak.
8 Transcript: Testimony of Denise Pilnak.
9 Transcript: Testimony of Robert Heidstra.
10 Transcript: Testimony of Robert Heidstra.
11 Transcript: Testimony of Robert Heidstra.
12 Transcript: Testimony of Steven Schwab.
13 Transcript: Testimony of Sukru Boztepe.

The Preliminary Hearing

1 It is set forth in detail on our website, TruthAboutTheOJSimp-
   sonTrial.com, together with psychiatric evaluations contained
   in the filings.
2 These scurrilous tapes are set forth word for ugly word on
   TruthAboutTheOJSimpsonTrial.com.
3 See Prosecution Preliminary Hearing Witness List at
   TruthAboutTheOJSimpsonTrial.com.

The Night of the Murders and What Happened Next

1 See Testimony from the preliminary hearing and trial at
   TruthAboutTheOJSimpsonTrial.com.
2 Fuhrman claimed he had Vannatter's blessing before he went
   over the wall, and Vannatter later said that was true. Anyone

who watched them both testify would have had the gravest of doubts about both.

3 Extremely odd that a junior detective would give direction to one many years his senior. Clearly, Fuhrman was up to something.

4 The call started with O. J. calling his assistant, Cathy Randa. She connected him with Hertz and Hertz then connected him with Thomas Cook Emergency Travel. This bouncing of connected calls made Ito rule there was no one to say that it was really O. J. (an unfair ruling).
See detailed transcript where Judge Ito makes his ruling at TruthAboutTheOJSimpsonTrial.com.

5 The audio version is located in its entirety on TruthAboutTheOJSimpsonTrial.com.

Pillars of Innocence

1 Not to be confused with Tom Lange, the LAPD detective. I believe Lang may have been the only witness to see the actual killer or killers that evening.

2 Despite his lack of appearance on the record, Lang's story is very well documented.

3 The deputy medical examiner for Los Angeles County, who conducted the autopsies, Dr. Irwin Golden, had suggested that the knife wounds could have been made by different cutting instruments. He was kept off the stand at trial.

4 As per Dr. Irwin Golden's autopsy report that he testified to at the preliminary hearing.

5 See testimony of Wayne Stansfield, captain, American Airlines.

6 See testimony of Jim Merrill, Hertz employee at TruthAbout-TheOJSimpsonTrial.com.

7 Simpson's recorded statement to police can be heard in its entirety.

8 Allen was then living in Kansas City. We served process on him there and had a hearing, asking that he be sent to Los Angeles to describe the incident. The Kansas judge turned us down.

Fuhrman Takes the Stand

1 *For the Defense*, Atheneum, 1975.

2 Kaelin actually testified that he heard the noise at between 10:40 and 10:45 p.m.

The "Fuhrman Tapes"

1   See testimony of Mark Fuhrman in Preliminary Hearing where he refers to the Bundy Drive glove as "them" at TruthAbout-TheOJSimpsonTrial.com.

Closing Arguments and Deliberation

1   Marcia Clark misstates the timing here. Kaelin testified the thumps he heard were around 10:40 to 10:45 p.m. He first saw O. J. Simpson with bags in the home's entry at 10:55 p.m. as the limo entered through the gate.
2   Again, Clark repeatedly distorted the actual witness testimony. Neither Allan Park nor Kato Kaelin said they saw Simpson walking up his driveway.

Author Biography

F. Lee Bailey is a former criminal defense attorney and noted author of more than twenty books. As a trial lawyer, Bailey's career is highlighted by such extraordinary cases as Dr. Sam Sheppard, Dr. Carl Coppolino, Albert DeSalvo, aka the Boston Strangler, Patty Hearst and O. J. Simpson. Among his previous books is the national bestseller, *The Defense Never Rests*. Today, Bailey is a consultant based in Atlanta, Georgia.